The Ultimate Kids Song Book

Over 300 Songs in Lead Sheet Format

Perfect for Children's Church,
Kids Worship,
Camps and VBS

BRENTWOOD-BENSON®
music publishing

A Haughty Heart

Words and Music by
JANET MCMAHAN-WILSON

Two-beat feel
Cm
A haugh - haugh - haugh - ty hah - hah - heart will cause you to
G7 Cm
fall down, cause you to fall down, cause you to
G Cm
fall down. A haugh - haugh - haugh - ty hah - hah - heart will
G7
cause you to fall down. So keep your hah - hah -
Cm7 Cm/C♯ C♯m
heart huh - huh - hum - ble.
F♯m C♯m/G♯ G♯7 C♯m
A haugh - haugh - haugh - ty hah - hah - heart will
G♯7
cause you to fall down, cause you to
C♯m G♯
fall down, cause you to fall down. A
C♯m
haugh - haugh - haugh - ty hah - hah - heart will cause you to

G♯7
fall down. So keep your hah - hah - heart huh - huh - hum -
C♯m7
C♯m/D Dm
Gm Dm/A A7
ble.
A
Dm
haugh - haugh - haugh - ty hah - hah - heart will cause you to
A7
fall down, cause you to fall down,
Dm
A
Dm
cause you to fall down. A haugh - haugh - haugh - ty
hah - hah - heart will cause you to fall down. So
A7
Dm
keep your hah - hah - heart huh - huh - hum - ble.
D° Dm A Dm
A7
Keep your hah - hah - heart huh - huh - hum -
Dm A Dm A Dm A Dm
ble.

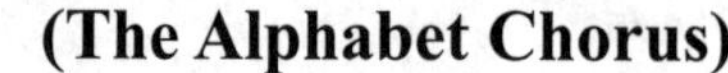

A-B-C-D-E-F-G

(The Alphabet Chorus)

Words and Music by
HUGH MITCHELL

F Am/C C7 Gm7 C7
A B C D E F G, Je - sus died for

Gm/F F F/C F G7sus
you and me; H I J K L M N,

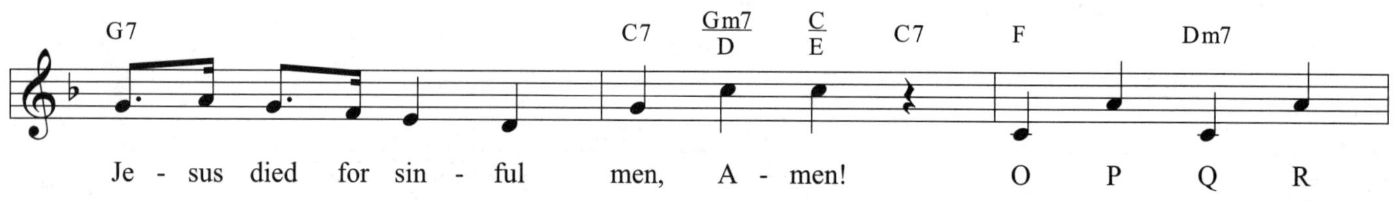
G7 C7 Gm7/D C/E C7 F Dm7
Je - sus died for sin - ful men, A - men! O P Q R

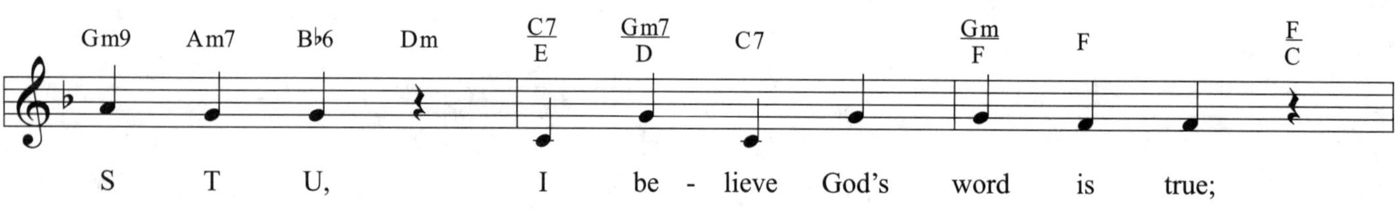
Gm9 Am7 B♭6 Dm C7/E Gm7/D C7 Gm/F F F/C
S T U, I be - lieve God's word is true;

F F7 B♭ Gm7 Am7 Dm7
U V dou - ble U, God has prom - ised you, X Y Z, a

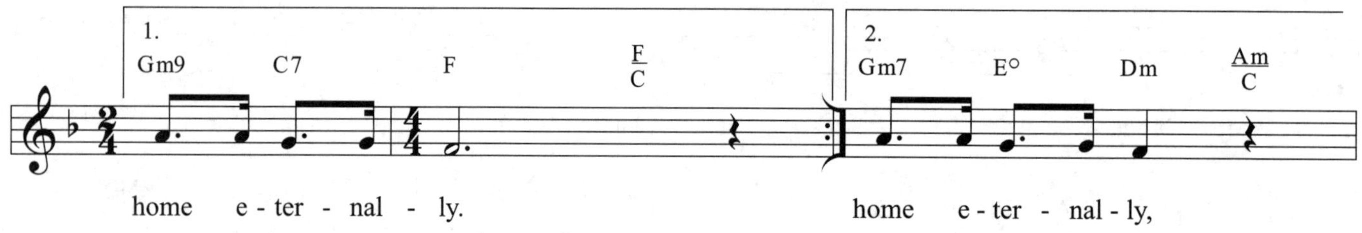
1. Gm9 C7 F F/C
home e - ter - nal - ly.
2. Gm7 E° Dm Am/C
home e - ter - nal - ly,

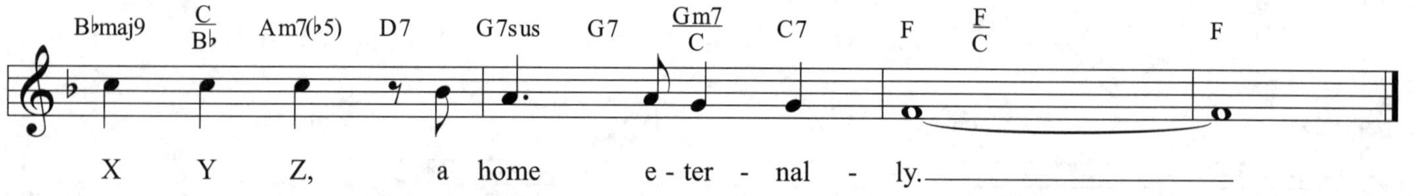
B♭maj9 C/B♭ Am7(♭5) D7 G7sus G7 Gm7/C C7 F F/C F
X Y Z, a home e - ter - nal - ly.

"Abundawonderful" Life in Jesus

Words and Music by
KATHIE HILL

There is a - bun - da - won - der - ful life in Je - sus, a -
bun - da - won - der - ful life that nev - er ends.
A - bun - da - won - der - ful hap - pi - ness, a -
3rd time to Coda
bun - da - won - der - ful friends, there's a - bun - da - won - der - ful life in Him.
1. Je - sus gives a rea - son for liv - ing; Je - sus gives you joy when you are
2. Je - sus gives you life ev - er - last - ing. Je - sus gives you love when you're a -
sad. He gives hope when days are drear - y, strength when you are wear - y.
lone. He gives peace when you are wor - ried, pa - tience when you're hur - ried.
Repeat twice
He can make life cheer - y e - ven when things look bad! There is a
When your day is blur - ry, He is still in con - trol!
CODA
Him. There's a - bun - da - won - der - ful life in Him. There's a -
bun - da - won - der - ful life in Him!

Adam, Adam

(To the tune of Reuben, Reuben)

Words and Music by
RHETT PARRISH, JODI HANNA and ED KEE

1. A - dam, A - dam, won't you tell us: How did you like par - a - dise? "God pro-vid-ed all I need-ed.
2. No - ah, No - ah, won't you tell us: How'd you ev - er build that boat? "God pro-vid-ed all I need-ed.
3. Mo-ses, Mo - ses, won't you tell us: How'd you ev - er part the seas? "God pro-vid-ed all I need-ed.

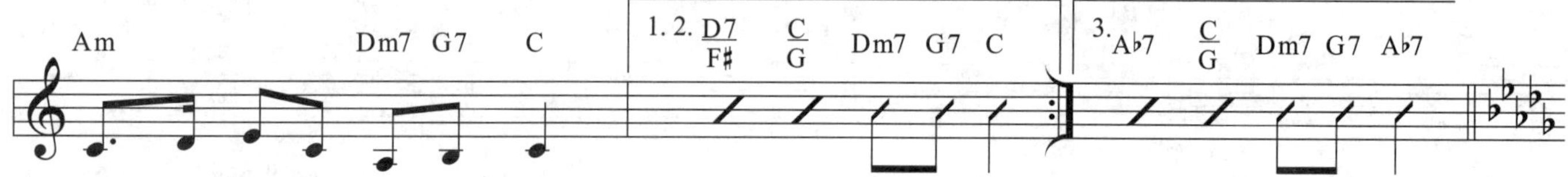

While it last - ed it was nice!"
Through the storm I stayed a - float."
With His help it was a breeze."

4. Da - vid, Da - vid, won't you tell us: How'd you kill that Phil - is - tine?
5. Shad - rach, Shad - rach, won't you tell us: How did you es - cape those flames?

"God pro-vid-ed all I need-ed with five peb-bles and a sling."
"God pro-vid-ed all I need-ed. All I did was call His name."

6. Dan - iel, Dan - iel, won't you tell us: How'd you face that li - on's den?
7. Jo - nah, Jo - nah, won't you tell us: How'd you live in - side that whale?

"God pro-vid-ed all I need-ed. Soon those cats be-came my friends."
"God pro-vid-ed all I need-ed, let me live to tell the tale."

Chris - tian, Chris - tian, let us tell you how to fin - ish an - y task.

God's pro - vid - ed all you need, so all you have to do is ask.

Ain't No Rock

Words and Music by
LAMARQUIS JEFFERSON

Ain't Gonna Let the Mountains Praise the Lord

Words and Music by
DOTTIE RAMBO

With enthusiasm (♩=112)
D♭ G♭ D♭
Ain't gon-na let the moun - tains praise the Lord.
A♭7
Ain't gon-na let the moun - tains praise the Lord. I'll
G♭ D♭ B♭m
shout it from the hills, "Ye moun-tains all stand still!" And I
D♭ A♭7 D♭ E♭m7 D♭/F
ain't gon-na let the moun - tains praise the Lord. My
G♭ D♭ G♭ D♭
hands were made to serve Him. My heart was made to love Him. My
G♭ D♭ G♭ D♭/A♭ A♭7 D♭ A7
voice was made to lift and raise and praise the Lord.
D G D
Ain't gon-na let the val - leys sing for me.
A7
Ain't gon-na let the val - leys sing for me. I'll
G D Bm
lift my voice and sing ho - san - nas to the King. And I

D A7 D B♭7
ain't gon-na let the val - leys sing for me.
E♭ A♭ E♭
Ain't gon - na let the rocks cry out for me.
B♭7
Ain't gon - na let the rocks cry out for me. I'll
A♭ E♭ Cm
lift my voice and shout so the rocks will not cry out. And I
E♭ B♭7 E♭ Fm7 E♭/G
ain't gon - na let the rocks cry out for me. My
A♭ E♭ A♭ E♭
hands were made to serve Him. My heart was made to love Him. My
A♭ E♭ A♭
1.2.
E♭/B♭ B♭7 E♭ Fm7 E♭/G
voice was made to lift and raise and praise the Lord. My
3.
E♭/B♭ B♭7 E♭
praise the Lord.

Ain't Nobody

Words and Music by
REGGIE COATES
Confidently (♩=106)
G F C G
SOLO CHOIR SOLO
Ain't no - bod - y (Ain't no - bod - y!) gon - na love me like Je - sus.
D C2
CHOIR SOLO
Ain't no - bod - y (Ain't no - bod - y!) gon - na love me like the Lord.
G F G
CHOIR SOLO
Ain't no - bod - y (Ain't no - bod - y!) gon - na love me like Je - sus.
Last time to Coda
D C 1. G 2. G
He's my Friend. Well,
C G C
I've had friends who have stood by my side, and I've had friends who have
G C Em
let me down. But Je - sus Christ is more than a friend. He's my
D D2 D D2
Mas - ter, He's my Mak - er. In Him I'm sat - is - fied. In
D D2 D
D.C. al Coda
Him I'm sat - is - fied. In Him I'm sat - is - fied.
CODA
G A(no3) G(no3) G♯(no3)
SOLO
Not my ma - ma, not my pa - pa.

A(no3)
CHOIR
D(no3)
C(no3)
A(no3)
SOLO
G(no3)
G♯(no3)
(Not my ma - ma, not my pa - pa.) Not my sis - ter, not my broth - er.
A(no3)
CHOIR
D(no3)
C(no3)
A(no3)
SOLO
G(no3)
G♯(no3)
(Not my sis - ter, not my broth - er.) Not my dog and not my cat.
A(no3)
CHOIR
D(no3)
C(no3)
A(no3)
SOLO
G(no3)
G♯(no3)
(Not my dog and not my cat.) Ain't no - bod - y gon - na love me like that.
A(no3)
CHOIR
B
SOLO
A
E
CHOIR
(Ain't no - bod - y gon' love me like that.) Ain't no - bod - y (Ain't no -
B
SOLO
F♯
CHOIR
bod - y!) gon - na love me like Je - sus. Ain't no - bod - y (Ain't no -
E2
SOLO
B
A
E
CHOIR
bod - y!) gon - na love me like the Lord. Ain't no - bod - y (Ain't no -
B
SOLO
F♯
E
bod - y!) gon - na love me like Je - sus. He's my Friend.
1. B
2. B
F♯
E
Don't you know that He's my Friend.
B
F♯sus
E2
B
Don't you know that He's my Friend.

Alice the Camel

Writer Unknown

Alive, Alive

Traditional

F F7 B♭ F F/A
A - live, a - live, a - live for - ev - er - more; my
C C7 C/B♭ F/A C F F7
Je - sus is a - live, a - live for - ev - er - more. A - live, a - live, a -
B♭ F C C7 F
live for - ev - er - more; my Je - sus is a - live. Sing Hal - le -
B♭ F C C7 C
lu - jah! Sing Hal - le - lu - jah! My Je - sus is a -
F C7/G F/A F B♭
live for - ev - er - more. Sing Hal - le - lu - jah! Sing Hal - le -
F C C7 1. F B♭/C
lu - jah! My Je - sus is a - live! A -
2. F F/A A♭o C9/G C9 C7 F
live! My Je - sus is a - live!

All God's Children

Words and Music by
JANET MCMAHAN-WILSON
and GRETA GARNER-HART

Big band swing (♩=144)
C Am7 Dm G
1. All God's chil - dren need the light of the Lord, the
2. All God's chil - dren need the love of the Lord, the
3. All God's chil - dren need the joy of the Lord, the
Dm G C G+
light of the Lord, the light of the Lord.
love of the Lord, the love of the Lord.
joy of the Lord, the joy of the Lord.
C Am7 Dm G
3rd time to Coda
All God's chil - dren need the light of the Lord to
All God's chil - dren need the love of the Lord to
All God's chil - dren need the joy of the Lord to
1. Dm7 G C G+
lead them ev - 'ry day.
2. Dm7 G C
guide them ev - 'ry day.
C B♭ A♭ G
Trust in Him with all your might and
A♭ G N.C.
D.C. al Coda
He'll be with you day and night.
CODA
Dm7 G C Am Dm7 G C
fill them ev - 'ry day. He'll guide you ev - 'ry day.
Am Dm7 G C
So let Him lead the way.

All Night, All Day

Traditional

Day is dy - in' in the west, an - gels watch - in' o - ver
me, my Lord. Sleep, my child, and take your rest,
an - gels watch - in' o - ver me. All night,
all day, an - gels watch - in' o - ver me, my Lord.
All night, all day, an - gels watch - in' o - ver
me. All night, all day,
an - gels watch - in' o - ver me, my Lord. All night,
all day, an - gels watch - in' o - ver
me. An - gels watch - in' o - ver me.

All Things Work Together

Words and Music by
TROY NILSSON and GENIE NILSSON

Moderate rock (♩=106)
G D/F♯ Em D C D G
Na na na na__ na na na na na na na na.__

D/F♯ Em D C D G
Na na na na__ na na na na na na na na.__

G D/F♯ Em D C D G
All things work to-geth - er for good to those who love God.__

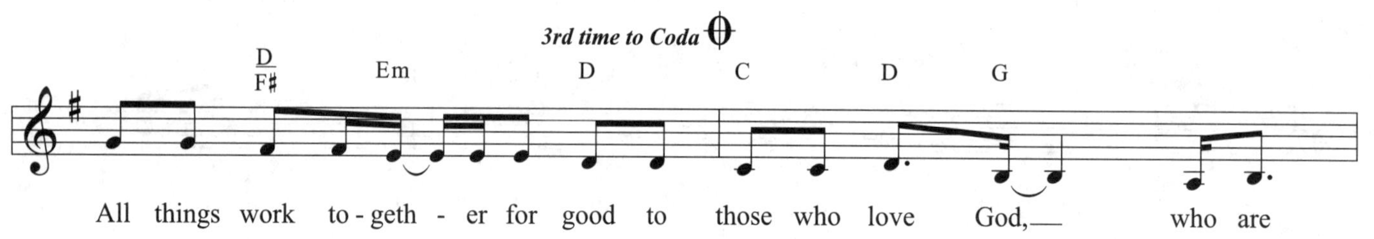
3rd time to Coda
D/F♯ Em D C D G
All things work to-geth - er for good to those who love God,__ who are

C D Em Bm7
called ac - cord - ing to His pur - pose, who are

C D 1. G 2. G
called ac - cord - ing to His pur - pose. - pose. That means

D C G
ev - 'ry - thing I'm wor - ried a - bout's__ gon - na work out in the end__ for your good,__

A7sus
A7
D
D.S. al Coda
not your bad.
You're gon - na be so glad!
CODA
C D G
E♭
those who love God.
When life won't go your way,
B♭
Fsus F
B♭
look on to a bright - er day,
'cause ev - 'ry - thing will turn out great says
C
D
G
D/F♯
Em
D
Ro - mans eight twen - ty eight.
C D G
D/F♯
Em
D
C
D
D♭
E♭
Ro - mans eight twen - ty eight.
A♭
E♭/G
Fm
E♭
D♭
E♭
A♭
All things work to - geth - er for good to those who love God.
E♭/G
Fm
E♭
D♭
E♭
A♭
All things work to - geth - er for good to those who love God. That means
E♭
D♭
A♭
ev - 'ry - thing I'm wor - ried a - bout's gon - na work out in the end for your good,

B♭7sus
B♭7
E♭
— not your bad. — You're gon - na be so glad!
A♭
E♭/G
Fm
E♭
D♭
E♭
A♭
All things work to - geth - er for good to those who love God. —
E♭/G
Fm
E♭
D♭
E♭
A♭
All things work to - geth - er for good to those who love God, — who are
D♭
E♭
Fm
Cm7
called ac - cord - ing to His pur - pose, who are
D♭
E♭
A♭
E♭/G
Fm
E♭
called ac - cord - ing to His pur - pose. Na — na na na
D♭
E♭
A♭
E♭/G
Fm
E♭
na na na na na. — Na na na na — na na na
D♭
E♭
A♭
A♭
E♭/G
Fm
E♭
na na na na na. — Na na na na — na na na
D♭
E♭
A♭
E♭/G
Fm
E♭
D♭
E♭
A♭
na na na na na. — Na na na na — na na na na na na na na. —

Amazing Grace

Words by
JOHN NEWTON

Early American Melody

1. A - maz - ing Grace! How sweet the sound, that saved a
(2. Through) man - y dan - gers, toils and snares, I have al -
wretch like me! I once was
read - y come; 'Tis Grace hath
lost, But now am found; Was blind, but
brought me safe thus far, And Grace will
now I see. 2. Through home. 3. When
lead me
we've been there ten thou - sand years, Bright
shin - ing as the sun; We've
no less days to sing God's praise, than when we
first be - gun! We've gun!

America the Beautiful

Words and Music by
SAMUEL A. WARD and KATHERINE LEE BATES

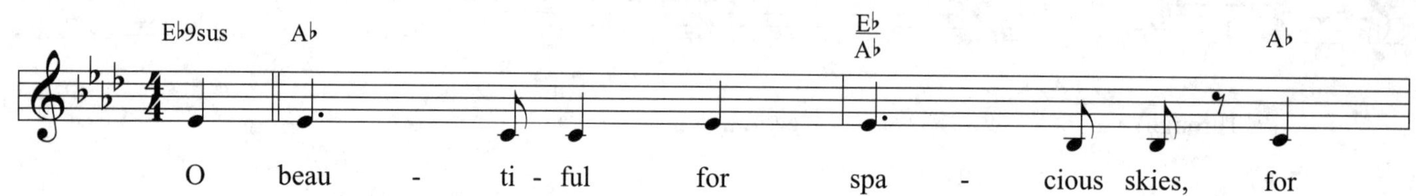
E♭9sus A♭ E♭/A♭ A♭
O beau - ti - ful for spa - cious skies, for

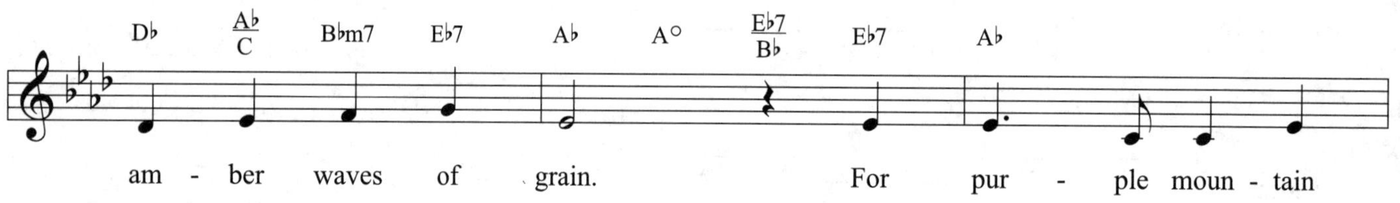
D♭ A♭/C B♭m7 E♭7 A♭ A° E♭7/B♭ E♭7 A♭
am - ber waves of grain. For pur - ple moun - tain

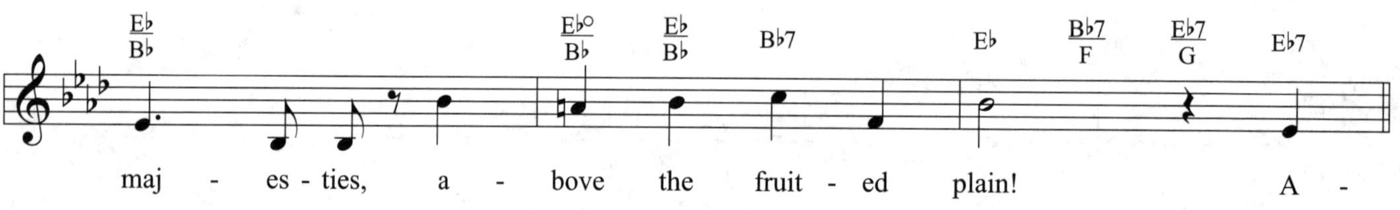
E♭/B♭ E♭°/B♭ E♭/B♭ B♭7 E♭ B♭7/F E♭7/G E♭7
maj - es - ties, a - bove the fruit - ed plain! A -

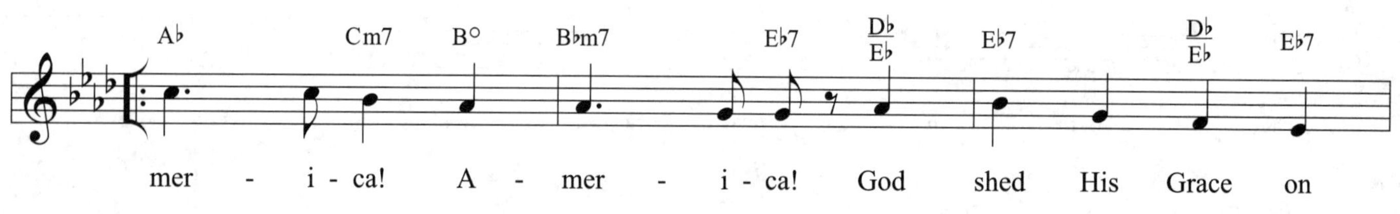
A♭ Cm7 B° B♭m7 E♭7 D♭/E♭ E♭7 D♭/E♭ E♭7
mer - i - ca! A - mer - i - ca! God shed His Grace on

A♭ B♭m7 B° A♭/C D♭ B♭m7 A♭/E♭
thee, And crown thy good with broth - er - hood, from

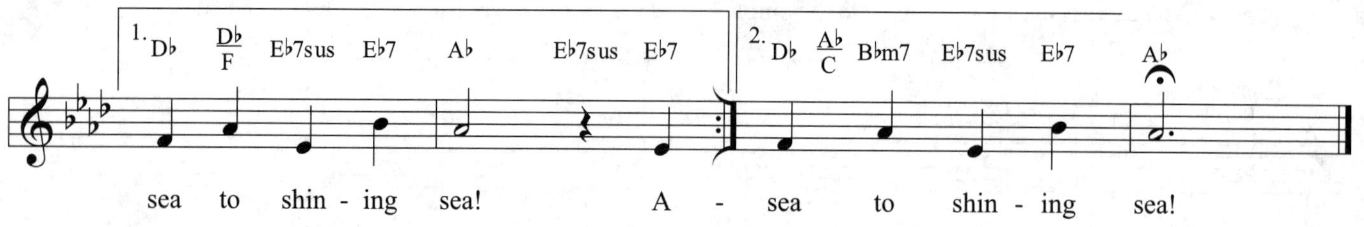
1. D♭ D♭/F E♭7sus E♭7 A♭ E♭7sus E♭7
2. D♭ A♭/C B♭m7 E♭7sus E♭7 A♭
sea to shin - ing sea! A - sea to shin - ing sea!

And This Is Eternal Life

Words and Music by
STEVE JONES

Bossa
A A/C♯ D Bm7
And this is e - ter - nal life
E7 D/A A A A/C♯
that they may know Thee, the on - ly true God and
D Bm7 E7 Bm7/E E7 1. A Bm7/E
Je - sus Christ, whom Thou hast sent.
2. A E♭/F B♭ B♭/D E♭ Cm7
sent. And this is e - ter - nal life
F7 E♭/B♭ B♭ E♭/F B♭ B♭/D
that they may know Thee, the on - ly true God and
E♭ Cm7 F7 Cm7/F F7 1. B♭ E♭6/F
Je - sus Christ, whom Thou hast sent.
2. B♭ Gm7 F7 Cm7/F F7 B♭
sent, whom Thou hast sent.

Ant Song

Words and Music by
JANET MCMAHAN-WILSON

Swing! (♩=152)
E6 C♯m7 F♯m7 F♯m7/B
Take a les - son from the ant.
E6 F♯9/A♯ B C B
You might learn a lot. An
E E7/D A/C♯ Am/C
ant can't work in the win - ter - time.
E/B B13 B E B/D♯ E7/D
Sum - mer's the on - ly shot. They know it's
A/C♯ Am/C
cra - zy to be la - zy. It's
E/B E B/D♯ E7/D
bet - ter to get things done, 'cause when the
A/C♯ Am/C
weath - er's get - tin' ha - zy the

B
A♯
B
B7
ants can have some fun.
C
F6
Dm7
Gm7
Gm7/C
Take a les - son from the ant.
F6
G9/B
C
D♭
C
You might learn a lot.
An
F
F7/E♭
B♭/D
B♭m/D♭
ant can't work in the win - ter - time.
F/C
C13
C
F
D7
Sum - mer's the on - ly shot.
Gm9
C13
C
F
D7
They give it all they've got.
Gm9
C13
C
F
They're read - y right on the dot.

Assurance March

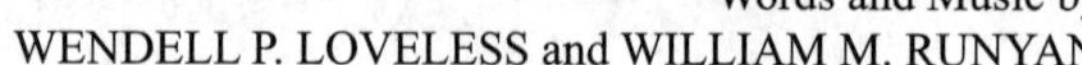
Words and Music by
WENDELL P. LOVELESS and WILLIAM M. RUNYAN

A♭ A♭/E♭ A♭6 A♭6/E♭ A♭ A♭6/E♭

1. Can we know that
2. We can know that

A♭ A♭/E♭ A♭/C B°

Je - sus saves us, can we
Je - sus saves us, we can

E♭7 E♭7/G E♭7 E♭°/F♯ E♭°

know?___ Be as -
know.___ Be as -

Cm/G E♭7 E♭7/B♭ D♭6/A♭ E♭7/G E♭7 E♭/G E♭7(♯5)

sured each mo - ment ev - 'ry - where we
sured each mo - ment ev - 'ry - where we

A♭ A♭/E♭ A♭° A♭°/E♭

go?___ Can we
go.___ We can

A♭ A♭6/E♭ A♭ A♭/E♭ A♭

know our sins are all for - giv - en,
know our sins are all for - giv - en,

E♭7/B♭ A♭7/C D♭ Cm7(4) F7

washed a - way?___
washed a - way,___

B♭m
B♭m(maj7)
D♭maj7
D♭m6
A♭/C
A♭
A♭°
A♭
That our path is lead - ing to God's
that our path is lead - ing to God's
B♭7
E♭7
2nd time to Coda
A♭
A♭
C
per - fect way? O yes,
per - fect way!
C7
Gm7
C7
Gm7
C
B♭m/D♭
we can know. Can know our sins are
Fm/D
C/E
Fm
B♭7
Fm7
B♭7
Fm7
washed a - way? We can know. Can
B♭7
A♭/C
B♭m6/D♭
B♭7/D
E♭
N.C.
know our sins are washed a - way: Chap - ter one, verse
twelve of John is the ground we stand up - on!
D.C. al Coda
E♭7
E♭°
E♭7
E♭°
E♭7
D♭6/F
G°
CODA
A♭
way.

Be Above It, Never Covet

Words and Music by
TROY NILSSON and GENIE NILSSON

Brightly (♩=152)
G
C
G
Nev - er cov-et, be a-bove it, Cov-et-ing will get the best of
D
G
C
you; Nev - er cov-et, be a-bove it, Re-
D
G G♯ A
D
mem-ber all that God has giv-en you, you, you! Greed-y Gus sees peo-ple's stuff and
Em A D A
real-ly starts to love it, C - O - V-E-T, C - O - V-E-T, C - O - V-E-T,
D
boy, he loves to cov - et. 'Cause when you want an-oth-er's stuff, that's what it means to cov - et,
Em A D A D
C - O - V-E-T, C - O - V-E-T, C - O - V-E-T, boy, he loves to cov - et.
Em
Greed-y Gus has got to learn God's tenth com-mand - ment, Don't C-O-V-E-T,
A D A
Don't C-O-V-E-T, Don't C-O-V-E-T, nev-er, nev-er cov - et.
G C G
Nev - er cov-et, be a-bove it, Cov-et-ing will get the best of

D G C D
you; Nev - er cov-et, be a-bove it, Re-mem-ber all that God has giv-en
G G♯ A D
you, you, you! If Gus does not get what he wants, he starts to scream and cry,
Em A D A
Waa, waa, waa, waa, waa, waa, waa, waa, waa, waa, waa, waa, waa, waa, waa, waa, waa, waa,
D
give it, give it, give it. He thinks if he can't have it all he will sure-ly die,
(fake crying) Em A D A D
boy, he loves to cov - et.
Em
So, don't be a Greed-y Gus, keep the tenth com-mand - ment: Don't C - O - V - E - T,
A D A D
Don't C - O - V - E - T, Don't C - O - V - E - T, nev-er, nev-er cov - et.
G C G D
Nev - er cov-et, be a-bove it, Cov-et-ing will get the best of you;
G C D 1. G 2. G
Nev - er cov-et, be a-bove it, Re-mem-ber all that God has giv-en you! you!

Be Cool

Words and Music by
STEVE KELLER

Shuffle eighths (♩=148)
E F#7 A2
La, la, la, la, la, la.__ La, la, la,__ la, la,__
E F#7
__ la, la.__ La, la, la, la, la, la.__
A2 E
La, la, la,__ la, la,__ la, la.__
E F#7
1. Pen - guins play all dressed__ in suits.__ They
2. Re - mem - ber, the next time you play and your
A2 E
wag - gle and wad - dle and look__ real__ cute__
tem - pers__ scream__ when you don't__ get your way,__
F#7
slip - pin' and slid - in' and chill - in' all day.__
take a deep breath,__ ____ count__ to ten,__
A2 E
It's fun to watch the pen - guins play.__
wheth - er you__ lose,__ wheth - er you win. If the
F#7
They all seem hap - py; they get a - long fine.__
tem - p'ra - ture's__ ris - in' and you're feel - in' hot,__ take a
A2 E
You nev - er hear a pen - guin whine.__
sec - ond or two__ and cool__ your - self off. Re -

F♯7
They may ar - gue, but they nev - er shout.
mem - ber that bird in the black and white suit;
A2
E
They al - ways seem to work it out. 'Cause they're cool
he's cool, and that's the truth. So be cool
E
F♯7
when they're hot.
when you're hot.
A2
E
Those an - gry words can hurt a lot. They think twice,
An - gry words can hurt a lot. So think twice
F♯7
A2
then they're nice.
and be nice.
They keep their
And keep your
1. E
2. E
tem - pers on ice. They're cool.
tem - per on ice. Be cool.
E
F♯7
La, la, la, la, la, la.
A2
E
La, la, la, la, la, la, la. La, la, la,
F♯7
A2
E
Repeat and fade
la, la, la. La, la, la, la, la, la, la.

Be Good

Words and Music by
JANET MCMAHAN-WILSON
and GRETA GARNER-HART

Bright shuffle (♩=126)
A♭ A♭6 A♭
Be good. Be good. Be good like you know that you
B♭m E♭7
should. Be good when you're all a - lone or
B♭m E♭7 B♭m E♭7
when you're with a friend, not just ev - 'ry
A♭ D♭/E♭ A♭ A♭6
now and then. Be good. Be good.
A♭ A♭7 D♭
Bet - ter nev - er ev - er for - get.
B°7 A♭/E♭ F7
Morn - ing, noon, and night - time, an - y - time's the right time. It's
B♭m D♭maj7 2nd time to Coda A♭2
al - ways good to be good.
B♭m E♭7 A♭2 B♭m E♭ D.S. al Fine
Be
CODA
A♭ F9 B♭m D♭maj7
good. It's al - ways good to be
A♭ F9 B♭ D♭maj7 A♭
good. It's al-ways good to be good.

Be Nice

Words and Music by
JANET MCMAHAN-WILSON and DEBRA BLACK

Steady two-beat (♩=116)
Dm A
1. When some - one is mean to you, there's on - ly one thing you should do.
2. When some - bod - y bursts your bub - ble, bet - ter not start mak - in' trou - ble.
A7 2nd time to Coda Dm
This is my ad - vice: (What is it?) Be nice. (Be
This is my ad - vice: (What is it?)
A Dm A Dm A Dm Gm
nice?) Be nice. Be nice. Be nice. 'Cause it's nice to be
Dm Gm
nice in all you do, not just
A Dm D7 Gm
when some - one's nice to you. If some - bod - y
Dm E
calls you names, don't go out and do the same. Re - mem - ber this ad -
A E
vice: (What is it?) Be nice. (Be nice?) Be
A E A E A E A E A D.C. al Coda
nice. Be nice. Be nice. Be nice. Be nice.
CODA
Dm A Dm A Dm A Dm A Dm
nice. Be nice. Be nice. Be nice. Be nice.

Be Thankful

Words and Music by
HERB OWEN

C C/G C7 F F/C F Dm7
We're thank - ful for our moth - er's love that guides us ev - 'ry day. We're
G7 G7/D G7 Dm7 G7 C C/G
thank - ful for a God a - bove who leads us in the way. We're
C Cmaj7/G C7 Gm7/D C7/E F F/C Dm(maj7) Dm7
thank - ful for e - ter - nal life that we re - ceive one day. We
G7 G7/D G7 Dm7 G7 C Dm7 D♯° C/E
dare not wait to ap - pre - ci - ate, but want to stand and say: Be
F F/C F F/G C Am7 Dm7 Em/G G7
(whistle)
thank - ful. Be thank - ful. His love a - maz - es,
C Dm7 D♯° C/E C F F/C F F♯° C/G Em7 A7(♭9)
fills with prais - es. Be thank - ful. Be thank - ful. Give
1. Dm7 G7 C C/G C Dm7 D♯° C/E
thanks to the Lord a - bove. Be
2. Dm7 G7
thanks to the Lord a -
C Am7 Dm7 G7 C
bove. Give thanks to the Lord a - bove.

Behold, Behold!

Traditional

Be - hold, be - hold! I stand at the door and
knock, knock, knock. Be - hold, be - hold! I
stand at the door and knock, knock, knock. If an - y girl hear My
voice, if an - y boy hear My voice, and will
o - pen, o - pen, o - pen the door, I will come in. Be -
will come in. I will
come in.

Be True to Your Mate, Mate

Words and Music by
TROY NILSSON and GENIE NILSSON

Stately (𝅗𝅥=69)

SOLO Recitative style

When you grow up big and strong— you'll be read-y to— set sail,
Out up-on— the seas— of life— and you will nev-er fail.—
When you find the hus-band or the wife— that God has planned— for you,—
SOLO 2 You'll nev-er cheat— and serve them well— and re-mem-ber to be true.
CHOIR Be true— to your

Faster triplet feel (♩=146)

mate, Mate, be true— to your mate,
Be true— to your mate, Mate, be true— to your mate;
'Cause life's a ship we're sail-in' on,— you need your mate— to keep you strong— so,
Be true, be true— to your mate.

SOLO 1

When the storms— of life— are try-in' to blow you o-ver-board,—
Don't for-get your prom-ise to your mate and to the Lord;—
SOLO 2 What

C C7 F C/E
God has joined to-geth - er let no man tear a-part, Re-
Dm Dm/C G/B Am G
DUET CHOIR
mem - ber this lit-tle song and sing it from the heart. Be true to your
C G
mate, Mate, be true to your mate, Be true to your
C Am G/B
mate, Mate, be true to your mate; 'Cause
C C/B♭ F/A F
life's a ship we're sail - in' on, you need your mate to keep you strong so,
G C N.C.
Be true, be true to your mate. Be true to your
D♭ A♭
mate, Mate, be true to your mate, Be true to your
D♭ B♭m7 A♭/C
mate, Mate, be true to your mate; 'Cause
D♭ D♭/C♭ G♭/B♭ G♭
life's a ship we're sail - in' on, you need your mate to keep you strong so,
A♭ D♭
Be true, be true to your mate, Mate!

Being Big

Words and Music by
HERB OWEN

Saul is might - y big, the big - gest fel - low in the ar - my,
but he is - n't big e - nough to lick the gi - ant in the
land. Da - vid's might - y small
com - pared to that Phil - is - tine sol - dier,
but he
licked him an - y - way be - cause he had the in - ward big - ness of a man.
You can be big on the out - side and not win the bat - tle.
Spir - i - tual vic - t'ries just aren't won that way. Be - in'
big on the in - side will give you the pow - er to win the big bat - tle if you
watch and pray. You can be watch and pray.

Boys and Girls for Jesus

Words and Music by
WENDELL P. LOVELESS

Boys and girls for Je - sus,
this our ear - nest prayer.
Boys and girls for Je - sus,
home, at school, at play, and ev - 'ry -
where we'll tell the world of life in
Je - sus. He is all our
song. There is
all you need in Je - sus. Won't you
come a - long?

Being Me

Words and Music by
DOTTIE RAMBO

Rhythmic (𝅗𝅥=120)
G
1. If I were a bird,
(2.) I were a bell
3. I am a light;
I could fly
I could chime,
I can shine.
high as the stars
"ring, ding - a - ling"
The light of the world,
in the sky.
all the time.
I can shine.
C G D7
But a bird I'll nev - er be, so I'm hap - py, you
But a bell I'll nev - er be, so I'm hap - py, you
Je - sus' love shines through me, so I'm hap - py, you
G D7 G
see, just be - ing me, be - ing me.
see, just be - ing me, be - ing me.
see, just be - ing me, be - ing me.
3rd time to Coda
C G
Be - ing me, be - ing free,
D G
be - ing all I can be,

C
G
D7
I can pass ev - 'ry test, 'cause I'll give it my
G
D7
best just be - ing me, be - ing
1. G
2. G
D.S. al Coda
me. 2. If me.
CODA
C
G
me, be - ing free, be - ing
D7
G
C
all I can be, I can pass ev - 'ry
G
D7
G
D7
test, 'cause I'll give it my best just be - ing me,
G
C
be - ing me. I can al - ways be my -
G
D7
G
1. D C D
self, bet - ter than an - y - bod - y else, just be - ing me.
C D C D
2. D C D
Be - ing me.
C D C D
G
Be - ing me!

Bless-a My Soul

Words and Music by
JANET MCMAHAN-WILSON

Spiritual
Dm
Bless - a my soul. Oh Lord, bless - a my
soul. Bless - a my soul. Oh Lord,
A
bless - a my soul. You
Dm A Dm
walk up - on the clouds up high and ride Your char - iot
A Dm
through the sky. Lord, Lord, Lord,
B♭m
bless - a my soul. Bless - a my
E♭m
soul. Oh Lord, bless - a my soul.
Bless - a my soul. Oh Lord, bless - a my
B♭ E♭m
soul. Cre - a - tion sees Your

B♭ E♭m B♭
might - y deeds. Lord, You sup - ply all of my needs.
E♭m
Lord, Lord, Lord, bless - a my soul.
Bm Em
Bless - a my soul. Oh Lord, bless - a my
soul. Bless - a my soul. Oh Lord,
B
bless - a my soul. You
Em B
formed the heav - ens with Your hand. The
Em B Em
earth was made at Your com - mand. Lord, Lord, Lord,
bless - a my soul. Bless - a my
soul. Bless - a my soul.

Bumble, Stumble, Fumble

Words and Music by
ELLEN TIFT

Shuffle (♩=138)
A
1. E - ven when I bum - ble, stum - ble, fum - ble, God won't let me
2. E - ven when I mum - ble, jum - ble, grum - ble, God will al - ways
(3.) if I ac - ci - dent - ly make a blun - der, I don't have to
E7
tum - ble.
teach me.
won - der.
On a
Bm
E7
E - ven when I tee - ter or I tot - ter, He won't let me
E - ven when I'm grouch - y or I'm grump - y, He wants me to
bad day or a glad day or a sad day, God is still the
A
A7
A7/C♯
fall.
learn.
same.
When I
When I
When I
D
D+
D6
land right on my face and I need a lit - tle grace, He'll
have a hard day and I seem to lose my way, He's
make a big mis - take, there is com - fort I can take; He'll
A
G
F♯7
nev - er cease to love me. Oh,
al - ways there to lead me. Oh,
nev - er cease to love me. So,

3rd time to Coda
Bm E Bm7 E7
bum - ble, stum - ble, tee - ter, tot - ter, tum - ble, fum - ble, He loves
grum - ble, grouch - y, grump - y, mum - ble, jum - ble, grum - ble, He loves
bum - ble, stum - ble, tee - ter, tot - ter,
1. A
me.
2. A
me.
A Bm7
Je - sus al - ways teach - es me to
E A
lis - ten and o - bey, be - cause He loves me
B7 E7
D.C. al Coda
end - less - ly. I like to live that way. 3. But
CODA
Bm E C♯m F♯
tum - ble, fum - ble, mum - ble, grum - ble, ev - 'ry time He's good to me, I
C♯m F♯7 Bm E
know it al - ways keeps me hum - ble. Bum - ble, stum - ble, fum - ble, mum - ble,
Bm7 E7 A
jum - ble, grum - ble, I love Him.

By the Rivers of Babylon

Words and Music by
JANET MCMAHAN-WILSON

Bright shuffle
C9(♯5) F
By the riv - ers of Bab - y - lon we
B♭ C7 F C9(♯5) F
hung our heads and cried. By the riv - ers of Bab - y - lon
G C7
we sat down at the wa - ter's side. We
F F7 B♭
hung our harps on the wil - low trees and talked of all those
D♭7 F/C F A/E D
"used to be's." Lord, we fell down on our knees by the
G C7 F B♭7
riv - ers of Bab - y - lon. Though we were in a
F
for - eign land, we still were in Je - ho - vah's hand. Our
B♭7 C7 D♭7
cap - tors could not keep us down. We kept on mak - ing a
C7
joy - ful sound. Glo - ry, glo - ry hal - le - lu - jah!

D♭
Glo - ry, glo - ry hal-le-lu - jah! By the riv-ers of
D♭9(♯5) G♭ B D♭7 G♭
Bab - y-lon we hung our heads and cried.
D♭9(♯5) G♭
By the riv-ers of Bab - y-lon we
A♭ D♭7 G♭
sat down at the wa-ter's side. We hung our harps on the
G♭7 B D7
wil-low trees and talked of all those "used to be's."
G♭/D♭ G♭ B♭/F E♭ A♭ D♭7 G♭
Lord, we fell down on our knees by the riv-ers of Bab-y - lon.
A♭ D♭7 G♭
By the riv - ers of Bab - y - lon,
A♭
Lord, we gath - ered and
D♭ A♭ D♭ G♭
sang our song by the riv-ers of Bab-y - lon.

Buildin' Up the Body of Christ

Words and Music by
PAM ANDREWS and JOHNATHAN CRUMPTON

In a shuffle (♩.=162)
We need our feet for walk - in'__ when we're stroll-in' down the beach.
We need our mouth for talk - in'__ and when we want to eat. We need our
mind for think-in' and our eyes for blink-in' and a heart to give a beat.
We're pump-in' up. We're pump-in' down. We're work-in' out. We're
run-nin' a-round. We're build - in' up the bod-y of Je - sus Christ. We're step-
- pin' up, step-pin' back, tak-in' ad-vice__ on us - ing ev-'ry part and
its a-bil - i - ty__ with-in the bod-y of Christ.
We need peo-ple for prais-
- in'__ to give glo-ry to the Lord. We need peo-ple for pray-

- in' to bring heal - ing to the world. We need teach - ers for teach - in' and
preach - ers for preach - in' the truth of God's great Word!
We're pump - in' up. We're pump - in' down. We're work - in' out. We're
run - nin' a - round. We're build - in' up the bod - y of Je - sus Christ. We're step -
- pin' up, step - pin' back, tak - in' ad - vice on us - ing ev - 'ry part and
its a - bil - i - ty with - in the bod - y of Christ.
Dem bones, dem bones, dem dry bones, dem bones, dem bones, dem
dry bones, dem bones, dem bones, dem dry bones, now hear the Word of the
Build gradually
Lord. The foot bone's con - nect - ed to the an - kle bone. The

E
F
an - kle bone's con - nect - ed to the leg bone. The leg bone's con - nect - ed to the
F♯
hip bone. The hip bone's con - nect - ed to the back bone. The
G
A♭
back bone's con - nect - ed to the neck bone. The neck bone's con - nect - ed to the
A
head bone. Now hear the Word of the Lord. Now
B♭7
E♭
hear the Word of the Lord. We're pump - in' up.
B♭
A♭
B♭
A♭
We're pump - in' down. We're work - in' out. We're run - nin' a - round. We're build -
E♭
B♭
E♭
A♭
E♭
- in' up the bod - y of Je - sus Christ. We're step - pin' up, step - pin' back,
B♭
E♭
A♭
E♭
B♭
E♭
A♭
tak - in' ad - vice on us - ing ev - 'ry part and its a - bil - i - ty
1. A♭/B♭
2. A♭/B♭
E♭
with - in the bod - y of Christ. with - in the bod - y of Christ.

Call on the Name of the Lord

(To the tune of Hickory Dickory Dock)

Words and Music by
JANET MCMAHAN-WILSON,
TED WILSON and ED KEE

Call on the name of the Lord. Call on the name of the Lord.

1. Like Dan - iel in the li - on's den, call on the name of the Lord.
2. Gol - i - ath's who Da - vid slew when he called on the name of the Lord.

3. Call on the name of the Lord. Call on the name of the Lord. The ra - vens fed E - li - jah bread when he called on the name of the Lord.
4. Paul in jail could nev - er fail when he called on the name of the Lord.

5. Call on the name of the Lord. Call on the name of the Lord. No - ah stayed dry when the storm filled the sky 'cause he called on the name of the Lord.

6. Call on the name of the Lord. Call on the name of the Lord. He's al - ways there to hear our prayer. Call on the name of the Lord.

Cartoons

Words and Music by
CHRIS RICE

E(no3) B(add4) A2 E(no3) B(add4)
Spoken: Cowabungalujah, dude!
Mu - tant Nin - ja Tur - tles
A2 E(no3) B(add4) A2
Spoken: Kermit the Frog here, singing:
Then there's "Hi - ho - la - lu -
E(no3) B(add4) A2 E(no3) B(add4)
- jah!" And that lit - tle bald guy, El -
A2 E(no3) B(add4) A2
mer Fudd, "How - wa - wuh - wah!"
E(no3) A2
I was think - ing the oth - er day, what if car - toons got saved?
E(no3) B(add4) A2 E(no3) B(add4)
They'd start sing - ing praise in a whole new way.
A2 E(no3) B(add4) A2
Oh, that big ol' moose and his friend Rock - ie, "Lew - ie - ga -
E(no3) B(add4) A2 E(no3) B(add4)
lu - jah!" And my fa - vorite bear named Yo -
A2 E(no3) B(add4) A2
- gi, "Ah, Boo - boo - la - lu - jah!" Then there's

E(no3) B(add4) A2 E A
all those lit - tle blue guys. La, la, la, la, la, la.
E B E(no3) B(add4) A2
La, la, la - le - lu - jah! How 'bout
E(no3) B(add4) A2 E(no3) B(add4)
Bea - vis and that oth - er guy? Nah!
A2 E(no3)
There's a point to this loon - ie tune;
A2 E(no3) B(add4)
I'm not an an - i - ma - ni - ac! There's a lot of prais - in' to do, and
A2 E(no3) B(add4)
car - toons weren't made for that. It's our job.
A2 E(no3) B(add4) A2
So let's sing, "Hal - le - lu - jah!" Hal - le - lu -
E(no3) B(add4) A2 E(no3) B(add4)
- jah! Hal - le - lu - jah!
A2 E(no3) B(add4) A2
Ya - ba - da - ba - lu - jah! Scoo - bie - doo - bie -
E(no3) B(add4) A2 E(no3) B(add4)
lu - jah! Ra - ra - ru - rah!

Cast Your Burden on the Lord

Words and Music by
JANET MCMAHAN-WILSON

Tenderly
D
F♯m
1. Cast your bur - den on the Lord, for He is near you.
(2.) bur - den on the Lord. He will sus - tain you.
Bm
A
G
D/F♯
Cast your bur - den on the Lord, be - cause He cares.
Cast your bur - den on the Lord, be - cause He cares.
G6
A
D
F♯m
Cast your bur - den on the Lord, for He will hear you.
Cast your bur - den on the Lord, for He has claimed you.
Bm
G
D/A
Bm/A
G/A
Cast your bur - den on the Lord in
Cast your bur - den on the Lord in
1. D
prayer. 2. Cast your
2. D
G
prayer. Cast your
D/A
rit.
Bm/A
D
bur - den on the Lord in prayer.

Celebration Song

Words and Music by
JANET MCMAHAN-WILSON

Swing feel
F
Dm
Gm7
C
Praise the Lord with the trum - pet sound,
F
Dm
C
for the Lord is great.
F
Dm
Gm7
C
Praise the Lord, ev - 'ry - one a - round.
F
B♭
F
Come on and cel - e - brate.
B♭7
Praise the Lord with the lute and flute.
F
Play your horn with a root - a - toot - toot.
B♭7
Crash the cym - bal. Clap your hands.

G
C
Shout hal - le - lu - jah! Come sing and dance.
D
Come sing and dance.
G
Em
Praise the Lord with the
Am7
D
G
Em
D
trum - pet sound, for the Lord is great.
G
Em
Praise the Lord, ev - 'ry -
Am7
D
G
C
G
one a - round. Come on and cel - e - brate,
C
G
for the Lord is great.
C
G
Come on and cel - e - brate!

Climb, Climb up Sunshine Mountain

Traditional

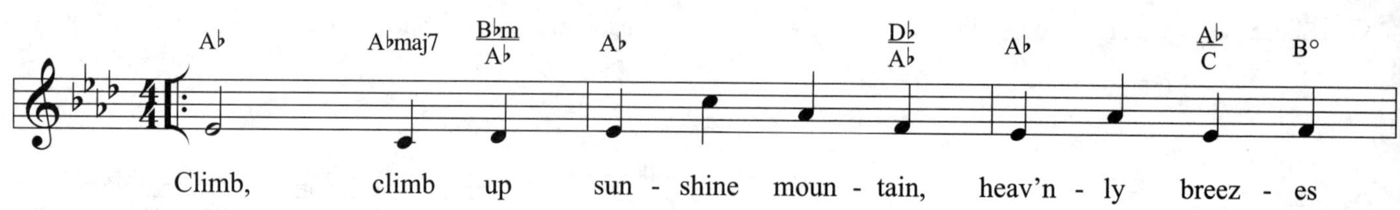
A♭
A♭maj7
B♭m/A♭
A♭
D♭/A♭
A♭
A♭/C
B°
Climb, climb up sun - shine moun - tain, heav'n - ly breez - es

E♭9/B♭
E♭7
A♭/E♭
E♭7
D♭/E♭
blow. Climb, climb up sun - shine moun - tain,

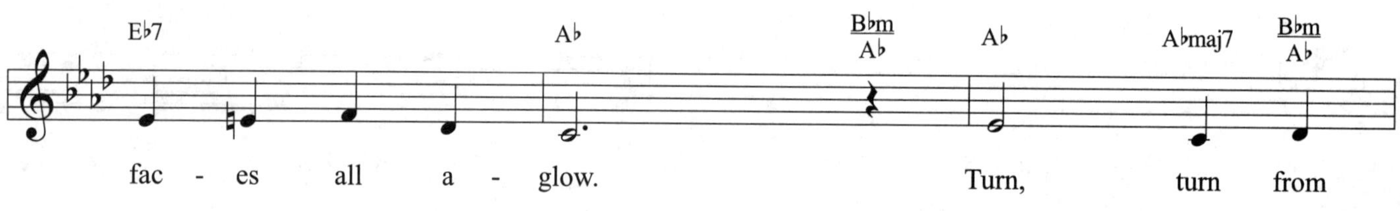
E♭7
A♭
B♭m/A♭
A♭
A♭maj7
B♭m/A♭
fac - es all a - glow. Turn, turn from

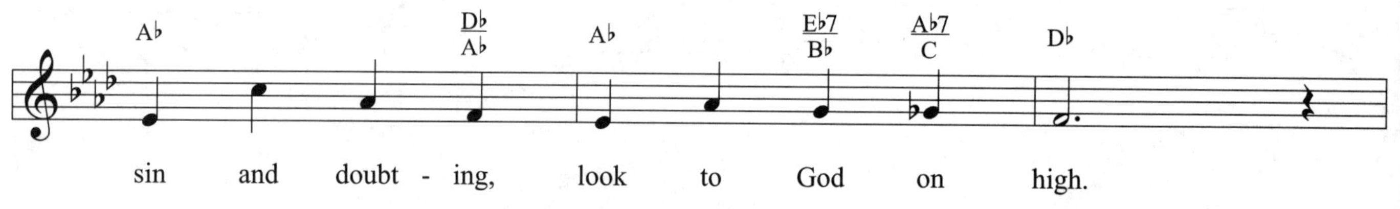
A♭
D♭/A♭
A♭
E♭7/B♭
A♭7/C
D♭
sin and doubt - ing, look to God on high.

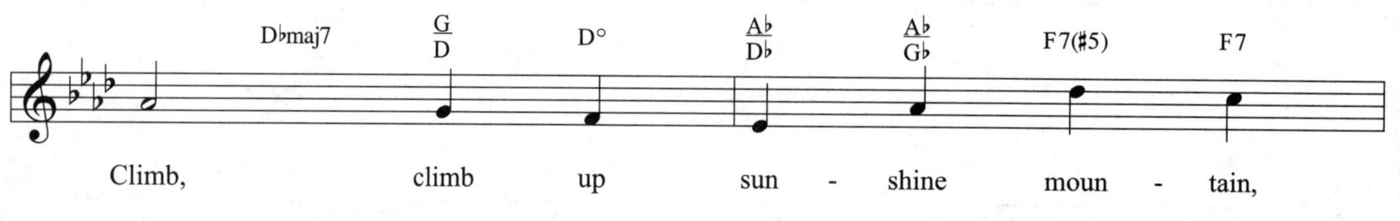
D♭maj7
G/D
D°
A♭/D♭
A♭/G♭
F7(♯5)
F7
Climb, climb up sun - shine moun - tain,

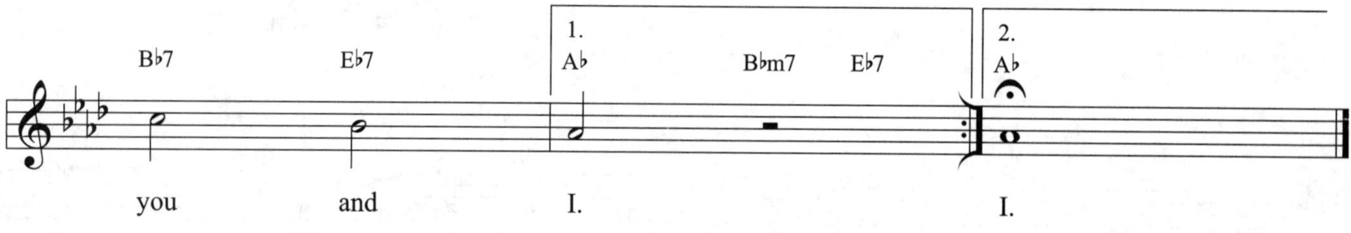
B♭7
E♭7
1.
A♭
B♭m7
E♭7
2.
A♭
you and I. I.

Come and Go with Me

Traditional

1. Come and go with me to my Fa - ther's house,
2. Je - sus is the way to my Fa - ther's house,
to my Fa - ther's house, to my Fa - ther's house.
to my Fa - ther's house, to my Fa - ther's house.
Come and go with me to my Fa - ther's house where there's
Je - sus is the way to my Fa - ther's house where there's
joy, joy, joy. joy.
joy, joy,
1.
2.
Come and go with me to my Fa-ther's house, to my Fa-ther's house,
to my Fa - ther's house. Come and go with me
to my Fa-ther's house where there's joy, joy, joy, where there's
joy, joy, joy.

Come Bless the Lord

Traditional

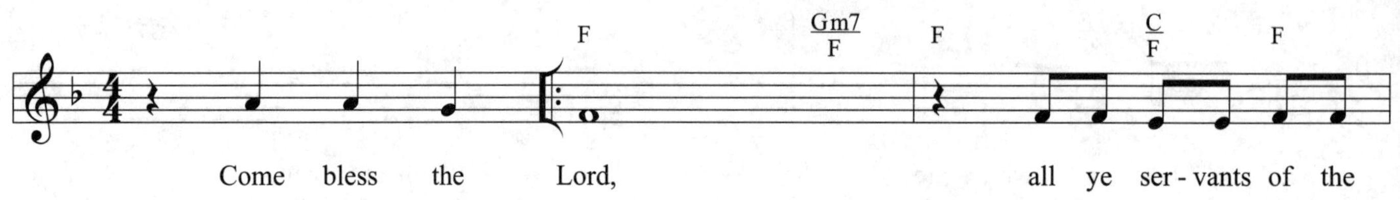
F Gm7/F F C/F F
Come bless the Lord, all ye ser-vants of the

Gm7 Gm9 C7 Gm7 Gm9
Lord, who stand by night

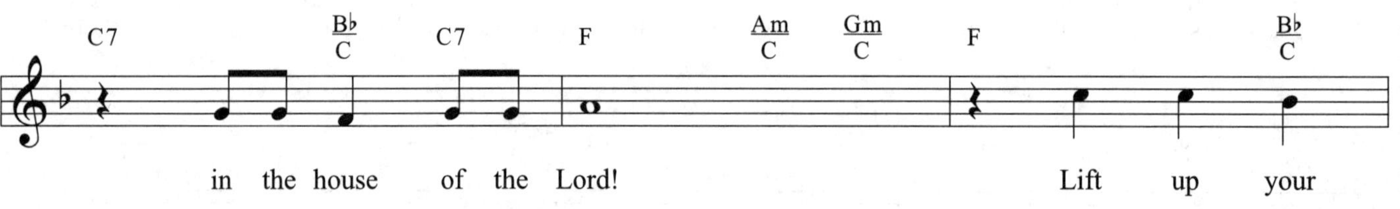
C7 B♭/C C7 F Am/C Gm/C F B♭/C
in the house of the Lord! Lift up your

F Gm7/C F7 Cm7/F F7 B♭ B♭/A
hands in the ho - ly place,

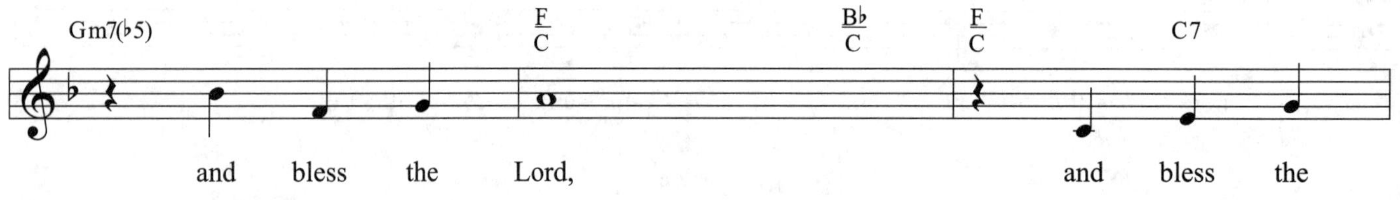
Gm7(♭5) F/C B♭/C F/C C7
and bless the Lord, and bless the

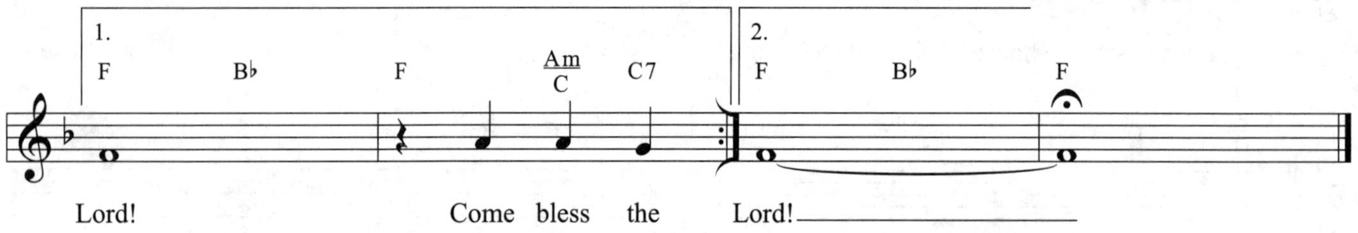
1. 2.
F B♭ F Am/C C7 F B♭ F
Lord! Come bless the Lord!

Come into His Presence Singing

Traditional

C
C/E
F
C
1. Come in - to His pres - ence sing - ing al - le - lu - ia,
2. Come in - to His pres - ence sing - ing Je - sus is Lord,

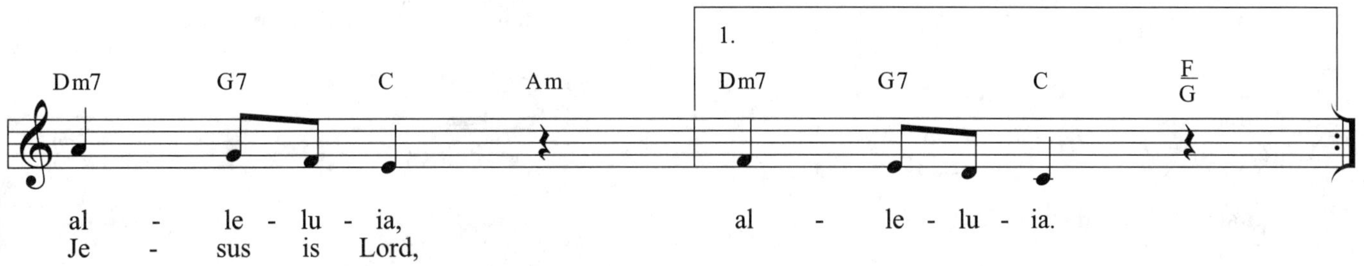
1.
Dm7
G7
C
Am
Dm7
G7
C
F/G
al - le - lu - ia,
Je - sus is Lord,
al - le - lu - ia.

2.
Dm7
G7
C
A♭7
D♭
A♭7/E♭
D♭/F
A♭7/E♭
Je - sus is Lord.
3. Praise the Lord to - geth - er, sing - ing
4. Praise the Lord to - geth - er, sing - ing

D♭
A♭7/E♭
D♭/F
D♭
G♭
D♭
B♭m7
wor - thy the Lamb,
glo - ry to God,
wor - thy the Lamb,
glo - ry to God,

1.
2.
E♭m7
A♭7
D♭
B♭m7
E♭m7
A♭7
D♭
G♭/A♭
E♭m7
A♭7
D♭
wor - thy the Lamb,
glo - ry to God,
wor - thy the Lamb.
glo - ry to God.

Come Praise the Lord

Words and Music by
STEPHEN ELKINS

B♭7 E♭ B♭ E♭ Gm7 G♭°
1. Day or night, (day or night) we will praise the Lord. Day or
(2.) shine, (rain or shine) we will praise the Lord. Rain or
Fm7 B♭7 A♭maj7/F B♭7 E♭ B♭7 E♭
night, (day or night) we will praise the Lord. Day or night, (day or night) we will
shine, (rain or shine) we will praise the Lord. Rain or shine, (rain or shine) we will
Fm7 E♭/G A♭ E♭/B♭ A♭maj7/F B♭7 1. E♭ B♭7
praise the Lord. All ye chil - dren, come praise the Lord! 2. Rain or
praise the Lord. All ye chil - dren, come praise the
2. E♭ E♭/D♭ B7 E B E G♯m7 G°
Lord! 3. Big or small, (big or small) we will praise the Lord. Big or
F♯m7 B7 Amaj7/F♯ B7 E B7 E
small, (big or small) we will praise the Lord. Big or small, (big or small) we will
F♯m7 E/G♯ A E/B Amaj7/F♯ B7 E B♯7
praise the Lord. All ye chil - dren, come praise the Lord! 4. Soft or
F C F Am7 A♭° Gm7 C
loud, (soft or loud) we will praise the Lord. Soft or loud, (soft or loud) we will
B♭maj7/G C F C7 F C7/E F/E♭ B♭/D
praise the Lord. Soft or loud, (soft or loud) we will praise the Lord. All ye
F/C B♭maj7/G C7 1. F B♭ B° 2. F
chil - dren, come praise the Lord! All ye Lord!

Creature Praise

Words and Music by
DAVID MATTHEWS

E♭ E♭/D♭ A♭/C C♭7 E♭/B♭ A♭/B♭ E♭
Large crea - tures, small crea-tures, short and tall crea - tures, come now and praise the Lord!
Gm7 F♯m7 Fm7 A♭/B♭ E♭ E♭/D♭ A♭/C C♭7
Young crea - tures, old crea - tures, hot and cold crea - tures,
E♭/B♭ A♭/B♭ E♭ E♭/B♭ E♭/C E♭/D E♭ E♭/B♭
come now and praise the Lord! Sing praise to the
A♭/E♭ E♭ E♭/B♭ E♭7 A♭ A♭/E♭ A♭ E♭ E♭/B♭ E♭/C E♭/D E♭ E♭/B♭
Fa - ther, sing praise to the Son, sing praise to the
A♭/E♭ E♭ E♭/B♭ Cm7 F7 B♭7 E♭ E♭/B♭
Spir - it Who makes all crea - tures one. Sing praise for the
A♭/E♭ E♭ E♭7/B♭ A♭ A♭m A♭m6/C♭
good - ness of what the Lord has done.
E♭/B♭ Cm Fm7(4) A♭/B♭ E♭ 1. E♭/C E♭/B♭
Let all crea - tures praise the Lord!
E♭ Gm7 F♯m7 Fm7 A♭/B♭ 2. E♭/B♭ E♭ E♭/D Cm Cm/B♭ Cm/A
E♭/B♭ Cm Fm7(4) A♭/B♭ E♭ Gm7 F♯m7 Fm7 A♭/B♭ E♭ E♭/B♭ E♭6/9
Let all crea - tures praise the Lord!

Creation Education

Words and Music by
MARY JORDAN and JANET MCMAHAN-WILSON

Triplet feel (♩=114)

There's no more a - maz - ing ed - u - ca - tion than to stud - y God's cre - a - tion. What a

great im - ag - i - na - tion it would take to make a star! It's an awe - some in - spi - ra - tion how He

made each con - stel - la - tion shine with bright il - lu - mi - na - tion from so far.

When I look up in the sky my heart is filled with won - der.

There's no won - der why. There's no more a - maz - ing ed - u - ca - tion than to

stud - y God's cre - a - tion. What a great im - ag - i - na - tion it would

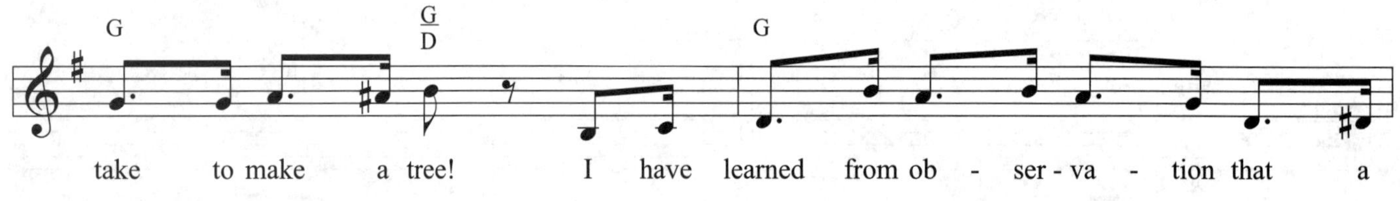

take to make a tree! I have learned from ob - ser - va - tion that a

seed at ger - mi - na - tion stores im - por - tant in - for - ma - tion per - fect - ly.

B
Em
A7
When I see a tree so tall my heart is filled with won - der from the
D7
D A7 D7 N.C.
G
won - der of it all. There's no more a - maz - ing ed - u - ca - tion than to
A7
A7/C♯
D7
stud - y God's cre - a - tion. What a great im - ag - i - na - tion it would
G
G/D
G
take to make a bug! They have great com - mu - ni - ca - tion, lots of
A7
A7/C♯
D7
G G/D G N.C.
legs for trans - por - ta - tion, man - y types of hab - i - ta - tion; one's a rug.
B
Em
A7
When I see a bug pa - rade, my heart is filled with won - der.
D7
D A7 D7 N.C.
G
They're so won - der - f'lly made. There's no more a - maz - ing ed - u - ca - tion than to
A7
A7/C♯
D7
stud - y God's cre - a - tion. What an awe - some rev - e - la - tion of His
G
A7
D7
G G/D G
love! What an awe - some rev - e - la - tion of His love!

Dance Just Like David

Words and Music by
DAVE HUNT

High energy (♩=120)
D(no3)
1. I'm saving up my energy until the time is right.
(2.) fun to dance a funky dance, moving to the beat.
F G D(no3)
I want to let my Jesus know that He is out of sight.
I love to use my energy getting down with happy feet.
G F D(no3)
He's worthy of this energy, and I want to let it show.
I'm dancing just like David danced when he danced before the Lord.
F G A7
My joy for Him is welling up and about to overflow.
There's overwhelming joy, and I can't contain it anymore.
Dm G Dm A7
Dance just like David; dance unto the Lord.
Dm G C F Dm
Dance just like David, 'til I can't dance anymore.
G D A7
Dance just like David; dance unto the Lord.
Dm G C F
1. D(no3)
Dance just like David, 'til I can't dance anymore.

2. It's
2. Dm
more.
It's
Dm F
start-ing to be-gin. I can bare-ly hold it in. I can feel it in my soul. I'm a-bout to lose con-trol. It's
Dm
start-ing to be-gin. I can bare-ly hold it in. I can feel it in my soul. I'm a-bout to lose con-trol. It's
start-ing to be-gin. I can bare-ly hold it in. I can feel it in my soul. I'm a-bout to lose con-
A7 Dm G
trol. Dance just like Da - vid;
Dm A7 Dm G
dance un - to the Lord. Dance just like Da - vid, 'til I
C F Dm G
can't dance an-y more. Dance just like Da - vid;
Dm A7 Dm G
dance un - to the Lord. Dance just like Da - vid, 'til I
1.2. C F Dm
can't dance an-y - more.
3. C F Dm
can't dance an-y - more.

Dare to Be a Daniel

Words and Music by
P. P. BLISS

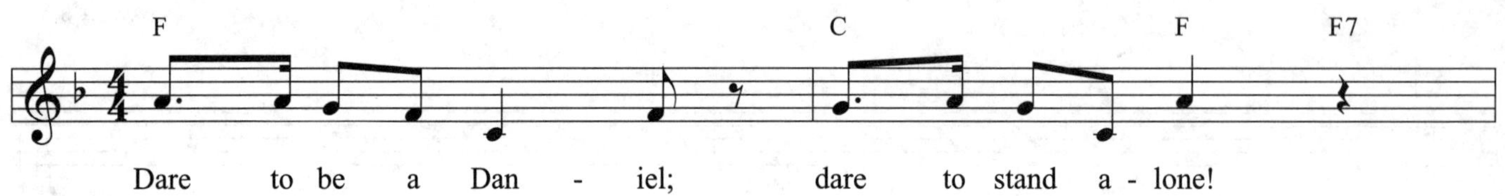
F
C
F
F7
Dare to be a Dan - iel; dare to stand a - lone!

2nd time to Coda
B♭
Gm
F/C
B♭maj7/C
C7
F
B♭/C
Dare to have a pur - pose firm; dare to make it known.

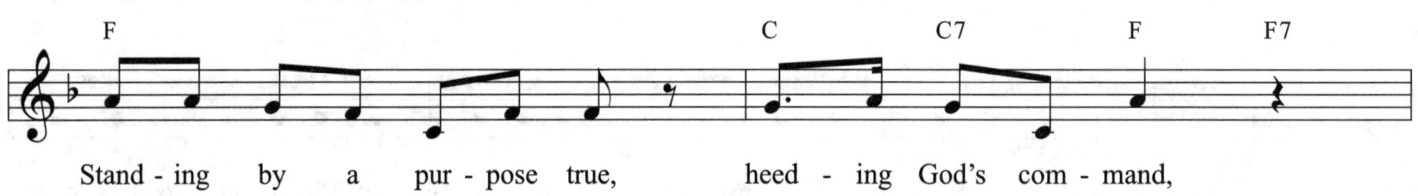
F
C
C7
F
F7
Stand - ing by a pur - pose true, heed - ing God's com - mand,

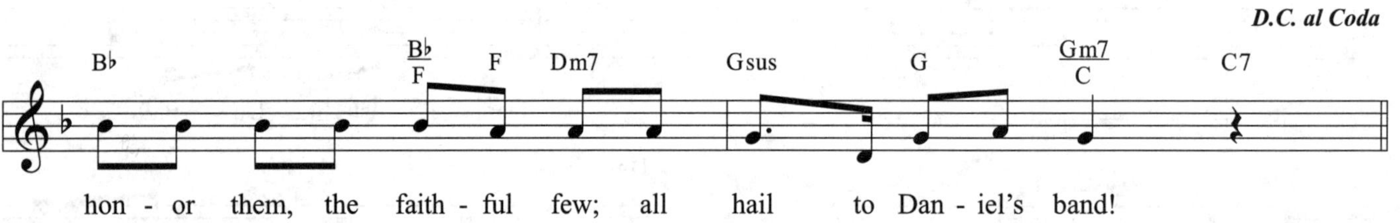
D.C. al Coda
B♭
B♭/F
F
Dm7
Gsus
G
Gm7/C
C7
hon - or them, the faith - ful few; all hail to Dan - iel's band!

CODA
F/C
B♭maj7/C
C7
F
C/D
D7
G
G/B
dare to make it known. Dare to be a Dan - iel;

Am7
D7
C
D/C
C
Am7(♭5)
G/D
Cmaj7/D
D7
G
dare to stand a - lone! Dare to have a pur-pose firm; dare to make it known.

Deep and Wide

Traditional

Moderato
A
Amaj7
E
A7
D
Dmaj7
A
D6
D
Deep and wide, deep and wide, there's a
A
F♯m7
Bm7
E7
Bm7
F♯
E7
foun - tain flow - ing deep and wide.
A
Amaj7
E
A7
D
Dmaj7
A
D6
D♯°
A
E
E7
Deep and wide, deep and wide, there's a foun - tain flow - ing deep and
1.
A
D
E
2.
A
A
G
F7
Cm7
G
F7
A
wide. wide.
B♭
B♭maj7
F
Fm7
B♭7
E♭
E♭maj7
B♭
E°
Deep and wide, deep and wide, there's a
B♭
F
Gm7
C7
B♭
D
C7
E
F7
E♭
G
F7
A
B♭
B♭maj7
F
Fm7
B♭7
foun - tain flow - ing deep and wide. Deep and wide,
E♭
E♭6
E°
B♭
F
F7
B♭
deep and wide, there's a foun - tain flow - ing deep and wide.

Deep in My Heart

Words and Music by
JANET MCMAHAN-WILSON

Waltz feel (♩.=60)
A Amaj7 A6 A♯°7
1. I've got the light of the Lord shin - ing deep in my heart,
(2.) love of the Lord liv - ing deep in my heart,
(3.) word of the Lord hid - den deep in my heart,
Bm7 E Am E A Amaj7
deep in my heart, deep in my heart, the light of the Lord shin - ing
deep in my heart, deep in my heart, the love of the Lord liv - ing
deep in my heart, deep in my heart, the word of the Lord hid - den
A6 A♯°7 Bm7 E7
3rd time to Coda
deep in my heart. And noth - ing can take it a -
deep in my heart. And noth - ing can take it a -
deep in my heart. And noth - ing can take it a -
1. A Amaj7 Bm7 E 2. A
way. 2. I've got the way.
E7 A F♯m
When I'm up and when I'm down, my
B7 E E° E
D.S. al Coda
Lord is al - ways a - round. 3. I've got the
CODA
A Amaj7 Bm7 E7 A Amaj7
way. Noth - ing can take it a - way.
Bm7 E7 A E A E A
Noth - ing can take it a - way.

Do Right

Words and Music by
JANET MCMAHAN-WILSON

Joyfully (♩=144)
Do right. Do what the Lord says. Do right.
Do what His word says. Do right. Ev - er - y day and
ev - er - y night, do right.
3rd time to Coda
right. Some - times when you're not sure what you should
do, just ask your - self what's good
and pure and true.
D.S. al Coda
CODA
right. Do right. Do what the Lord says.
Do right. Do what His word says. Do right.
Ev - er - y day and ev - er - y night, do right.

Deep, Deep

Writer Unknown

SOLO
Do you love your Je - sus deep down in your heart?
CHOIR
Yes, I love my Je - sus deep down in my heart.
SOLO
Well, do you love your Je - sus deep down in your heart?
CHOIR
Yes, I love my Je - sus deep down in my heart.
SOLO
Well,
CHOIR & SOLO
Deep, deep, whoa, deep down, down, deep down in my heart I love You, Je - sus.
Deep, deep, whoa, deep down, down, deep down in my heart.
Deep, deep, whoa, deep down, down, deep down in my heart I love You, Je - sus.
Deep, deep, whoa, deep down, down, Deep down in my heart.
Deep down in my heart. Deep down in my heart.

Do Lord

Traditional

G
G/D
C/D
G
G/D
Am/D
G
G/D
Am/D
Do Lord, oh, do Lord, oh, do re - mem - ber
G
Gsus/A
G7/B
C
C/G
D/G
C
C/G
me. Do Lord, oh, do Lord, oh,
C
G
G
G/D
C/D
do re - mem - ber me. Do Lord, oh,
G
G/D
Am/D
G
B7/F♯
Em
Cm6/E♭
do Lord, oh, do re - mem - ber me
G/D
Gmaj7/D
Am7
D7
C/D
G
C/G
C/D
way be - yond the blue.
G
G/D
G
G/D
G
G/D
G
G/B
1. I've got a home in Glo - ry - land that out - shines the sun.
2. I took Je - sus as my Sav - ior; you take Him, too.
C
C/G
C
C/G
C
I've got a home in Glo - ry - land that out - shines the
I took Je - sus as my Sav - ior; you take Him,

G G/D G G/D
sun. I've got a home in Glo - ry - land that
too. I took Je - sus as my Sav - ior;
G B7 B7/D♯ Em Cm6 G/D Am7 D7
out - shines the sun way be - yond the
you take Him, too, while He's call - ing
1. G C/D 2. G D♭/E♭
blue. you!
A♭ A♭/E♭ D♭/E♭ A♭7 D♭/E♭ A♭ B♭m7/E♭ A♭ A♭sus/B♭ A♭/C
Do Lord, oh, do Lord, oh, do re - mem - ber me.
D♭ D♭/A♭ E♭/A♭ D♭7 D♭7/A♭ D♭7 A♭ D♭/E♭
Do Lord, oh, do Lord, oh, do re - mem - ber me.
A♭ D♭/F A♭7 D♭/E♭ A♭ Gm7 C7 Fm D♭m6/E
Do Lord, oh, do Lord, oh, do re - mem - ber me
A♭/E♭ A♭maj7/E♭ B♭m7 E♭7 Fm Fm/E♭ Dm7(♭5)
way be - yond the blue,
A♭/E♭ A♭maj7/E♭ D♭maj7/E♭ E♭7 D♭/E♭ A♭sus A♭
way be - yond the blue.

Don't Bow Down to Idols

Words and Music by
TROY NILSSON and GENIE NILSSON

(♩=112)
TRIO
Cm
In the old - en days peo - ple used to bow and pray to the
Fm
G
i - dols tall, fat, med - i - um and small. They would bow and grov - el down
on their knees, slob - ber on their i - dols and kiss their feet. What a
Cm
Fm
sil - ly sight, you can see it did no good! For the stat - ues were made of
G
met - al, rocks and wood, And bend - ing down kiss - ing i - dol's toes, they
might as well been wor - ship - ping their play - dough! So,
Cm
TRIO
CHOIR
Don't bow down to i - dols, i - dols don't love you.
TRIO
CHOIR
Don't bow down to i - dols, that's com - mand - ment num - ber two.
TRIO
CHOIR
Don't bow down to i - dols, i - dols are a joke.

TRIO
ALL
Don't bow down to i - dols, they'll go up in smoke!
ALL
May - be we don't bow down to
i - dols made of stone, but we don't al - ways love
Fm
God and God a - lone. 'Cause we love our stuff and our -
G
selves and our things and we i - dol - ize peo - ple on T V! So,
Cm
Don't bow down to i - dols, i - dols don't love you.
Don't bow down to i - dols, that's com - mand - ment num - ber two.
Don't bow down to i - dols, i - dols are a joke.
1.
2.
Don't bow down to i - dols, they'll go up in smoke! they'll go up in smoke!

Down in My Heart
(I've Got the Joy)

Words and Music by
GEORGE W. COOKE

B♭ B♭maj7 E♭ B♭ B♭/F F7 B♭
1. I've got the joy, joy, joy, joy down in my heart, (Where?)
Cm7 F7 B♭ F7sus F7
down in my heart, (Where?) down in my heart. I've got the
B♭ B♭maj7 E♭ B♭ B♭/F F7 B♭
joy, joy, joy, joy down in my heart, (Where?)
2nd time to Coda
Cm7 F7 B♭ E♭ B♭/D Cm7 F7
down in my heart to stay! 2. I've got the
B♭ Dm7 E♭ B♭ B♭/F F7 B♭ B♭/D
love of Je - sus, love of Je - sus down in my heart, (Where?)
(3.) peace that pass - eth un - der - stand - ing down in my heart, (Where?)
Cm7 F7 B♭ F7sus F7
down in my heart, (Where?) down in my heart. I've got the
down in my heart, (Where?) down in my heart. I've got the
B♭ Dm7 E♭ B♭ B♭/F D7/F♯ Gm
love of Je - sus, love of Je - sus, down in my heart, (Where?)
peace that pass - eth un - der - stand - ing down in my heart, (Where?)

Cm7 F7 B♭ E♭ B♭/D Cm7 F7
down in my heart to stay! 3. I've got the
down in my heart to stay! 4. I've got the
B♭ Dm7 E♭ B♭
(4.) won - der - ful love of my bless - ed Re - deem - er way
B♭/F F13 B♭ B♭/D Cm7 F7
down in the depths of my heart, (Where?) down in the depths of my heart, (Where?)
B♭ F7sus F7
down in the depths of my heart. I've got the
B♭ Dm7 E♭ B♭
won - der - ful love of my bless - ed Re - deem - er way
B♭/F D7/F♯ Gm Cm7 F7
down in the depths of my heart, (Where?) down in the depths of my heart to
D.S. al Coda
B♭ E♭ B♭/D Cm7 F7
stay! I've got the
CODA
B♭
stay!

Doxology

Words and Music by
THOMAS KEN and LOUIS BOURGEOIS

F C Dm Am Dm C F
Praise God, from whom all bless - ings flow; Praise

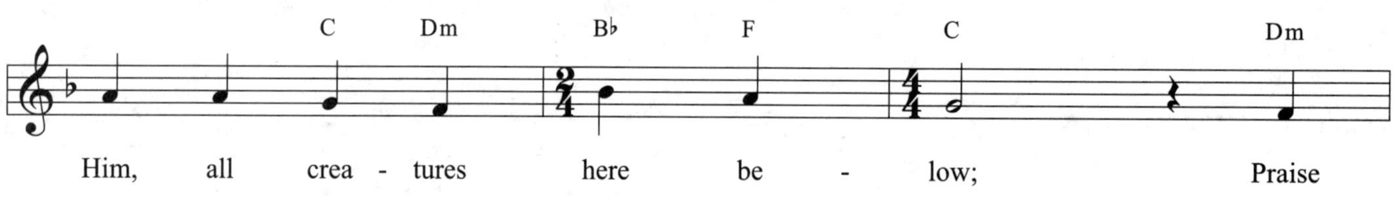
C Dm B♭ F C Dm
Him, all crea - tures here be - low; Praise

C/E F C Dm B♭ C7 Dm C/E
Him a - bove, ye heav'n - ly host; Praise

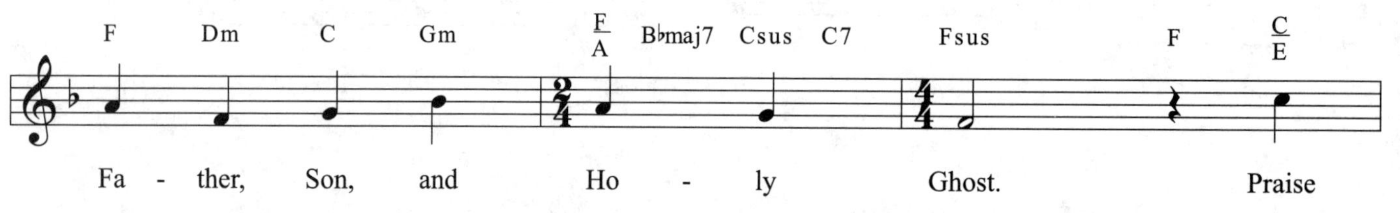
F Dm C Gm F/A B♭maj7 Csus C7 Fsus F C/E
Fa - ther, Son, and Ho - ly Ghost. Praise

F/E♭ B♭/D B♭m6/D♭ F/C C7 F B♭/F F
Fa - ther, Son, and Ho - ly Ghost. A - men.

Escaping in a Basket

(To the tune of A Tisket, a Tasket)

Words and Music by
RUTH ELAINE SCHRAM

C Dm7 G Dm7 G
Da - mas - cus, Da - mas - cus, the Gov - 'nor of Da - mas - cus want - ed Paul put in jail for
Dm7 G7 C C
preach - ing in Da - mas - cus, Da - mas - cus, Da - mas - cus, for preach - ing in Da - mas - cus. He
Dm7 G Dm7 G Dm7 G C Dm7 G7 C A♭7
want - ed Paul put in jail for preach - ing in Da - mas - cus. A
D♭ E♭m7 A♭ E♭m7 A♭
bas - ket, a bas - ket, they put him in a bas - ket. That's how Paul went down the wall, es -
E♭m7 A♭7 D♭ D♭
cap - ing in a bas - ket, a bas - ket, a bas - ket, es - cap - ing in a bas - ket.
E♭m7 A♭ E♭m7 A♭ E♭m7 A♭7 D♭ E♭m7 A♭7 D♭ A7
That's how Paul went down the wall, es - cap - ing in a bas - ket. He's
D Em7 A Em7 A
preach - ing. He's preach - ing. He's free a - gain and preach - ing. The world will know God loves them so. Of
Em7 A7 D D
Je - sus he is preach - ing. He's preach - ing. He's preach - ing. Of Je - sus he is preach - ing. The
Em7 A Em7 A Em7 A7 D Em7 A7 D
world will know God loves them so. Of Je - sus he is preach - ing.

Encouraging Words

Words and Music by
MARY JORDAN, TOM MCBRYDE
and JANET MCMAHAN-WILSON

In six
E/B E E/G# A Am
S - P - E - L - L, I am learn - ing to spell spec - ial
E F#7 F#m A6 B B/C# B7/D# E E/G#
words like G - L - A - D! J - E - S - U - S brings
A A9 E/B B E/B B7 E B A/C# B7/D#
me hap - pi - ness in - side my H - E - A - R - T.
E B7 E E/B E F#7
Words, won - der - ful words, I L - O - V - E what they
F#m B B/C# B7/D# E E/G# A D9
say. When - ev - er there's heard an en - cour - ag - ing word, there's
2nd time to Coda
E/B B E/B B7 E B A/C# B7/D# E E/G#
H - O - P - E on the way. Be a N - I - C - E F - R -
A Am E F#7 F#m A B B/C# B7/D#
I - E - N - D. Lend a H - A - N - D when you can. You'll
D.S. al Coda
E E/G# A D9 E/B B E/B B7 E B A/C# B7/D#
find J - O - Y. Just give it a try. It's P - A - R - T of God's plan.

CODA
E C Bb/D C7/E F F/A Bb Bbm
way. "T - H - A - N - K Y - O - U," you should say ev-'ry
F G7 Gm Bb C C/D C7/E F F/A
day to the L - O - R - D. He loves us S - O. Yes, we
Bb Eb9 F/C C F/C C7 F F/C
know that it's so when we read the B - I - B - L - E.
F C7 F F/C F G7
Words, won - der - ful words, I L - O - V - E what they
Gm Bb C C/D C7/E F F/A Bb Eb9
say. When - ev - er there's heard an en - cour - ag - ing word, there's
F/C C F/C C7 F F/C F F/A
slowing
H - O - P - E on the way. When - ev - er there's heard an en -
Bb Eb9 F/C C F/C C7 F F/C F/A F
a tempo
cour - ag - ing word, there's H - O - P - E on the way.

Every Day in Every Way

Words and Music by
HERB OWEN

C C6/G C Em/G G7
1. Ev - 'ry day in ev - 'ry way I love my Je - sus more and more.
2. Ev - 'ry time the dev - il finds me Je - sus fills me with His love,
G9 G7 F/C C
Ev - 'ry time I seem to find more rea - sons than I had be - fore.
nev - er leav - ing, al - ways be - ing all that I was dream - ing of.
Cmaj7/G C7 B♭/D C7/E F
He's the One who makes life fun and nev - er ev - er is a bore.
He is with me and will give me lots of pow - er from a - bove.
F♯°7 C/G Am 1. Dm7 G7
Ev - 'ry day in ev - 'ry way I love my Je - sus
Ev - 'ry day in ev - 'ry way I
C C6/G Cmaj7 C6/G 2. Dm7 G7 C G♭/A♭ A♭
more. love my Je - sus more.
D♭ B♭m/A♭ D♭maj7 E♭m7 A♭7
3. Ev - 'ry time I ask I find that He will hear me when I pray.
4. Take a look in - to the book and soon you'll start to un - der - stand
E♭m E♭maj7/B♭ E♭m7 A♭7 G♭/D♭ D♭
He is near me and will hear me ev - 'ry min - ute, ev - 'ry day.
all the glo - ry of the sto - ry: God, the Son, be - came a man!
Fm/A♭ A♭m7 C♭/D♭ D♭ G♭
How He un - der - stands I won - der, yet He loves me an - y - way!
You can be e - ter - nal - ly ex - act - ly just what He has planned.

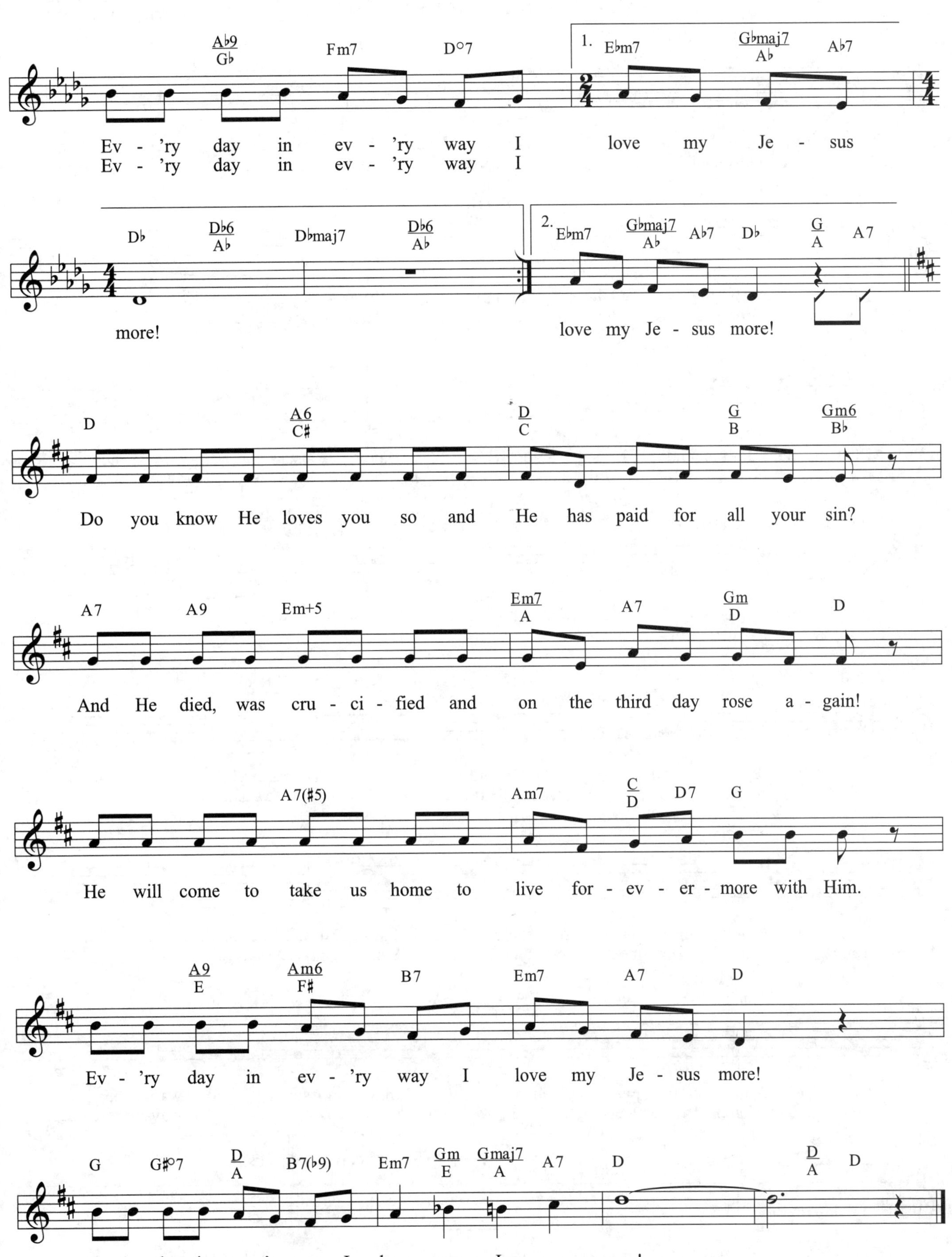
Ab9/Gb Fm7 D°7
1. Ebm7 Gbmaj7/Ab Ab7
Ev - 'ry day in ev - 'ry way I love my Je - sus
Ev - 'ry day in ev - 'ry way I
Db Db6/Ab Dbmaj7 Db6/Ab
2. Ebm7 Gbmaj7/Ab Ab7 Db G/A A7
more! love my Je - sus more!
D A6/C# D/C G/B Gm6/Bb
Do you know He loves you so and He has paid for all your sin?
A7 A9 Em+5 Em7/A A7 Gm/D D
And He died, was cru - ci - fied and on the third day rose a - gain!
A7(#5) Am7 C/D D7 G
He will come to take us home to live for - ev - er - more with Him.
A9/E Am6/F# B7 Em7 A7 D
Ev - 'ry day in ev - 'ry way I love my Je - sus more!
G G#°7 D/A B7(b9) Em7 Gm/E Gmaj7/A A7 D D/A D
Ev - 'ry day in ev - 'ry way I love my Je - sus more!

Every Day of the Week

(To the tune of Crawdad Hole)

Words and Music by
RUTH ELAINE SCHRAM

1. I'll read the Bi - ble and I'll say a prayer, Mon - day.
2. I'll sing a - bout His ten - der care, Wednes - day.
I'll read the Bi - ble and I'll say a prayer, Tues - day.
I'll sing a - bout His ten - der care, Thurs - day.
I'll read the Bi - ble and I'll say a prayer. I know Je - sus is al - ways there,
I'll sing a - bout His ten - der care. I know Je - sus is al - ways there,
ev - 'ry day of the week. week.
ev - 'ry day of the
3. I've got love and joy to share, Fri - day.
4. You go to church. I'll meet you there, Sun - day.
I've got love and joy to share, Sat - ur - day.
You go to church. I'll meet you there, Sun - day.
I've got love and joy to share. I know Je - sus is al - ways there,
You go to church. I'll meet you there. I know Je - sus is al - ways there,
ev - 'ry day of the week. week.
ev - 'ry day of the

Every Ounce of Me

Words and Music by
DAVID HUNT

Two-beat feel (♩.=164)
C
faster and faster each time
F
C
I will praise You. I will praise You with ev - 'ry ounce of
G
C
F
me. I lift my heart up to the Lord and
C
G
F
praise You with my hands, (hands!) feet, (feet!)
G
F
G
mouth, (ah!) nose, (snort!) tongue, (blah!)
F
1.
toes.
2.
D
G
I will praise You. I will praise You with
D
A
D
ev - 'ry ounce of me. I lift my heart up
G
D
A
to the Lord and praise You with my hands, (hands!)
G
A
G
feet, (feet!) mouth, (ah!) nose, (snort!)

A
G
tongue,
(blah!)
toes.
1. A
2.
E
A
E
I will praise You. I will praise You with ev - 'ry ounce of
B
E
A
me. I lift my heart up to the Lord and
E
B
A
praise You with my hands, (hands!) feet, (feet!)
B
A
B
mouth, (ah!) nose, (snort!) tongue, (blah!)
A
Last time to Coda
1. B
toes.
2.
E
slowing 3rd & 4th times
A2
1.2. Spin a - round, spin a - round, spin a -
(3.4.) down, slow - ing down, slow - ing
E
B
E
round, spin a - round; jump up and down, up and
down, slow - ing down, we're slow - ing down, squat - ting

A2 B 1.2.3.

down, up and down.
down to the ground.

2. Spin a -
3.4. Slow - ing

4.

E *accel. to end* A E

I will praise You. I will praise You with ev - 'ry ounce of

B E A

me. I lift my heart up to the Lord.

1. 2.

Spin a -

E A2 E

round, spin a - round, spin a - round, spin a -

B E A2

round; jump up and down, up and down, up and

B 1. 2. *D.S. al Coda* 𝄋

down. Spin a -

𝄌 **CODA**

E

Every Word of the Lord Is True

Words and Music by
JANET MCMAHAN-WILSON

Brightly (♩=120)
D
Bm
Em7
A
Ev - 'ry word of the Lord is true. Ev - 'ry
Em7
A
D
D7
word of the Lord is true. God
G
A
G
F♯m
B
Gm
wrote them in the Bi - ble for me and you. Ev - 'ry
2nd time to Coda
D
A7
D
D7
word of the Lord is true. So
Em7
A
F♯m
A
E7
A
keep His words deep in your heart. They'll be with you where -
Asus
A
Asus
A
D.S. al Coda
ev - er you are. Ev - 'ry
CODA
Bm
E7
G♯
Gm
D
A7
D
true. Ev - 'ry word of the Lord is true.

Everybody Ought to Know

Traditional

Ev - 'ry - bod - y ought to know, ev - 'ry - bod - y ought to
know, ev - 'ry - bod - y ought to know
who Je - sus is. Ev - 'ry - bod - y ought to know,
ev - 'ry - bod - y ought to know, ev - 'ry - bod - y ought to
know who Je - sus is.
He's the lil - y of the val - ley;
He's the bright and morn - ing star.
He's the fair - est of ten thou -
sand; ev - 'ry - bod - y ought to know.

Everybody Ought to Love Jesus

Words and Music by
HARRY DIXON LOES

1. Ev - 'ry - bod - y ought to love Je - sus,
2. Ev - 'ry - bod - y ought to go to Sun - day School,
Je - sus, Je - sus. He died on the cross to
Sun - day School, Sun - day School. The men and the wom - en and the
save us from sin. Ev - 'ry - bod - y ought to love Je -
boys and the girls, ev - 'ry - bod - y ought to go to Sun - day
sus.
School.
Ev - 'ry - bod - y ought to keep smil - ing, smil - ing,
smil - ing. If you have a lit - tle frown turn it up - side down.
Ev - 'ry - bod - y ought to keep smil - ing. Ev - 'ry - bod - y ought to keep
smil - ing.

Everything's Better with a Friend

Words and Music by
JANET MCMAHAN-WILSON and DEBRA BLACK

Happily
C
Dm
G7
Dm
G7
We are friends, for - ev - er friends. You're al - ways there. I'll
2nd time to Coda
C
C9
F
G
F
Em
A
al - ways care. We are friends, for - ev - er friends.
Dm7
Em
F
F
G
G
C
C9
Ev - 'ry - thing's bet - ter with a friend. A
F
C
E
Am
friend is a gift, a life - long lift. A
D
F
G
G
F
A
D7
G
D.C. al Coda
friend is some - one you share things with.
CODA
Dm7
Em
F
F
G
G
C
A7
Ev - 'ry - thing's bet - ter with a friend.
Dm7
Em
F
F
G
G
C
A7
Dm
Em
F
F♯m
Ev - 'ry - thing's bet - ter with a friend. Ev - 'ry - thing is
G
F
G
G
G+
C
C6
bet - ter with a friend.

Everything

Words and Music by
HERB OWEN

Southern Gospel
E♭ A♭ E♭ A♭/B♭
He's the Al - pha and O - me - ga, the Be - gin - ning and the End. He's the
E♭ Cm F B♭
Cap - tain of Sal - va - tion and the Door for sin - ful men. He's our
E♭ A♭ E♭ A♭/B♭
Ev - er - last - ing Fa - ther, First Be - got - ten of the dead. Of His
E♭ Cm7 Fm7 B♭7 E♭ Fm7(4) E♭/G
sheep, He's the Great Shep - herd; of His church, He is the Head. He's Im -
A♭ A♭/B♭ E♭ A♭ A♭/E♭ E♭
man - u - el, God with us, Je - sus Christ, our Sav - ior, seen as
A♭ A♭/E♭ E♭ Cm F B♭
King of kings, the Lamb of Glo - ry, Might - y God, the Naz - a - rene, our
E♭ A♭ E♭
peace and our Phy - si - cian, quick - 'ning Spir - it from a - bove, our Re -
Cm F B♭
deem - er, Son of Da - vid and the Truth that God is love. He's a

E♭ A♭ E♭
gift that is un - speak - a - ble,___ the ver - y Christ, the Way. He's ex -
Cm Fm7 B♭7 E♭ Fm7(4) E♭/G
act - ly what I need - ed, and Yesh - u - a, Zi - on's praise. He's
A♭ E♭ A♭ E♭ B♭ A♭2/C B♭/D E♭ Fm7(4) E♭/G
ev - 'ry - thing, ev - 'ry - thing, He's ev - 'ry - thing from A to Z. I
A♭ E♭ A♭ E♭ F9 B♭ E♭7
love Him. He's ev - 'ry - thing, this Man from Gal - i - lee. He's
A♭ E♭ A♭ E♭ B♭ A♭2/C B♭/D E♭ Fm7(4) E♭/G
ev - 'ry - thing, ev - 'ry - thing, He's ev - 'ry - thing a God could be. I
A♭ E♭ A♭ E♭ 1. B♭ E♭
love Him. He's ev - 'ry - thing; He's ev - 'ry - thing___ to me. He's
2. B♭ E♭ Fm7 B♭7 E♭ Cm
ev - 'ry - thing___ to me. He's ev - 'ry - thing___ to me. He's
Fm7 B♭ B♭7 E♭ B♭7sus E♭
ev - 'ry - thing to me.___

F-R-I-E-N-D

Words and Music by
JANET MCMAHAN-WILSON and DEBRA BLACK

Lively (♩=120)
G A
Oh, I'm so glad that you're my F - R - I - E - N - D, my
D7 F♯m G
ver - y spe - cial F - R - I - E - N - D. And I pray ev - 'ry day that you will
A D7
2nd time to Coda
al - ways be my ver - y spe - cial F - R - I - E -
Cm6 G D Amaj7 D Cm6 G
N - D. I'll
C G
do my best to nev - er let you down.
A7 D Em D A7(♭5) D
D.S. al Coda
An - y - time you need me I'll be a - round. Oh, I'm so
CODA
Cm6 G D7
N - D. My ver - y spe - cial F - R - I - E -
Cm6 G D7 Cm6 G D7 G
N - D. You're my ver - y spe - cial F - R - I - E - N - D.

Father Abraham

Traditional

Eb
Eb6/Bb
Ebmaj7
Fa - ther A - bra - ham had man - y sons, man - y
Ab/Eb
Gm/Bb
Bb7
Bb7/F
sons had Fa - ther A - bra - ham. I am one of them, and so are
Bb
Ab/C
Bb7/D
1.
Eb/Bb
you, so let's just praise the Lord, right arm. Fa - ther
2.
3.
Lord, right arm, left arm. Fa - ther Lord, right arm, left
4.
arm, right foot. Fa - ther Lord, right arm, left arm, right foot, left
5.
foot. Fa - ther Lord, right arm, left arm, right foot, left
6.
foot, chin up. Fa - ther Lord, right arm, left arm, right foot, left
7.
foot, chin up, turn a - round. Fa - ther Lord, right arm, left
Eb6 9/Bb
Eb6
arm, right foot, left foot, chin up, turn a - round, sit down!

Fear Not!
Words and Music by
TROY NILSSON and GENIE NILSSON
With a beat (♩=120)
Fear— not. Fear— not.
Fear— not. Fear— not.
3rd time to Coda
Fear— not. Fear not. Fear not. Fear not. Fear not. Fear
not. Fear not. Fear not. Fear not. Fear not.
E-ven though I walk through the val-ley of the shad-ow of death, I will fear no
e-vil, for You are with me. Our God— did not give us a
spir-it of fear, but of pow - er and love— and a sound mind. Fear—
When you hear of wars— and rev - o - lu-tions, don't be fright-ened; your
God is right there by your side.— Do— not let your heart— be trou-bled;

D.S. al Coda
C/G
G♯m7(♭5)
Am7
Am/D
trust in God. For if God is for us, who can be a - gainst us? Fear
CODA
D
Em
G
F♯
Spoken: The Lord is my Shepherd; I shall not want. He makes me lie down in
Fear not.
E♭
green pastures. He leads me beside still waters. He restores my soul. He leads me
C
in paths of righteousness for His name's sake. Even though I walk through
A♭
E
the valley of the shadow of death, I will fear no evil, for You are with me.
G/E
Am
Fear not.
1.
2.
Fear
Fear not.

Fill in the Blanks

Words and Music by
DOTTIE RAMBO and DAVID HUNTSINGER

Out in the sea, in the mid-dle of the deep blue sea, a
great big whale was swim-min' by, and boy was he in for a big sur-prise! He
o-pened his mouth and what do you think? He swal-lowed broth-er (whoop!) as
quick as a wink. You got-ta fill in the blanks. You got-ta
close your eyes and think.
1. It was just like be-in' in a jail down in the bel-ly of the whale.
2. Who did Zac-che-us wan-na see from the top of the syc-a-more
2nd time to Coda
(spoken) "Who was it?" "Jo-nah!"
Up in a tree, in the top of a syc-a-more tree,
sat a lit-tle man on a limb so high. He
heard that (whoop!) would be pass-in' by. He was so short that he

A6 Amaj7 A E/G♯ F♯m A6 B A/B E B7sus/E E D.S. al Coda
could not see, and that's why he climbed up a syc - a-more tree. You got - ta
CODA E E/B E E/D B♭/C F C7 F
tree? (spoken) "Who was it?" "Je - sus!" Down in the den, in the
C7 F B♭/C F F7 B♭ B♭/D
bot-tom of the li - on's den, the king threw (whoop!) to the hun - gry beasts. The
C7 B♭/C A/C♯ C♯° Dm F F7 B♭6 Am Gm7 B♭
li-on's get-tin' read-y for a great big feast. They smacked their mouths and they licked their paws, but
C B♭/C F C7sus/F F C7 F F/C F
God closed their mouths and locked their jaws. You got - ta fill in the blanks. You got - ta
C C♯° Dm F7/C B♭ F F7 F7/C Bm7(♭5) B°
close your eyes and think. Tell me now if you can.
F/C C7 F F/C F F/C
Who was in the li - on's den? (spoken) "Who was it?" "Dan - iel!"
F F/A F7/A B♭ B♭6 B° F/C C7
Who did Zac - che - us wan - na see from the top of the syc - a - more
F F/C F F7 B♭ B♭6 B°
tree? "Je - sus!" Ev - 'ry - bod - y give a yell!
F/C C7 F F/C F C C7 F F/C F
Who was in the bel - ly of the whale? "Jo - nah!"

Fishers of Men

Words and Music by
HARRY D. CLARK

Brightly!
"I will make you fish - ers of men, fish - ers of men,
fish - ers of men. I will make you fish - ers of men, if you
fol - low Me. If you fol - low Me, if you
fol - low Me; I will make you
fish - ers of men, if you fol - low Me."
Hear Christ call - ing, "Come un - to Me, come un - to Me, come un - to Me."
Hear Christ call - ing, "Come un - to Me, I will give you rest. I will
give you rest, I wll give you rest;
Hear Christ call - ing, "Come un - to Me, I will give you rest."

For Me

Words and Music by
HERB OWEN

Hymn-like
Dm Am B♭ A7 Dm Am B♭ C
1. See Him dy - ing on a tree; can it be He dies for me?
3. Heav - en's gates are o - pened wide, for the blood has been ap - plied.
2nd time to Coda
F C/E B♭/D C7sus C7 F Dm Gm7 C F
2nd time: rit.
Nev - er thought that I would see such as this for me.
I shall one day stand in - side, when He comes for me.
Dm Am B♭ A7 Dm Am B♭ C
2. As the Fa - ther looks up - on this, His on - ly, dy - ing, Son,
F C/E B♭/D C7sus C7 F Dm Gm7 C Dm C/E
sees He now the work is done, fin - ished now for me.
F B♭ C A/C♯ Dm Dm9/C B♭ C/B♭
For this mo - ment He was born long a - go on
F/A G Csus C B♭2/D C7/E F B♭6 D7/A Gm
Christ - mas morn. Dy - ing, He ful - filled God's plan,
C7/E F Dm Gm7 C7 F
D.C. al Coda
pay - ing for the sins of man.
CODA
Fsus F
me.

For He's a Wonderful Savior

(To the tune of For He's a Jolly Good Fellow)

Words and Music by
RUTH ELAINE SCHRAM

G C F/C C G
1. For He's a won - der - ful Sav - ior. For He's a won - der - ful
(2. For) He's the God of cre - a - tion. For He's the God of cre -
C F/G C F F♯°
Sav - ior. For He's a won - der - ful Sav - ior
a - tion. For He's the God of cre - a - tion and
G C C F C
ev - 'ry - one ought to know. And ev - 'ry - one ought to know. Yes,
F/G C C
ev - 'ry - one ought to know. For He's a won - der - ful
For He's the God of cre -
F/C C G C F/G
Sav - ior. For He's a won - der - ful Sav - ior. For
a - tion. For He's the God of cre - a - tion. For
C F F♯°
He's a won - der - ful Sav - ior
He's the God of cre - a - tion and
G 1. C 2. C A♭7
ev - 'ry - one ought to know. 2. For know. 3. So,

D♭ G♭/D♭ D♭ A♭
tell your friends a - bout Je - sus. So, tell your friends a - bout
D♭ G♭ G°
Je - sus. So, tell your friends a - bout Je - sus,
A♭ D♭
for ev - 'ry - one ought to know. And
D♭ G♭ D♭ G♭/A♭ D♭ G♭/A♭
ev - 'ry - one ought to know. Yes, ev - 'ry - one ought to
D♭ G♭/D♭ D♭
know. So, tell your friends a - bout Je - sus. So,
A♭ D♭ G♭/A♭ D♭
tell your friends a - bout Je - sus. So, tell your friends a - bout
G♭ G° A♭ D♭
Je - sus, for ev - 'ry - one ought to know.

Optional Lyrics: *For He's the rock of the ages. . .*
For He's the Lord of salvation. . .

Forever

Words and Music by
CHRIS TOMLIN

Driving rock (♩=126)
E
1. Give thanks to the Lord, our God and King. His
2. From the ris - ing to the set - ting sun, His
F♯m/E A/E E A2
love en - dures for - ev - er. For He is good; He is a -
love en - dures for - ev - er. And by the grace of God we will
F♯m/A A A/E E
bove all things. His love en - dures for - ev - er. Sing
car - ry on. His love en - dures for - ev - er.
B A2/C♯
praise. Sing praise. Sing
B A2
praise. Sing praise. For - ev -
Esus E Esus E C♯m7
- er God is faith - ful. For - ev - er God is
B
strong. For - ev - er God is with us. For - ev -
A2 3rd time to Coda 1. Esus E
- er and ev - er. For - ev - er.

Esus E Esus E
2.
D.S. al Coda
er. For - ev -
CODA
E
- er. For - ev - er.
E$^{4}_{2}$ E2 B
Sing praise. Sing
A2/C♯ B
praise. Sing praise. Sing
A2 N.C. Esus E
praise. For - ev - er God is faith -
Esus E C♯m7
- ful. For - ev - er God is strong. For - ev -
B A2
- er God is with us. For - ev - er and ev -
1. 2. E
- er. For - ev - - er. For - ev - er.

Fruit of the Spirit

Writer Unknown

Csus C 1. F 2. F
gen-tle-ness and self-con - trol. Oh, the trol. Oh, the
C
fruit of the Spir-it's not a straw-ber-ry. The fruit of the Spir-it's not a straw-ber-ry. If you
F B♭ F C F
wan-na be a straw-ber-ry, you might as well hear it, you can't be a fruit of the Spir-it. 'Cause the fruit is
B♭ F Csus F
love, joy, peace, pa-tience, kind-ness, good-ness, faith-ful-ness, gen-tle-ness and self-con-trol,
B♭ F Csus C F
love, joy, peace, pa-tience, kind-ness, good-ness, faith-ful-ness, gen-tle-ness and self-con - trol.
O - kay! The
C F
fruit of the Spir-it's not a grape. The fruit of the Spir-it's not a grape. If you wan-na be a grape,
B♭ F C F
you might as well hear it, you can't be a fruit of the Spir-it. 'Cause the fruit is
B♭ F Csus F
love, joy, peace, pa-tience, kind-ness, good-ness, faith-ful-ness, gen-tle-ness and self-con-trol,
B♭ F Csus C F Repeat 2 times and fade
love, joy, peace, pa-tience, kind-ness, good-ness, faith-ful-ness, gen-tle-ness and self-con-trol. Well, the fruit is

Freedom

Words and Music by
HERB OWEN

Military
E♭
A♭/E♭
E♭
I___ was locked_ with - in a
pris - on house_ of sin, held
cap - tive by_ the sin that I had loved a - gain and a -
B♭
Cm7(4)
B♭/D
F
gain. Then___ I saw_ a ray of
light___ that seemed_ to say, "You soon shall be a soul set
Fm7(4)
E♭/G
A♭
Fm7
B♭7
free to live for Me."
Christ, my Sav - ior, set me free___ from all_ my
Cm

E♭ B♭/D Cm7
sin; free to do the things that count for
B♭ E♭ B♭ B♭7 E♭
Him a-gain and a-gain. I have been re-
E♭7 A♭ Gm7 Fm7
leased, giv-en love and joy and peace. I am
E♭/B♭ Fm7 B♭ E♭ A♭
free to live for Him who gives me life!
E♭ F B♭/F F
Has
B♭/F F B♭/F
it oc-curred to you that you're a pris-on-er
F B♭/F F C/E Dm7(4)
too, a cap-tive to the sin that you have
C G C F B♭/F
loved a-gain and a-gain? Lis-ten, you will

F
B♭/F
F
Gm7(4)
F/A
bear a voice of love and cheer, tell - ing
B♭
Gm7
C7
F
B♭/F
you He loves you too, and He'll set you free.
F
B♭
C
F
B♭
F
Dm
C
Christ, my Sav - ior, set me
F
B♭
F
free from all my sin; free to do the
C/E
Dm7
C
F
C
C7
things that count for Him a - gain and a - gain.
F
F7
B♭
Am7
I have been re - leased, giv - en love and joy and
Gm7
F/C
Gm7
C
peace. I am free to live for Him who gives me
F
B♭/F
F
B♭/F
F
B♭/F
C/F
F
life!

Give and Go

(To the tune of Lightly Row)

Words and Music by
RUTH ELAINE SCHRAM

D Em7 A D Asus A
Give and go, give and go, so that all the world may know.
D Em7 A D A D
Give and go, give and go, Je - sus loves them so.
A Em7 A7 D A7 D
Ev - 'ry na - tion, ev - 'ry land, they must hear and un - der - stand.
D Em7 A D A D B♭7
Give and go, give and go, Je - sus loves them so.
E♭ Fm7 B♭ E♭ Fm7 B♭
Give and go, give and go, so that all the world may know.
E♭ Fm7 B♭ E♭ B♭ E♭
Give and go, give and go, Je - sus loves them so.
B♭ Fm7 B♭ E♭ B♭7 E♭
Ev - 'ry na - tion, ev - 'ry land, they must hear and un - der - stand.
E♭ Fm7 B♭ E♭ B♭sus B♭ E♭
Give and go, give and go, Je - sus loves them so.

Germs

(My Invisible Dog)

Words and Music by
DOTTIE RAMBO

With imagination (♩=112)

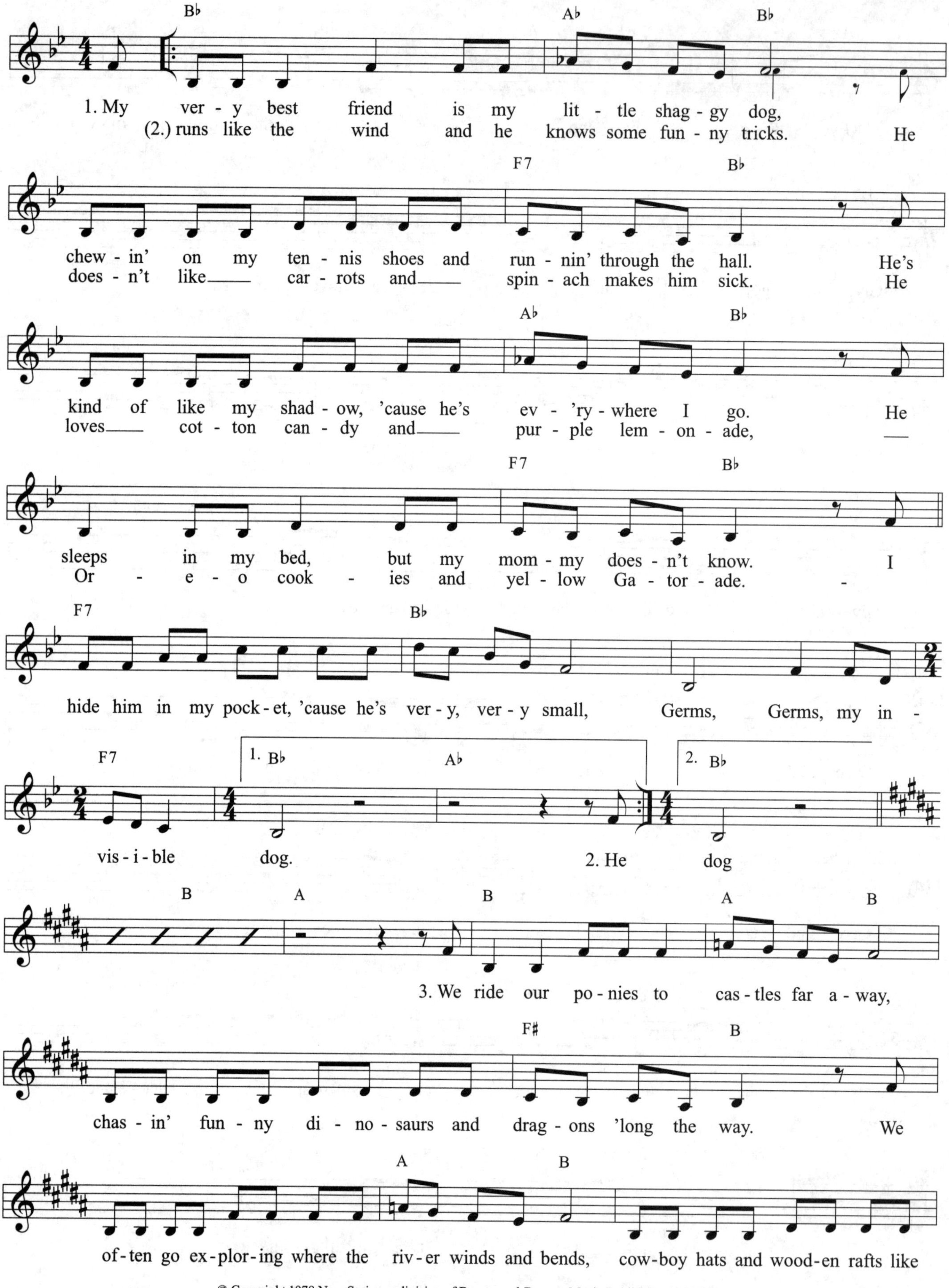

B♭ A♭ B♭

1. My ver - y best friend is my lit - tle shag - gy dog,
(2.) runs like the wind and he knows some fun - ny tricks. He

F7 B♭

chew - in' on my ten - nis shoes and run - nin' through the hall. He's
does - n't like___ car - rots and___ spin - ach makes him sick. He

A♭ B♭

kind of like my shad - ow, 'cause he's ev - 'ry - where I go. He
loves___ cot - ton can - dy and___ pur - ple lem - on - ade, ___

F7 B♭

sleeps in my bed, but my mom - my does - n't know. I
Or - e - o cook - ies and yel - low Ga - tor - ade. -

F7 B♭

hide him in my pock - et, 'cause he's ver - y, ver - y small, Germs, Germs, my in -

F7 1. B♭ A♭ 2. B♭

vis - i - ble dog. 2. He dog

B A B A B

3. We ride our po - nies to cas - tles far a - way,

F♯ B

chas - in' fun - ny di - no - saurs and drag - ons 'long the way. We

A B

of - ten go ex - plor - ing where the riv - er winds and bends, cow - boy hats and wood - en rafts like

F♯ B F♯ B
Huck - le - ber - ry Finn. I hide him in my pock - et, 'cause he's ver - y, ver - y small,
F♯ B A
Germs, Germs, my in - vis - i - ble dog. 4. I
B A B
take him to church, but no - bod - y ev - er sees this lit - tle shag - gy, spot - ted dog
F♯ B A B
sit - tin' on my knee. He's learn - in' Bi - ble vers - es and he loves the hap - py songs, but he
of - ten falls a - sleep when the ser - mon is too long! I
F♯7 B
hide him in my pock - et, 'cause he's ver - y, ver - y small,
1. F♯7 B 2. F♯7 B
Germs, Germs, my in - vis - i - ble dog. I vis - i - ble dog.
F♯7 B
Germs, Germs, my in - vis - i - ble dog. Germs, Germs, my in -
F♯7 B rit. F♯7 B
vis - i - ble dog. Germs, Germs, my in - vis - i - ble dog.

GIGO

(Garbage in - Garbage out)

Words and Music by
STEVE KELLER

Laid back (♩=90)

Em Am
Gar - bage in, gar - bage out.

Em Am
Gar - bage in, gar - bage out. A

Em Am
goat will eat an - y - thing. Trash can be a meal. Your

Em Am
shirt might be the main course, for des - sert, a ba - na - na peel.

Em Am
You can learn a les - son from the di - et of a goat: What

Em Am N.C.
goes in comes right back out. Just re - mem - ber this lit - tle quote: Gar - bage

𝄋 Em7 Am
in, gar - bage out. It

Em7 Am
does - n't take a ge - nius to know what I'm talk - in' a - bout. Gar - bage

Em7 Am
in, gar - bage out. Gar - bage

2nd time to Coda 𝄌

Em7 Am N.C. Em
in, gar - bage out.

Am
Em
Am
Em
Am
Some peo - ple say you are what you eat.
Em
Am
One per - son's trash is an - oth - er one's treat. Be
Em
Am
care - ful what you put in - to your mind and in your mouth. When you
Em
Am
N.C.
D.S. al Coda
put gar - bage in, gar - bage comes right back out. Gar - bage
CODA
Em
Am
out. Fill your heart with good - ness.
Em
Am
Fill your heart with truth. Fill your heart with God's love.
Em
Am
It will come back to you. It's a sim - ple rule, but
Em
Am
one that's wise to fol - low. You are what you eat.
N.C.
Spoken: Be careful what you swallow.
Em7
Guess what comes out?
You put love in.

Am
Em7
It does-n't take a ge - nius to
Am
Em7
And love comes out.
know what I'm talk-in' a-bout. You put love in.
Am
Em7
Am
N.C.
Em7
Love in, love out. Be
Am
Em7
care-ful what you put in your mind and in your mouth.
Am
B
N.C.
You put gar-bage in, gar-bage comes right back out. Gar-bage
Em7
Am
in, gar-bage out. It
Em7
Am
does-n't take a ge - nius to know what I'm talk-in' a-bout. Gar-bage
Em7
Am
in, gar-bage out. Gar-bage
Em7
Am
N.C.
Em7
Am
in, gar-bage out. Gar-bage
Repeat several times
Last time
Em7
Am
in, gar-bage out. Gar-bage out.

Give Me Oil in My Lamp

Traditional

D♭ D♭maj7/A♭ D♭7 G♭ G♭/D♭ G♭ A♭7sus
Give me oil in my lamp, keep me burn - ing. Give me
D♭ B♭m7 E♭9 E♭m7 A♭7 D♭ D♭maj7/A♭ D♭7
oil in my lamp, I pray; Give me oil in my lamp, keep me
G♭ G♭/D♭ G♭ D♭ D♭/F G♭ D♭/A♭ A♭7 D♭ G♭ D♭/F E♭m7 E♭m7/A♭
burn - ing. Keep me burn - ing 'til the break of day.
D♭ D♭/A♭ D♭ D♭7 G♭ G♭/D♭ G♭ E♭m7 A♭7 A♭7/E♭ A♭7
Sing, "Ho - san - na." Sing, "Ho - san - na." Sing, "Ho - san - na to the
D♭ G♭/D♭ D♭ G♭/A♭ D♭ D♭/A♭ D♭ D♭7 G♭ G♭/D♭ G♭ E♭m7
King of kings!" Sing, "Ho - san - na." Sing, "Ho - san - na."
A♭7 A♭7/E♭ A♭7 1. D♭ A♭13 2. D♭ G/A A7
Sing, "Ho - san - na to the King!" Give me King!"
D Dmaj7/A D7 G G/D Em7 E7 A7 A7/E A7
Sing, "Ho - san - na." Sing, "Ho - san - na." Sing, "Ho - san - na to the
D G/D D G/A D Dmaj7/A D7 C/E D7/F♯
King of kings!" Sing, "Ho - san - na."
G Em7 E7 A7 D G/D D
Sing, "Ho - san - na." Sing, "Ho - san - na to the King!"

Give Me a "J"

Writer Unknown

Raucous celebration (♩=134)
SOLO
CHOIR
Give me a J (J,— you got yo J, you got yo J), give me an
E (E,— you got yo E, you got yo E), give me an S (S,— you got yo
S, you got yo S), give me a U (U,— you got yo U, you got yo U), give me an
S (S,— you got yo S, you got yo S). What's that—
E7
A7
3rd time to Coda
—spell? King of kings! Lord of lords! Who's com - in'
Je - sus! Je - sus! Je - sus!
1. A7
2. A7
back? back? What's that— spell? King of
Je - sus! Je - sus! Je - sus!
kings! Lord of lords! Who's com - in' back?
Je - sus! Je - sus! Je - sus!

E7
A7
E7
A7
E7
A7
E7
A7
SOLO
D.S. al Coda
Give me a
CODA
A7
E7
A7
back? What's that spell? King of kings! Lord of
Je - sus! Je - sus! Je - sus!
E7
A7
E7
lords! Who's com - in' back? Je - sus!
Je - sus! Je - sus!
A7
E7
A7
Je - sus! Yeah, yeah, Je -
Je - sus! Je - sus!
E7
A7
E7
A7
- sus! Je - sus!
Je - sus! Je - sus!
E7
Vocal: 1st time only
A7
E7
A7
Repeat 2 times and fade

Giving My Heart to Jesus

(To the tune of Skip to My Lou)

Words and Music by
RUTH ELAINE SCHRAM

Country Hoe Down

D A A7
Heart, heart, giv - in' my heart, heart, heart, giv - in' my heart,

D A7 A/C♯ D
heart, heart, giv - in' my heart, giv - in' my heart to Je - sus.

D A A7
1. Lost in sin. Now, what - 'll I do? Lost in sin. Now, what - 'll I do?

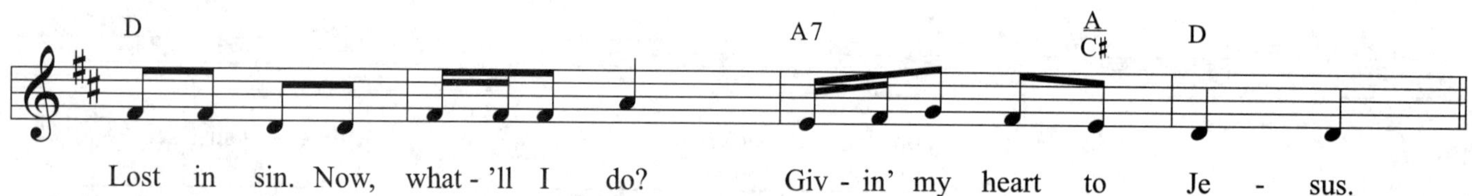
D A7 A/C♯ D
Lost in sin. Now, what - 'll I do? Giv - in' my heart to Je - sus.

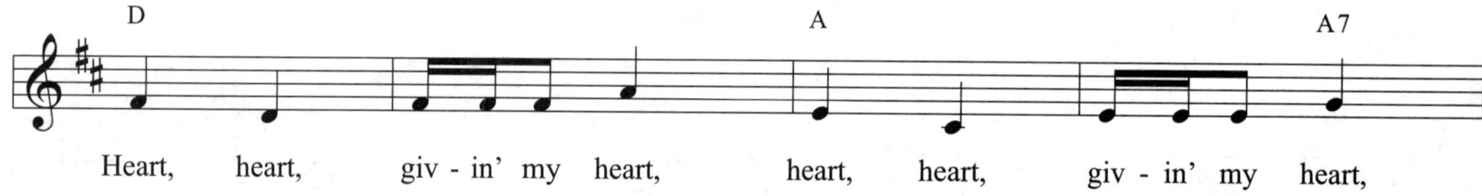
D A A7
Heart, heart, giv - in' my heart, heart, heart, giv - in' my heart,

D A7 A/C♯ D B♭7
heart, heart, giv - in' my heart, giv - in' my heart to Je - sus.

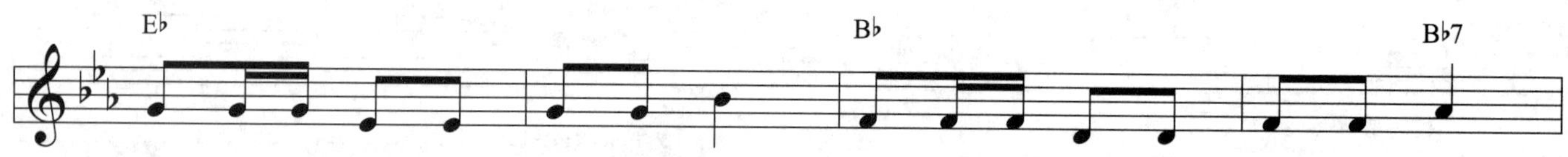
E♭ B♭ B♭7
2. He's gon - na make my heart brand new. He's gon - na make my heart brand new.

E♭ B♭7 B♭/D E♭
He's gon - na make my heart brand new. Giv - in' my heart to Je - sus.

E♭ B♭ B♭7
Heart, heart, giv - in' my heart, heart, heart, giv - in' my heart,
E♭ B♭ B♭/D
heart, heart, giv - in' my heart, giv - in' my heart to
E♭ E♭ C B♭/D C/E
Je - sus.
F C C7
3. Goin' to heav - en, how 'bout you? Goin' to heav - en, how 'bout you?
F C7 C/E
Goin' to heav - en, how 'bout you? Giv - in' my heart to
F F C
Je - sus. Heart, heart, giv - in' my heart, heart, heart,
C7 F
giv - in' my heart, heart, heart, giv - in' my heart,
C C/E F F C F
giv - in' my heart to Je - sus.

Glory Be to God on High

Traditional

D G/D D
1. Glo - ry be to God on High, Al - le -
(2.) Fa - ther, Spir - it, Son, Al - le -

G D D/F♯ G Bm/G♯
lu - ia, Glo - ry be to God on
lu - ia, Praise the God - Head, Three in

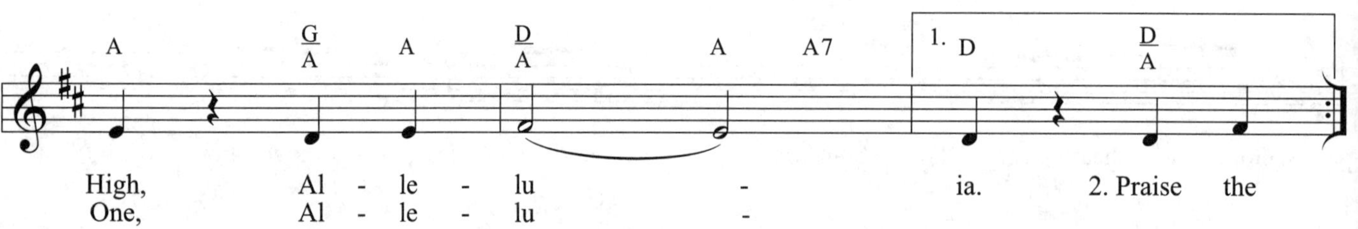
A G/A A D/A A A7 1. D D/A
High, Al - le - lu - ia. 2. Praise the
One, Al - le - lu -

2. D B♭7 A♭/B♭ E♭ B♭7/F E♭/G E♭
ia. 3. Sing we prais - es un - to Thee, Al - le -

A♭ B♭9/A♭ E♭/G B♭7/F E♭ Gm7 A♭ Cm/A
lu - ia. For the truth that sets us

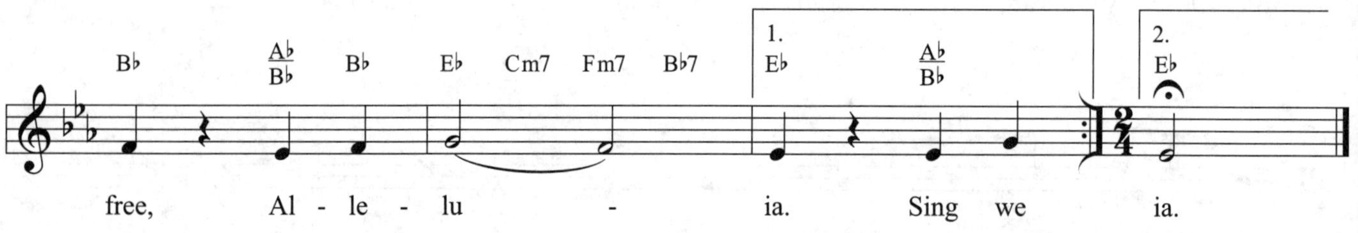
B♭ A♭/B♭ B♭ E♭ Cm7 Fm7 B♭7 1. E♭ A♭/B♭ 2. E♭
free, Al - le - lu - ia. Sing we ia.

Go Tell It on the Mountain

Spiritual

Go, tell it on the moun - tain, O - ver the hills and
ev - 'ry - where; Go, tell it on the moun - tain That
Je - sus Christ is born!
1. While shep - herds kept their watch - ing O'er si - lent flocks by night, Be - hold, through - out the heav - ens There shone a ho - ly light.
2. Down in a low - ly man - ger The hum - ble Christ was born, And brought us God's sal - va - tion That bless - ed Christ - mas morn.
Go, tell it on the moun - tain, O - ver the hills and ev - 'ry - where; Go, tell it on the moun - tain That Je - sus Christ is born, That Je - sus Christ is born, That Je - sus Christ is born!

Glow in the Dark

Words and Music by
GARY FORSYTHE

E♭
Fm
Glow in the dark. Glow in the dark. I
B♭7
E♭
want my life to glow in the dark. If
A♭
E♭/G
A♭o
A♭o/B
Cm
ev - 'ry - one could see it, then may - be they'll be - lieve and
3rd time to Coda
Fm
B♭7
E♭
they can live e - ter - nal - ly.
E♭
Fm7
1. See that lit - tle fi - re - fly;
2. See the moon in out - er space
B♭
E♭
makes no noise as he flys by.
shin - ing from its spe - cial place
A♭
E♭/G
Cm
Yet with - in the black - est night
with a light that's not its own,

F7
B♭
we can see His flash - ing light.
but the sun's re - flect - ed glow.
E♭
Fm
Just like that old fi - re - fly,
Like the moon that lights the night,
B♭
E♭
peo - ple watch as I pass by.
I must shine with bor - rowed light,
A♭
E♭/G
Cm
In this world of dark - est days,
light that comes from God a - bove
F
B♭
D.C. (twice) al Coda
I must glow with hope and praise.
born in me to share in love.
CODA
B♭7
A♭
E♭/G
ter - nal - ly. If ev - 'ry - one could see it, then
A♭o
A♭o/B
Cm
Fm
may - be they'll be - lieve and they can live e -
B♭7
E♭
ter - nal - ly.

Go!!

Words and Music by
TROY NILSSON and GENIE NILSSON

With energy (♩=194)
A D E
Repeat as desired
Go! Go! Go! Go! Go! Go! Go! Go!
A D E
Go and make dis - ci - ples of ev - 'ry na -
A D
- tion, bap - tiz - ing them in the name of the Fa - ther and the
E A
Son and the Ho - ly Spir - it. Go and teach
D E
them to ob - serve all I've com - mand - ed. And
D E A
I'll be with you 'til the end of the age.
1. E 2.3. E E
You've got the green
light. Go pedal's on the right.
D E
Step on the gas; go fast. Bap - tize and make dis - ci -
A E
2nd time to Coda
- ples. Go on your skate - board

or on your surf - board or in your big
D E A
fat Ford. Bap - tize and make dis - ci - ples.
A D E
Mat - thew twen - ty - eight: nine - teen and twen - ty: That's the great
A/C♯ D
com - mis - sion. Mat - thew twen - ty - eight; nine - teen and
E 1. 2. E/F♯ E/G E/G♯ A
D.S. al Coda
twen - ty says to go soul fish - in'. go, go, go, go!
CODA
Go in your big fat Ford. Burn rub - ber
D E A
for the Lord. Bap - tize and make dis - ci - ples.
A D E
Mat - thew twen - ty - eight; nine - teen and twen - ty: That's the great
A/C♯ D
com - mis - sion. Mat - thew twen - ty - eight; nine - teen and
E 1. 2. E/F♯ E/G E/G♯ A
twen - ty says to go soul fish - in'. go, go, go, go!

God Gave Us a Special Book
(To the tune of B-I-N-G-O)
Words and Music by
RHETT PARRISH, JODI HANNA
and TRISH MENDOZA
E♭ A♭ E♭/G Fm7 B♭ E♭
God gave us a spe - cial book. The Bi - ble is its name.
E♭ Fm7 B♭sus B♭ E♭ Cm Cm7 F7
B - I - B - L - E, B - I - B - L - E, B - I - B - L - E, the
B♭7 E♭ E♭ E♭/D♭ Bsus B
Bi - ble is its name.
E A E/G♯ F♯m7 B7 E
1. God gave us a spe - cial book. The Bi - ble is its name.
2. God gave us a spe - cial book. The Bi - ble is its name.
E F♯m7 Bsus B E C♯m C♯m7 F♯
(clap) - I - B - L - E, (clap) - I - B - L - E, (clap) - I - B - L - E, the
(clap, clap) - B - L - E, (clap, clap) - B - L - E, (clap, clap) - B - L - E, the
1. B7 E
Bi - ble is its name.
2. B7 E C7
Bi - ble is its name.
F B♭ F/A Gm7 C F
3. God gave us a spe - cial book. The Bi - ble is its name.
4. God gave us a spe - cial book. The Bi - ble is its name.

F Gm7 C7sus C7 F
(clap, clap, clap) - L - E, (clap, clap, clap) - L - E,
(clap, clap, clap, clap) - E, (clap, clap, clap, clap) - E,
Dm Dm7 G7
1. C7 F
2. C7 F D♭7
(clap, clap, clap) - L - E, the Bi - ble is its name. Bi - ble is its name.
(clap, clap, clap, clap) - E, the
G♭ C♭ G♭/B♭ A♭m7 D♭ G♭
God gave us a spe - cial book. The Bi - ble is its name.
A♭m7 D♭sus D♭ G♭
(clap, clap, clap, clap, clap), (clap, clap, clap, clap, clap),
E♭m E♭m7 A♭ D♭7 G♭ D7
(clap, clap, clap, clap, clap), the Bi - ble is its name.
G C G/B Am7 D G Am7
God gave us a spe - cial book. The Bi - ble is its name. B - I - B - L - E,
Dsus D7 G Em Em7 A7 D7 G
B - I - B - L - E, B - I - B - L - E, the Bi - ble is its name.

God Is Bigger

Words and Music by
KURT HEINECKE and PHIL VISCHER

Slowly and freely
BOB
Cm
Fm6
You were ly - ing in your bed; you were feel - ing kind of sleep - y, but you

G
Cm
could - n't close your eyes be - cause the room was get - ting creep - y. Were those

Fm
Cm
eye - balls in the clos - et? Was that God - zil - la in the hall? There was

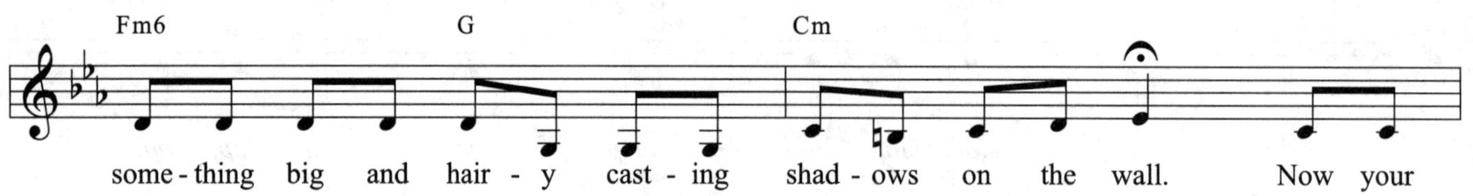
Fm6
G
Cm
some - thing big and hair - y cast - ing shad - ows on the wall. Now your

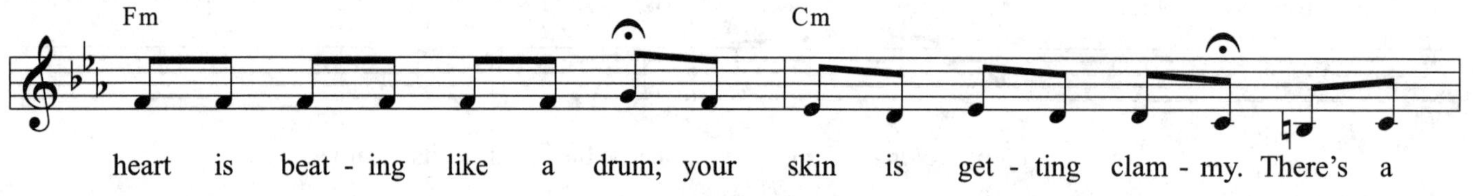
Fm
Cm
heart is beat - ing like a drum; your skin is get - ting clam - my. There's a

Fm
G7
hun - dred ti - ny mon - sters jump - ing right in - to your jam - mies.

In tempo (♩=116)
F
C
G
God is big - ger than the boog - ie man. He's big - ger than God - zil - la or the

C F
mon - sters on T. V. Oh, God is big - ger than the
2nd time to Coda
C Dm G C F/A C
boog - ie man, and He's watch - ing out for you and me.
Freely, as at the beginning
JUNIOR
Fm
So, when I'm ly - ing in my bed and the
Cm G
fur - ni - ture starts creep - ing, I'll just laugh and say, "Hey, cut that out!" and
Cm Fm
accel.
get back to my sleep - ing, 'cause I know that God's the big - gest and He's
Cm G7
rit.
watch - ing all the while. So, when I get scared, I'll think of Him and
a tempo
D.S. al Coda
close my eyes and smile.
CODA
C F/A C F
MONSTER
JUNIOR
MONSTER
me. So, are you fright - ened? No, not real - ly. Are you
C G
JUNIOR
wor - ried? Not a bit. I know what - ev - er's gon - na hap - pen, that

FRANKENCELERY
God can han - dle it. I'm sor - ry that I scared you when you
JUNIOR
rit.
saw me on T. V. Well, that's o - kay, 'cause now I know that God is
a tempo
tak - ing care of me. God is big - ger than the boog - ie man. He's
big - ger than God - zil - la or the mon - sters on T. V. Oh,
God is big - ger than the boog - ie man, and He's
watch - ing out for you and me.
me. He's watch - ing out for you and
me. Watch - ing, watch - ing, watch - ing
out for you and me.

God Is So Good

Folk Song

Slow 4
1. God is so good. God is so good. God is so good. He's so good to me.
2. God loves me so. God loves me so. God loves me so. He's so good to me.
God an - swers prayer. God an - swers prayer.
God an - swers prayer. He's so good to me.
God is so good. God is so good. God is so good. He's so good to me.
God is so good. He's so good to me.

God Is Love
Words and Music by
TROY NILSSON and GENIE NILSSON
Freely
F C/F F Csus B♭2
First John four: six - teen says, "God is love."
F C/F F Csus B♭2
First John four: six - teen says, "God is love."
F C/F F2
In tempo (♩=92)
Gm7
God is love.
F Gm7
God is love. God is love.
F
God is love, love, love.
G C
Faith, hope, and love:
D G D/F♯ Em7 C
These nev - er change. These three re - main, but the
D G G/F G C
great - est of these is love. Faith, hope, and love:
D G D/F♯ Em7 C
3rd time to Coda
These nev - er change. These three re - main, but the

D
G
Gm7
great - est of these is love.
Love, love,
love.
Love, love, love.
(God is love.)
F
Gm7
Love, love,
love.
Love, love, love, love,
(God is love, love,)
1.
F
Gm7
love.
His love is high.
His love is deep.
His love is
wi - ee - i - ee - i - ee - i - ee - i - ee - i -
ee - i - ee - i - ee - i - ee - ide.
2.
D.S. al Coda
love.
CODA
D
Gm7
great - est of these is
love, love, love.
God is love.
God is
love.
God is love, love, love.
F
Gm7

God Is Number One!

Words and Music by
TROY NILSSON and GENIE NILSSON

Lightly (♩=88)
C F/C G/C F/C
God is num - ber One, have no oth - er gods be - fore Him.
C F/C G/C F/C
He's the Might - y One, have no oth - er gods be - fore Him.
Same tempo, bouncy 4 (♩=♩)
C G7
God's num - ber One! He won't be num - ber two. He
C
loves you more than an - y - bod - y else can ev - er do.
C7 F Dm7
God's num - ber One, so here's what you can do: Just
G7 C
love Him with all your heart and mind and soul and mus - cle too.
C F/C G/C F/C
God is num - ber One, have no oth - er gods be - fore Him.
C F/C G/C F/C
He's the Might - y One, have no oth - er gods be - fore Him.
C G7
God's num - ber One! He's the Lord of all, the

C
ev - er - last - ing Ru - ler of both big and small.
C7 F Dm7
God's num - ber One! He is on the throne; There
G7 C
is no oth - er god like Him for He is God a - lone.
D A7
God's num - ber One! He won't be num - ber two. He
D
loves you more than an - y - bod - y else can ev - er do.
D7 G Em7
God's num - ber One, so here's what you can do: Just
A7 D
love Him with all your heart and mind and soul and mus - cle too.
D G/D A/D G/D
God is num - ber One, have no oth - er gods be - fore Him.
D G/D A/D G/D D2
Sing 4 times
He's the Might - y One, have no oth - er gods be - fore Him.

God Knows Everything

Words and Music by
HERB OWEN

Bouncy 2 beat
F F/A B♭ Gm C B♭/D C/E
If God knows how man - y hairs are on my
F E7 E♭7 D7
head, I don't have to wor - ry 'bout
Gm C7 F B♭ F/A Gm7(4)
an - y - thing, but trust in Him in - stead.
F F/A B♭ Gm C B♭/D C/E
For He must know ev - 'ry - thing, He is wise and
F E7 E♭7 D7
smart; He will show you how to live
Gm C7 B♭/D C/E F Gm7(4) F/A
joy - ful - ly if He is in your heart!
B♭ C F Gm7 B♭/C C F Gm7(4) F/A
Ask me how I know, why I'm cer - tain that it's so, and
2nd time to Coda
B♭ C F Gm7 C7 F B♭/C
then His prais - es I will sing, 'cause God knows ev - 'ry - thing!
F F/A B♭ Gm C7 B♭/D C/E
Man - y times I won - der who will care for

F E7 E♭7 D7
me, who will see that I be - come
Gm C7 F B♭ F/A Gm7(4)
ev - 'ry - thing that God wants me to be;
F F/A B♭ Gm C B♭/D C/E
who can look be - yond and tell where my life should
F E7 E♭7 D7
go? Then I hear a lov - ing voice
D.S. al Coda
Gm7 C7 B♭/D C/E F Gm7 F/A
tell - ing me "Fol - low me; the way I know."
CODA F Dm7 G C D G
thing! Ask me how I know,
Am7 C/D D G Am7(4) G/B C D
why I'm cer - tain that it's so, and then His prais - es
G Am7 D7 G Em Am7 D7
I will sing, 'cause God knows ev - 'ry - thing. Yes, God knows ev - 'ry -
G Em Am7 Cmaj7/D D7 G D G
thing. Yes, God knows ev - 'ry - thing!

God Loves Chickens, Too

Words and Music by
TOM STEINMAN and JAY TYLER

Upbeat country (♩=128)
C G D
God loves chick - ens, too. All the oth - er an - i - mals
G C G
know it's true. You hear 'em talk - in' down at the zoo.
D G G
God loves chick - ens, too.
1. God must love watch - in' all the chick - ens. They sure seem to have a lot of fun
2. God must love feed - in' all the chick - ens. They sure seem to have a lot to eat.
3. God must love talk - in' with the chick - ens. They must have a whole lot to say.
D G
flap - pin' their wings, danc - in' and a - scratch - in', stick - in' their necks out,
There must be a mil - lion piec - es of chick - en food all a -
They all seem to know the same sto - ry, pass - in' it a - round fresh
3rd time to Coda
1. D G
yell - in' at the sun.
2. D G
round their feet. They're peck - in' and scratch - in' and
danc - in' and a - walk - in', stick - in' their necks out, yell - in' at the sun,
D G

eat - in' and drink - in', sit - tin' and a - talk - in'. The chick - en's day is a
D G G Instrumental
lot of fun.
D G
2nd time: D.S. al Coda
D G
CODA
D G C G
ev - 'ry day. God loves chick - ens, too.
D G C
All the oth - er an - i - mals know it's true. You hear 'em talk - in'
1. 2.
G D G G D G
down at the zoo. God loves chick - ens, too. too.

God of Wonders

Words and Music by
STEVE HINDALONG and MARC BYRD

Heavy acoustic feel (♩=80)
C2 Dm B♭2
1. Lord of all cre - a - tion,
2. Ear - ly in the morn - ing,
C2 Dm B♭2
of wa - ter, earth, and sky,
I will cel - e - brate the light.
C2 Dm B♭2
the heav - ens are Your tab - er - nac - le.
When I stum - ble in the dark - ness,
C2 Dm B♭2
Glo - ry to the Lord on high!
I will call Your name by night.
F Csus C
God of won - ders be - yond our gal - ax - y, You are
B♭maj9
ho - ly, ho - ly. The
F Csus C
u - ni - verse de - clares Your maj - es - ty. You are

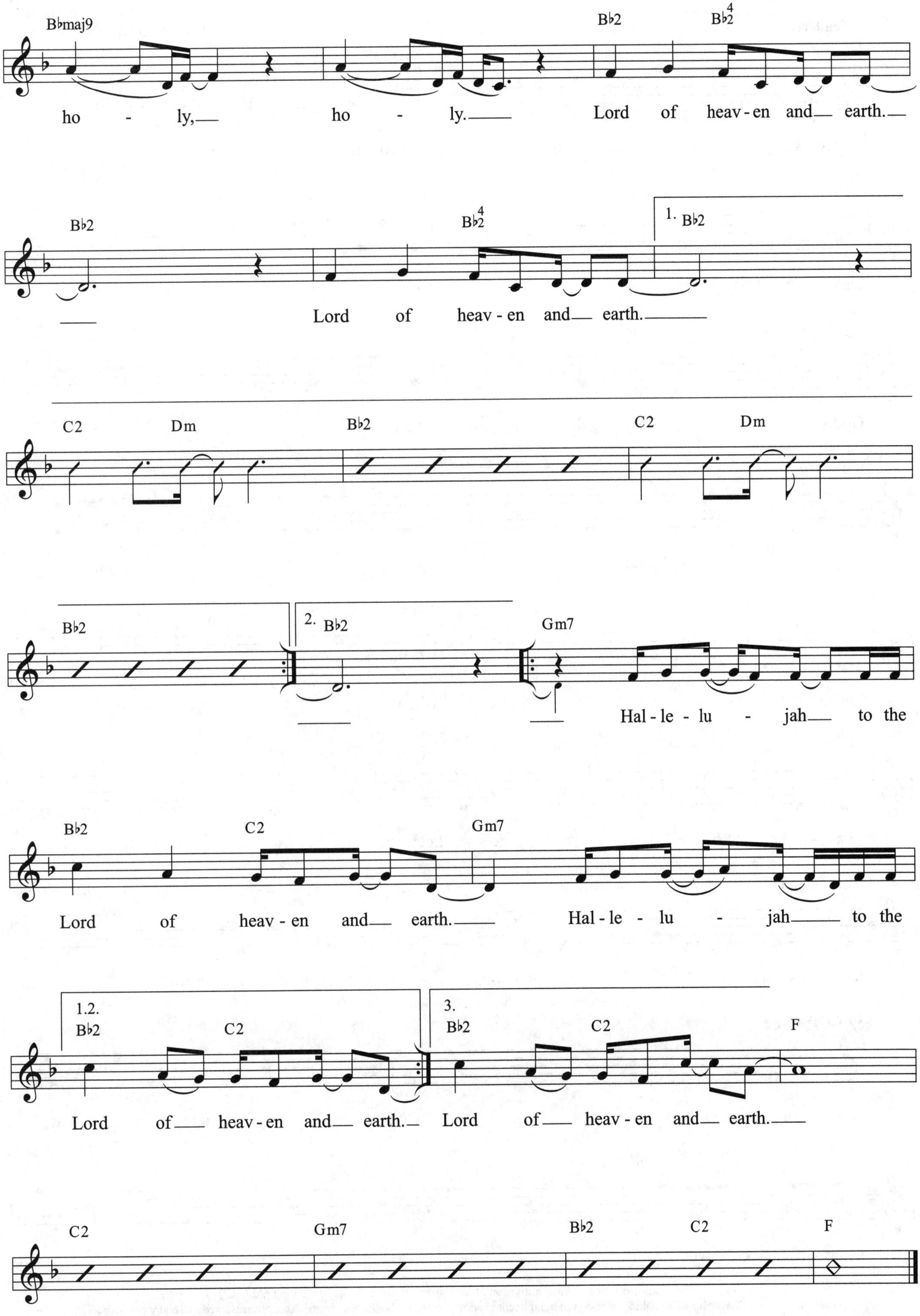
B♭maj9
ho - ly, ho - ly.
B♭2 B♭2 4
Lord of heav-en and earth.
B♭2 B♭2 4 1. B♭2
Lord of heav-en and earth.
C2 Dm B♭2 C2 Dm
B♭2 2. B♭2 Gm7
Hal-le-lu - jah to the
B♭2 C2 Gm7
Lord of heav-en and earth. Hal-le - lu - jah to the
1.2. B♭2 C2 3. B♭2 C2 F
Lord of heav-en and earth. Lord of heav-en and earth.
C2 Gm7 B♭2 C2 F

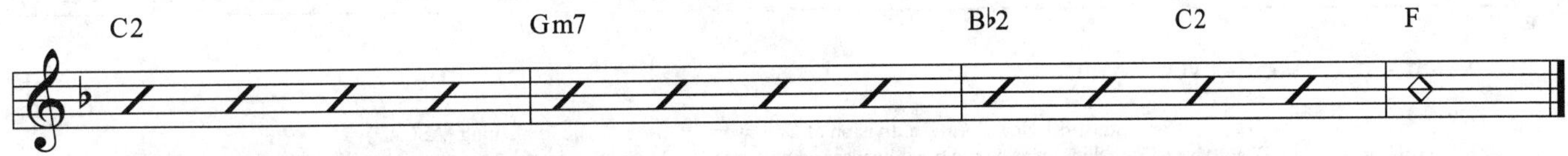

God's Angels Are Watchin' Over You

Words and Music by
JANET MCMAHAN-WILSON

Tenderly
F
Dm
B♭
Gm
God's an - gels are watch - in' o - ver you,
B♭
Gm
F
C
watch - in' o - ver you, watch - in' o - ver you.
F
Dm
B♭
A
God's an - gels are watch - in' o - ver you
B♭
Gm
2nd time to Coda
F
day and night. While
Dm
C/E
Fsus
F
F/A
F
you're a - wake and when you sleep, your
B♭
C/E
Fsus
F/A
F
B♭
C
Fa - ther has His an - gels keep you in their
Dm
C
G/B
C
D.C. al Coda
con - stant care all the time, ev - 'ry - where.
CODA
F
night. God's an - gels are
Gm
Dm
watch - in' o - ver you.

God's Top Ten

Words and Music by
TROY NILSSON and GENIE NILSSON

Brightly (♩=152)
C G/C D7/A G
God's top 10 com - mand - ments give us long and hap - py days.
G7 C
God's top 10 com - mand - ments make us hap - py to o - bey.
F
God's top 10 com - mand - ments, they're God's work of art. God
D13 C/G A7 Dm G7 C
wrote them on the tab - lets, and He writes them on our hearts. It will go
Gsus G Am7/G G F
well with you if you wor - ship God a - lone.
C Gsus G Am7/G G F
It will go well with you if you don't bow down to i -
C F C/E
- dols and you hon - or God's name and His ho - ly day
Dm7 C F
and your mom and dad. Don't kill. Be true to your
C/E Dm7 1. C 2. C
mate. Don't steal. Don't lie and nev - er cov - et. It will go - et.

God's Holy Day

Words and Music by
TROY NILSSON and GENIE NILSSON

Joyously (𝅗𝅥=108)
Hey, hey, hey, it's God's ho-ly day. We can sing and pray on God's ho-ly day, A day of rest, a day of peace, spend-ing time with fam-i-ly, On God's ho-ly day, Hey, hey, hey!
It's a great day to love your neigh-bor, it's a great day to serve your Sav-ior, It's a great day to rest from all your work, aah; It's a great day to read your Bi-ble, it's a great day to have re-viv-al, It's a great day to see your friends at church.
Hey, hey, hey, it's God's ho-ly day, We can sing and pray on God's ho-ly day, A day of rest, a day of peace, spend-ing time with fam-i-ly, On God's ho-ly day, Hey, hey, hey! When God fin-ished
C G7 C F Dm7 C G2 G C G C G C F♯/E G C G7 C F Dm7 C G2 G C

G
C
His cre - a - tion, He made time for re - lax - a - tion, By giv - ing us the Sab - bath
G
C
G
day; He said, "It's a great day for cel - e - bra - tion, rest - ing and re -
C
F♯
E
G
A♭7
ju - ve - na - tion, It's a great day to dance your blues a - way." It's
D♭
A♭
a great day to love your neigh - bor, it's a great day to serve your Sav - ior,
D♭
A♭
D♭
It's a great day to rest from all your work, It's a great day to
A♭
D♭
read your Bi - ble, it's a great day to have re - viv - al, It's a great day to
G
F
A♭
D♭
see your friends at church. Hey, hey, hey, it's
A♭7
D♭
God's ho - ly day, We can sing and pray on God's ho - ly day,
G♭
A day of rest, a day of peace, spend - ing time with
E♭m7
D♭
A♭2
A♭
D♭
fam - i - ly, On God's ho - ly day, Hey, hey, hey!

God's Name Is Holy

Words and Music by
TROY NILSSON and GENIE NILSSON

Lightly in two (𝅗𝅥=70)
C G7sus G G7
God's name is ho - ly.__ God's name is
C F
ho - ly.__ God's name is ho - ly.__
G7 C C
Ho - ly is His name. Treat God's name in a
Gsus G C
spe - cial way.__ Nev - er say__ God's name in vain.__
C F G7sus G7
Say what you mean and mean what you pray. Treat God's name in a
C G7sus G
spe - cial way.__ God's name is ho - ly.__
G7 C
God's name is ho - ly.__ God's name is
F G7 C
ho - ly.__ Ho - ly is His name.

Gsus G
Treat God's name in a spe - cial way.__ Nev - er say__ God's
C F
name in vain.__ Say what you mean and mean what you pray.
G7sus G7 C D♭
Treat God's name in a spe - cial way.__ Treat God's name in a
A♭sus A♭ D♭
spe - cial way.__ Nev - er say__ God's name in vain.__
G♭ A♭7sus A♭7
Say what you mean and mean what you pray. Treat God's name in a
D♭ D♭ A♭7sus A♭
spe - cial way.__ God's name is ho - ly.__
A♭7 D♭
God's name is ho - ly.__ God's name is
G♭ A♭7 D♭
ho - ly.__ Ho - ly is His name.
A♭7 D♭ A♭7 D♭
Ho - ly is His name. Ho - ly is His name.

God's Wacky Animals

Words and Music by
BEN RYAN, TOM STEINMAN and JAY TYLER

Jungle rap
Em
God's wack - y an - i - mals. God's wack - y
N.C.
an - i - mals.
1. Do your dance. Swing through the trees limb to limb; hang from your knees
2. Do your dance from the heart. Nev - er ev - er stop once you start.
up - side down, up in the out - side. Grab a friend; slip down the down - slide.
Make some noise. Don't be sneak - y. Hug some - bod - y cheek to cheek - y.
Up a - gain, dance on the ceil - ing; raise the roof. Show what you're feel - ing.
Share the life that you're giv - en. Let your - self go; shed your skin.
Shake it up to the next lev - el. Shout to God. Sing it to heav - en.
Do your dance. Show your re - la - tion. Jump up and join in God's cre - a - tion.
Em G Em
God's wack - y an - i - mals. God's wack - y
G Em A
an - i - mals. The an - i - mal king - dom looks cra - zy,
B Em
go - ing ba - na - nas, get - tin' nuts, but God's wack - y
G Em 1. 2.
an - i - mals know what's up. up.
Em Repeat several times G Em Last time G Em
God's wack - y an - i - mals. an - i - mals.

Grace Is Bigger

Words and Music by
KAREN DEAN

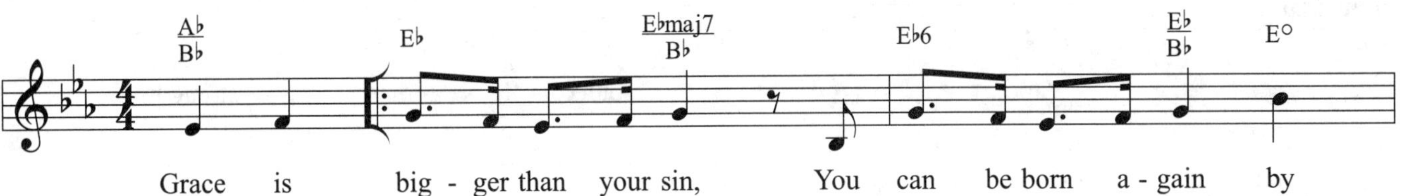
A♭/B♭ E♭ E♭maj7/B♭ E♭6 E♭/B♭ E°
Grace is big - ger than your sin, You can be born a - gain by

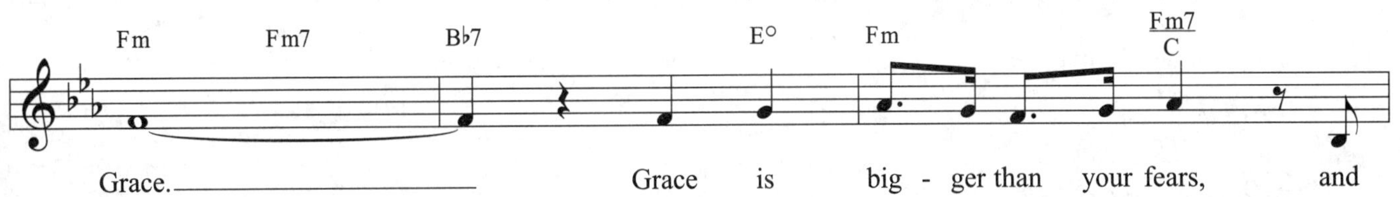
Fm Fm7 B♭7 E° Fm Fm7/C
Grace. Grace is big - ger than your fears, and

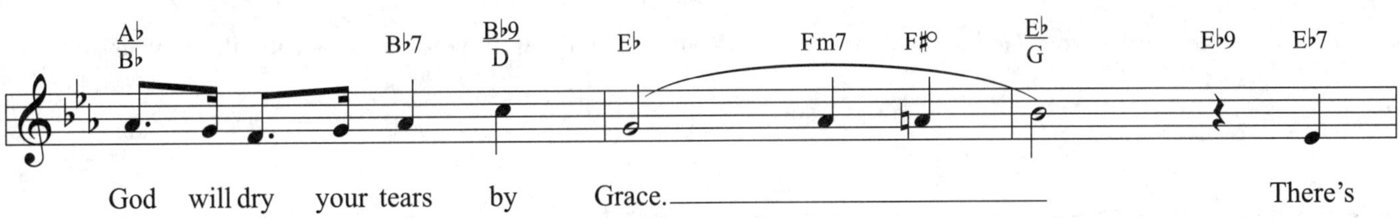
A♭/B♭ B♭7 B♭9/D E♭ Fm7 F♯° E♭/G E♭9 E♭7
God will dry your tears by Grace. There's

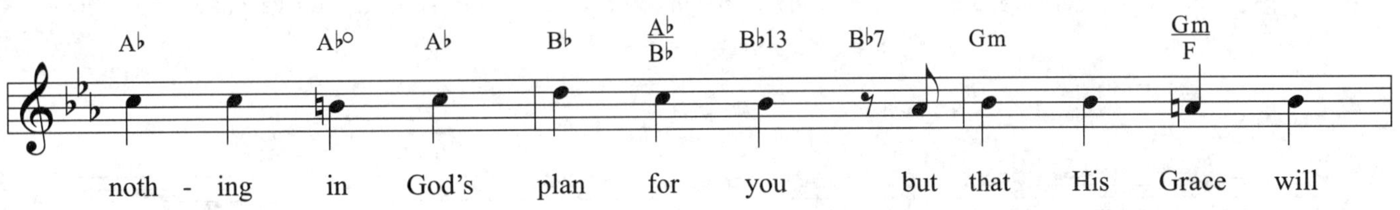
A♭ A♭° A♭ B♭ A♭/B♭ B♭13 B♭7 Gm Gm/F
noth - ing in God's plan for you but that His Grace will

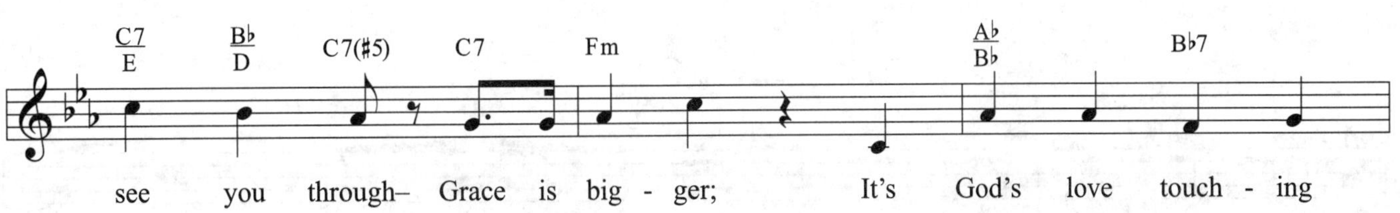
C7/E B♭/D C7(♯5) C7 Fm A♭/B♭ B♭7
see you through– Grace is big - ger; It's God's love touch - ing

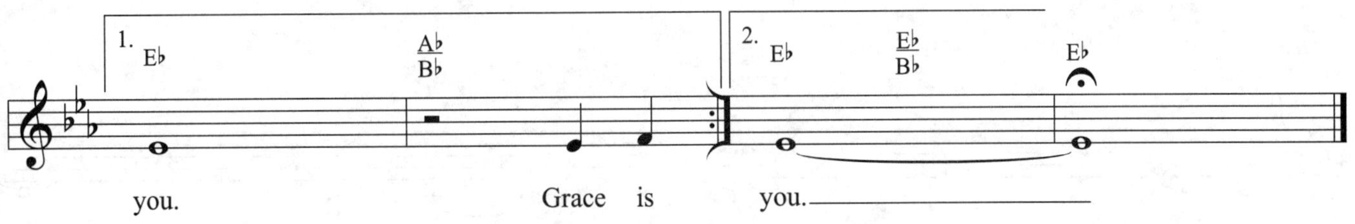
1. E♭ A♭/B♭ 2. E♭ E♭/B♭ E♭
you. Grace is you.

Greatest Commandments

Words and Music by
TROY NILSSON and GENIE NILSSON

Moderately (♩=72)
C G/B Am G C G/B
Love, God, heart, soul, mind, strength,

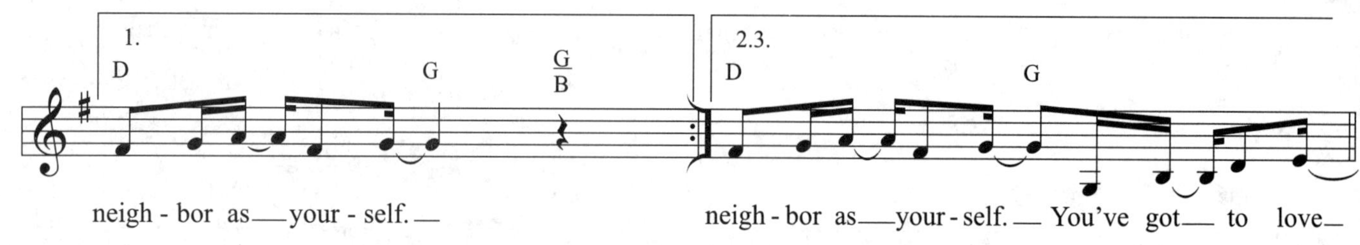
1.
D G G/B
neigh - bor as your - self.
2.3.
D G
neigh - bor as your - self. You've got to love

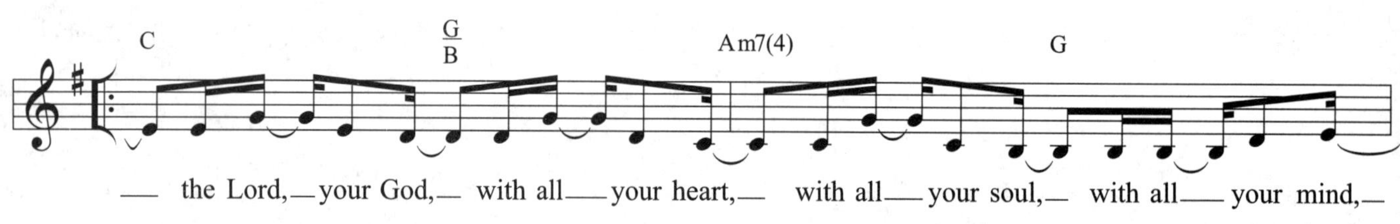
C G/B Am7(4) G
the Lord, your God, with all your heart, with all your soul, with all your mind,

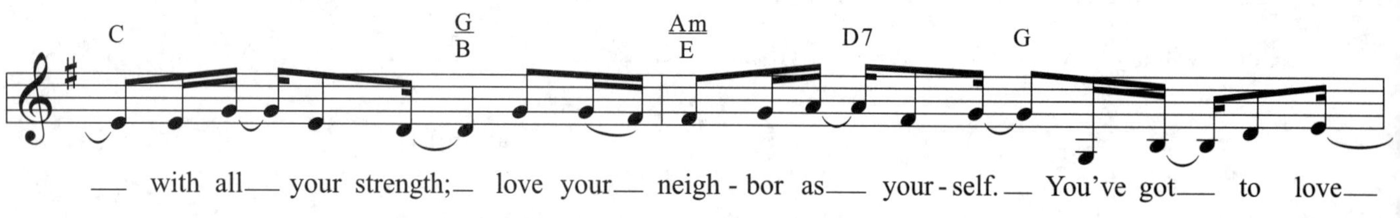
C G/B Am/E D7 G
with all your strength; love your neigh - bor as your - self. You've got to love

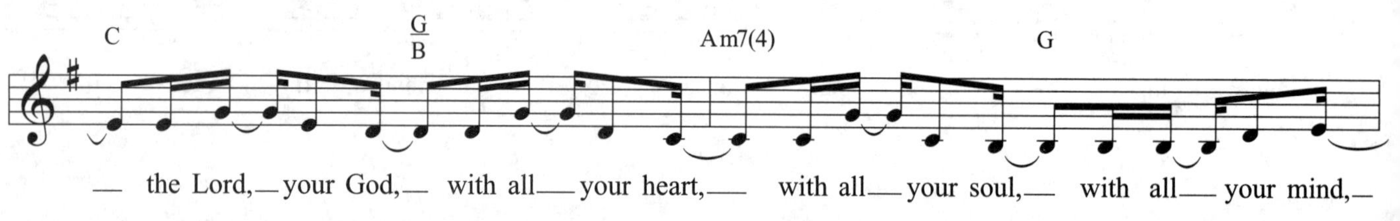
C G/B Am7(4) G
the Lord, your God, with all your heart, with all your soul, with all your mind,

3rd time to Coda
C G/B Am/E D7 G
with all your strength; love your neigh - bor as your - self. These two,

B♭ F F♯ G G/A
they're the great - est com - mand - ments. These two,

B♭ F F♯ 1. G G/B
they're the great - est com - mand - ments. You've got to love
2. G G/A G/B G/C D
- ments. There is no com - mand - ment that is
C G A7
great - er than these. There is no com - mand - ment that is
D7 D.C. al Coda
great - er than these.
CODA
Am D7 G
neigh - bor as your - self. These two,
B♭ F F♯ G
they're the great - est com - mand - ments. Mark twelve: thir - ty and thir - ty - one.
B♭ F F♯ G
They're the great - est com - mand - ments. Mark twelve: thir - ty and thir - ty - one.
B♭ F F♯ G
They're the great - est com - mand - ments. Mark twelve: thir - ty and thir - ty - one.
B♭ F rit. F♯ G
They're the great - est com - mand - ments.

Growin' the Fruits of the Spirit

Words and Music by
RUTH ELAINE SCHRAM

Happy two!
Like fruit we eat at snack time, like ap - ples, grapes, and pears, the
Spir - it of the Lord has fruit that we a - lone can bear. A
love for one an - oth - er, a love we can - not hide, a
joy that comes from know - ing God is al - ways on our side. Grow - in' the
fruits of the Spir - it, grow - in' the fruits of the
Spir - it, grow - in' the fruits of the Spir - it with -
in the heart of me. Like gen - tle - ness and
kind - ness, like faith and self - con - trol, like peace that pass - es
un - der - stand - ing deep down in my soul. Grow - in' the

fruits of the Spir - it, grow - in' the fruits of the
Spir - it, grow - in' the fruits of the Spir - it with -
in the heart of me.
Now, I be - long to Je - sus. I
want to live for Him. The Spir - it of the Lord took o - ver
when I let Him in. Grow - in' the fruits of the Spir - it, grow - in' the
fruits of the Spir - it, grow - in' the fruits of the Spir - it with -
in the heart of me. Grow - in' the in the heart of
me.

Grumblers

Words and Music by
THORO HARRIS

In coun - try, town or cit - y some peo - ple can be found Who
spend their lives in grum - bling at ev - 'ry - thing a - round. O
yes, they al - ways grum - ble, no mat - ter what we say, For
these are chron - ic grum - blers, and they grum - ble night and day. O they
grum - ble on Mon - day, Tues - day, Wednes - day, Grum - ble on Thurs - day, too;
Grum - ble on Fri - day, Sat - ur - day, Sun - day, Grum - ble the whole week through.
Grum - ble the whole week through. They grum - ble on Mon - day, Tues - day, Wednes - day,
Grum - ble on Thurs - day, too; Grum - ble on Fri - day, Sat - ur - day, Sun - day,
Grum - ble the whole week through! Grum - ble the whole week through!

H-O-P-E

Words and Music by
JANET MCMAHAN-WILSON
and DEBRA BLACK

Brightly (♩=126)
He gives me H - O - P - E, hope in my H - E - A - R - T.
H - O - P - E, hope is a - live in - side of me. And I tru - ly T - R -
U - S - T Him ev - 'ry sin - gle day. For I have H - O - P - E, hope down
in my heart to stay.
He gives me H - O - P - E,
hope in my H - E - A - R - T. H - O - P - E, hope is a -
live in - side of me. And I tru - ly T - R - U - S - T Him ev - 'ry sin - gle
day. For I have H - O - P - E, hope down in my heart to
stay.

Ha-La-La-La

Words and Music by
DAVID GRAHAM

Ha-le-la-le-lu-jah!

Words and Music by
JANET MCMAHAN-WILSON

With energy!
C C#°7 Dm G+
The Lord led Mo - ses out of E - gypt's land.___ He
C C°7 Dm G+
brought him out from un - der ol' Pha - raoh's hand.___ With a
C C7/B♭ F/A Fm/A♭ G
cloud by day___ and a fire by night,___ Je - ho - vah God guid - ed the
C
Is - ra - el - ites.___ He freed them from their fright - ful plight.___
F C Dm
Hal - le, hal - le - la - le - lu - jah, hal -
G C F C
- le - lu - jah! Let us all___ pro - claim, hal - le, hal -
Dm G C
- le - la - le - lu - jah, hal - le - lu - jah! Praise the Lord.___
A♭
___ The
D♭ D°7 E♭m A♭+
Lord took Mo - ses to the moun - tain - top.___ He

D♭
D°7
E♭m
A♭+
showed him all the "shalts" and the "thou shalt nots." Then He
D♭
D♭7
B
G♭
B♭
G♭m
A
sent them birds and bread to eat. The
A♭
quail and the man - na were quite a treat.
D♭
Yum, yum, eat 'em up. It can't be beat.
G♭
D♭
E♭m
Hal - le, hal - le - la - le - lu - jah, hal -
A♭
D♭
G♭
D♭
- le - lu - jah! Let us all pro - claim, hal - le, hal -
E♭m
A♭
D♭
- le - la - le - lu - jah, hal - le - lu - jah! Praise the Lord.
A
The
D
D♯°7
Em
A+
Lord is watch - in' o - ver me and you like

D D♯°7 Em A+
He did for Mo - ses and his trav - 'lin' crew. So
D D7/C G/B Gm/B♭
sing a song and say a prayer to
A
thank your heav'n - ly Fa - ther for His care. Je -
D G D
ho - vah is with you ev - 'ry - where. Hal - le, hal -
Em A D
- le - la - le - lu - jah, hal - le - lu - jah! Let us all pro - claim,
G D Em
hal - le, hal - le - la - le - lu - jah, hal -
A D Bm Em
- le - lu - jah! Praise the Lord. Hal -
A D Bm Em
- le - lu - jah! Praise the Lord. Hal -
A D
- le - lu - jah! Praise the Lord.

Hallelu, Hallelujah!

Traditional

G G/B C Am7
Hal - le - lu, Hal - le - lu, Hal - le - lu, Hal - le - lu - jah!
G/D D7 G C/G G D7/A G/B
Praise ye the Lord! Hal - le - lu, Hal - le - lu, Hal - le-
C Am7(♭5) G/D D7
lu, Hal - le - lu - jah! Praise ye the
G C/D G D
Lord! Praise ye the Lord, Hal - le - lu - jah!
D7 G G7/B
Praise ye the Lord, Hal - le - lu - jah! Praise ye the
Am/C E/B Am G/D D7 G G/F E♭7 D♭/E♭
Lord, Hal - le - lu - jah! Praise ye the Lord!
A♭ A♭/G Fm7 B♭9 B♭m7 E♭7 E♭ E♭/D♭
Praise ye the Lord, Hal - le - lu - jah! Praise ye the
A♭/C E♭/B♭ A♭ D♭/E♭ A♭ A♭7 B♭m/D♭ F/C B♭m D♭m6
Lord, Hal - le - lu - jah! Praise ye the Lord, Hal - le - lu - jah!
E♭9sus E♭7 1. A♭ D♭/E♭ 2. A♭
Praise ye the Lord! Lord!

Happy All the Time

Words and Music by
A. B. SIMPSON

I'm in - right, out - right, up - right, down - right, hap - py all the time. I'm
in - right, out - right, up - right, down - right, hap - py all the time. Since Je - sus Christ came in and
cleansed my heart from sin, I'm in - right, out - right, up - right, down - right,
hap - py all the time! I'm hap - py all the time! I'm
in - right, out - right, up - right, down - right, hap - py all the time. I'm
in - right, out - right, up - right, down - right, hap - py all the time. Since
Je - sus Christ came in and cleansed my heart from sin, I'm
in - right, out - right, up - right, down - right, hap - py all the time! I'm
in - right, out - right, up - right, down - right, hap - py all the time!

Hallelujah, Praise the Lord

Words and Music by
JANET MCMAHAN-WILSON

Slow two
Em
1. Lift your voic - es to the sky.
2. Lift your voic - es to the sky.
3. Lift your voic - es to the sky.
Am7
B7
Hal - le - lu - jah! Praise the Lord. Our
Hal - le - lu - jah! Praise the Lord. Our
Hal - le - lu - jah! Praise the Lord. Our
Em
God Je - ho - vah reigns on high.
God Je - ho - vah reigns on high.
God Je - ho - vah reigns on high.
B
Em
Hal - le - lu - jah! Praise the Lord. He
Hal - le - lu - jah! Praise the Lord. He
Hal - le - lu - jah! Praise the Lord. It's
C7
freed us from ol' Pha - raoh's hand,
o - pened up that big Red Sea,
just like it was way back then.
Em
led us 'cross the des - ert sand. With a
swal - lowed up the en - e - my. Then He
God will do the same a - gain. Put your
C7
cloud by day and the fire by night, He
gave the "shalts" and the "thou shalt nots" way
faith in Him and He'll lead your way. He'll

B C7 B
saved us from our fright - ful plight.
up there on that moun - tain - top.
be right with you ev - 'ry day.
Am7 B
Sing, sing, glo - ry hal - le - lu - jah.
Em
Am7 B Em
Hal - le - lu - jah! Praise the Lord.
B Em
Hal - le - lu - jah! Praise the Lord.
Am7 B
Sing, sing hal -
Am7 B
- le - lu - jah! Praise the Lord.
Am7 B Em
Sing, sing hal - le - lu - jah! Praise the Lord.
(whisper)
Hal - le - lu - jah! Praise the Lord.

Have Mercy on Me, Lord

Words and Music by
JANET MCMAHAN-WILSON and LORI CASTEEL

Calypso feel

G
C
1. Cre - ate in me a clean heart.
(2.) blot out all my e - vil.
D
G
Help me make a new start.
Soothe my soul's up - heav - al.
C
Wash me 'til I'm whit - er than snow. Fill me
Hide Your face from all of my sin. Let Your
D
G
'til I o - ver flow. Have
Spir - it live with - in.
C
G
D
mer - cy on me, Lord. Have mer - cy and re - store
G
C
G
the joy of sal - va - tion. Let all cre - a - tion
D
1. G
sing of Your mer - cy, oh Lord.

D
2. Lord,
2. G
C
G
Lord. Have mer - cy on me, Lord. Have
D
G
C
mer - cy and re - store the joy of sal - va - tion.
G
D
Let all cre - a - tion sing of Your mer - cy, oh
G
D
G
Lord, sing of Your mer - cy, oh Lord,
D
sing of Your mer - cy, oh
G
C
G
Lord.

He Is Always There

Words and Music by
JANET MCMAHAN-WILSON

Tenderly (♩.=50)

D
God takes care of you day and night.
You are al - ways in His sight.
G D/F♯ Em A D Em A
An - y - time, an - y - where, He is al - ways
D 1. 2. Em A D
rit.
there.

He Is Lord

Traditional

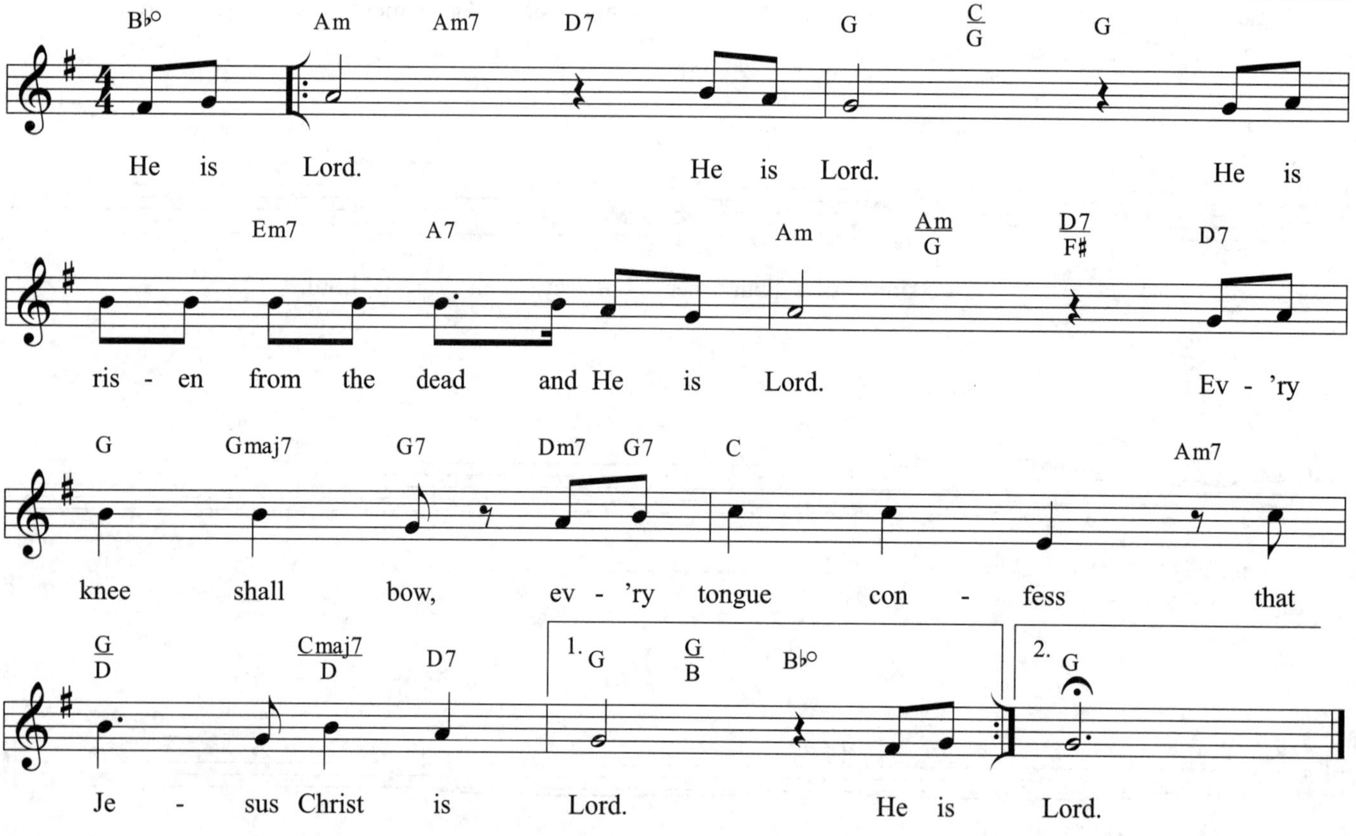

B♭o Am Am7 D7 G C/G G
He is Lord. He is Lord. He is
Em7 A7 Am Am/G D7/F♯ D7
ris - en from the dead and He is Lord. Ev - 'ry
G Gmaj7 G7 Dm7 G7 C Am7
knee shall bow, ev - 'ry tongue con - fess that
G/D Cmaj7/D D7 1. G G/B B♭o 2. G
Je - sus Christ is Lord. He is Lord.

He L-O-V-E-S Me

Words and Music by
JANET WILSON and TED WILSON

Verse
1. Since Je - sus filled me with His L - O - V - E, now it's all so clear to see. He is the J - O - Y in - side my H - E - A - R - T. He gave His L - I - F - E as a G - I - F - T just for M - E. Now I want to T - E - L - L all the world.
(2. If you will) B - E - L - I - E - V - E He'll give you ev - 'ry - thing you need, He'll be the J - O - Y in - side your H - E - A - R - T. He'll give you L - I - F - E as a G - I - F - T. And you'll S - E - E, you'll
He
Chorus
L - O - V - E - S M - E. He L - O - V - E - S M - E. Yes, I know J - E - S - U - S L - O - V - E - S me.
He said He L - O - V - E - S M - E. He L - O - V - E - S M - E, and I know He L - O - V - E - S
1.
Y - O - U, too.
to Verse
2. If you will
2.
Repeat Chorus
Y - O - U, too. He
3.
loves you, too.

He Is the Rock

Words and Music by
TROY NILSSON and GENIE NILSSON

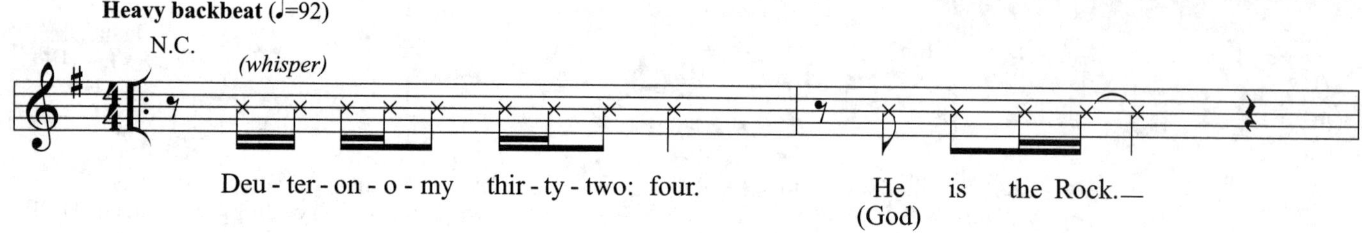
Heavy backbeat (♩=92)
N.C.
(whisper)
Deu - ter - on - o - my thir - ty - two: four.
He is the Rock.
(God)

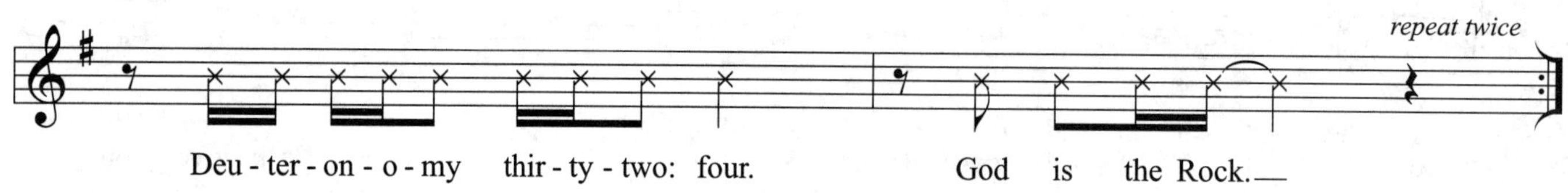
repeat twice
Deu - ter - on - o - my thir - ty - two: four.
God is the Rock.

E(no3)
(shout)
Who is the Rock ex - cept our God?
He is the Rock.

Who is God be - sides the Lord?
He is the Rock.

E(no3)
Who is the Rock? He is the Rock.
Who is the Rock? He is the Rock.

Fine
Who is the Rock? He is the Rock.
God is the Rock!

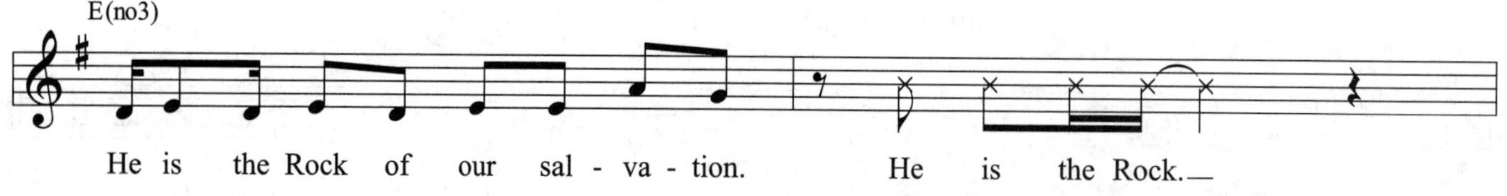
E(no3)
He is the Rock of our sal - va - tion.
He is the Rock.

He is the Rock, the Rock of ag - es. He is the Rock.

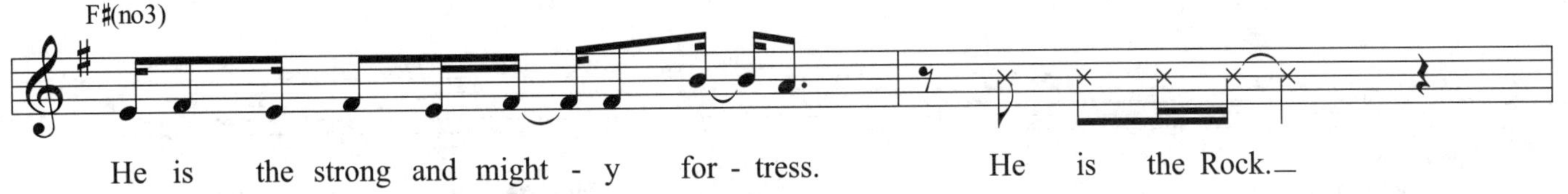
F♯(no3)
He is the strong and might - y for - tress. He is the Rock.

G(no3)
A(no3)
B(no3)
He is the war - rior fight - ing for us. He is the Rock. The

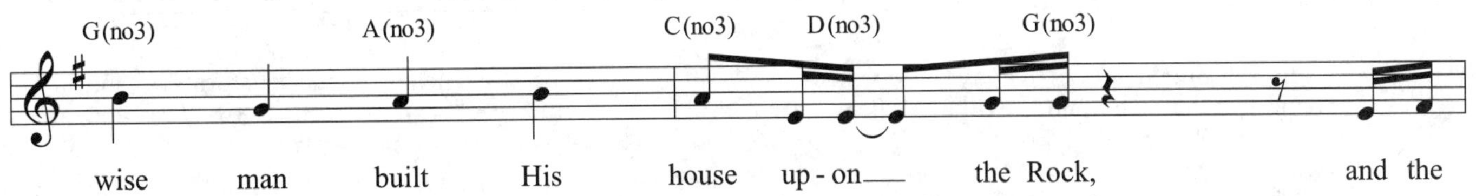
G(no3)
A(no3)
C(no3)
D(no3)
G(no3)
wise man built His house up - on the Rock, and the

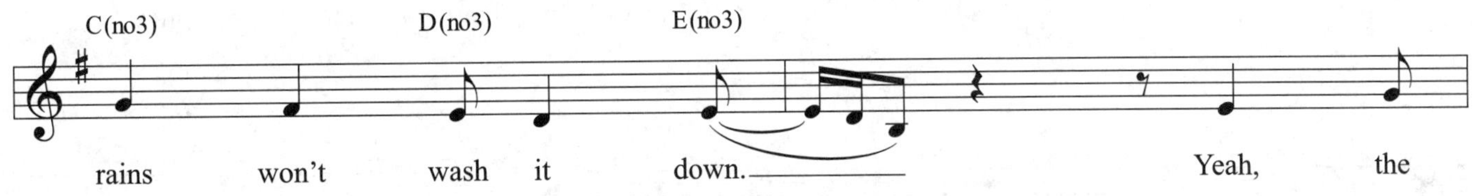
C(no3)
D(no3)
E(no3)
rains won't wash it down. Yeah, the

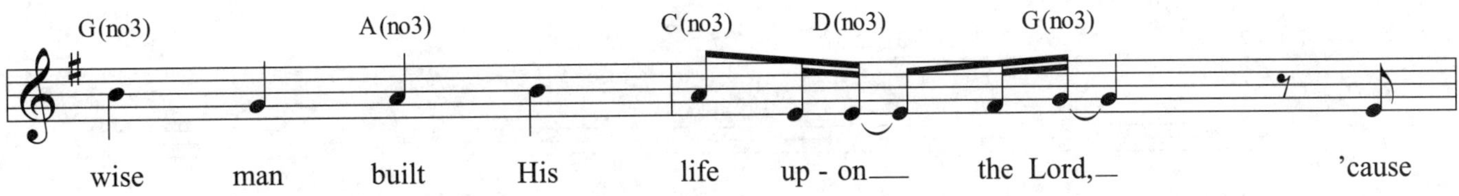
G(no3)
A(no3)
C(no3)
D(no3)
G(no3)
wise man built His life up - on the Lord, 'cause

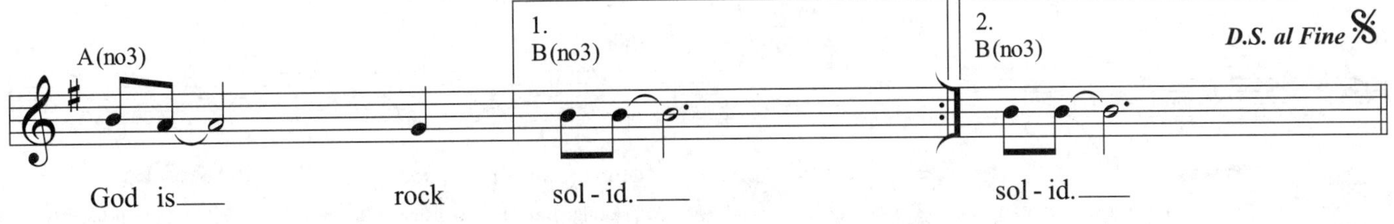
A(no3)
1.
B(no3)
2.
B(no3)
D.S. al Fine
God is rock sol - id. sol - id.

He Plants Me Like a Seed

Words and Music by
DOTTIE RAMBO and DAVID HUNTSINGER

Slowly (♩=66)
G♭ A♭/G♭
1. He plants me like a seed and
(2.) plants me like a seed be -
C♭m/G♭ G♭
watch - es as I grow. He wa - ters me with
neath the fer - tile land. My roots grow strong and
A♭/G♭ C♭m/G♭ G♭
love and shields me from the cold. My
deep while tend - ed by His hand. And
B♭m7 C♭maj7 B♭m7
2nd time to Coda
ten - der leaves may bend be - neath the storms and
soon the branch will bear the har - vest sweet and
C♭maj7 G♭
wind, but comes the morn - ing
A♭/G♭ C♭m/G♭ D♭7/G♭ G♭
D.S. al Coda
sun; I'm grow - ing strong a - gain. 2. He
CODA
C♭ C♭maj7 G♭
fair. The Mas - ter smiles to
A♭/G♭ C♭m/G♭ D♭7/G♭ G♭
see the fruit from one small seed.

He's Got the Whole World in His Hands

Traditional

He's Alive

(And the Tomb Is Empty Now)

Words and Music by
HERB OWEN
Lively
I came to the tomb of Je - sus, where
once His bod - y lay; they'd oft - en told me sto - ries that
thrilled me day by day. They told me how He suf - fered and
died on Cal - va - ry; and though I knew that it was true I
want - ed now to see that He's a - live and the
tomb is emp - ty now! He rose a - gain by His
grand tri - um - phant pow'r. He's seat - ed now at the
2nd time to Coda
Fa - ther's own right hand; the war is won, the work is done and He's a -

G
live! While
Em D/F♯ G
Je - sus walked a - mong us some prom - is - es were made; He
D A7 D D7
told us He'd re - mem - ber them the way that He had said. The
G Em D/F♯ G G/B
dead can't keep their prom - is - es, and He was cru - ci - fied; but
C G/B Em G/D D7 G
D.S. al Coda
all that He has prom - ised me will one day all be mine, for He's a -
CODA
G/D C G/D B7 Em Em/D C
won, the work is done and He's a - live! The war is
G/D C G/D Am7/D D7
won, the work is done and He's a -
G Am7 G/B C G/D D7 G D G
live!

He's Still Workin' on Me

Words and Music by
JOEL HEMPHILL

He's still work - in' on me, to make me what I ought to
be. It took Him just a week to make the moon and stars, the
sun and the earth and Ju - pi - ter and Mars. How lov - ing and pa - tient He must
2nd time to Coda
be! He's still work - in' on me! There
real - ly ought to be a sign up - on my heart: "Don't judge him yet, there's an
un - fin - ished part." But I'll be per - fect just ac -
D.C. al Coda
cord - ing to His plan, fash - ioned by the Mas - ter's lov - ing hand.
CODA
me! He's still work - in' on
me! He's still work - in' on me!

He's My Savior

(To the tune of Are You Sleeping?)

Words and Music by
STEVE TANNER

** Round begins on repeat*

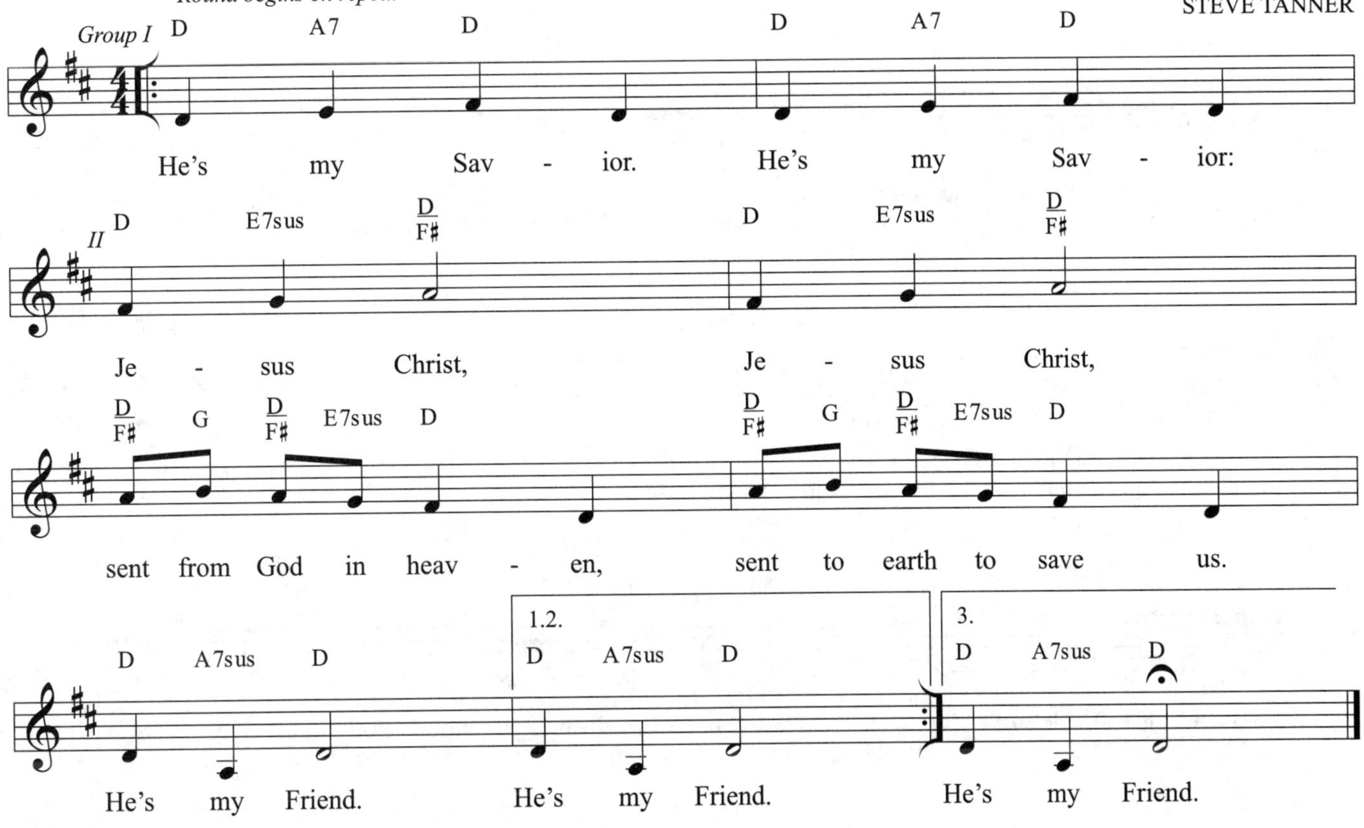

Group I D A7 D D A7 D

He's my Sav - ior. He's my Sav - ior:

II D E7sus D/F# D E7sus D/F#

Je - sus Christ, Je - sus Christ,

D/F# G D/F# E7sus D D/F# G D/F# E7sus D

sent from God in heav - en, sent to earth to save us.

D A7sus D | 1.2. D A7sus D | 3. D A7sus D

He's my Friend. He's my Friend. He's my Friend.

** Each group will sing the song three times.*

Only One Way

Words and Music by
LENNY WISEHART

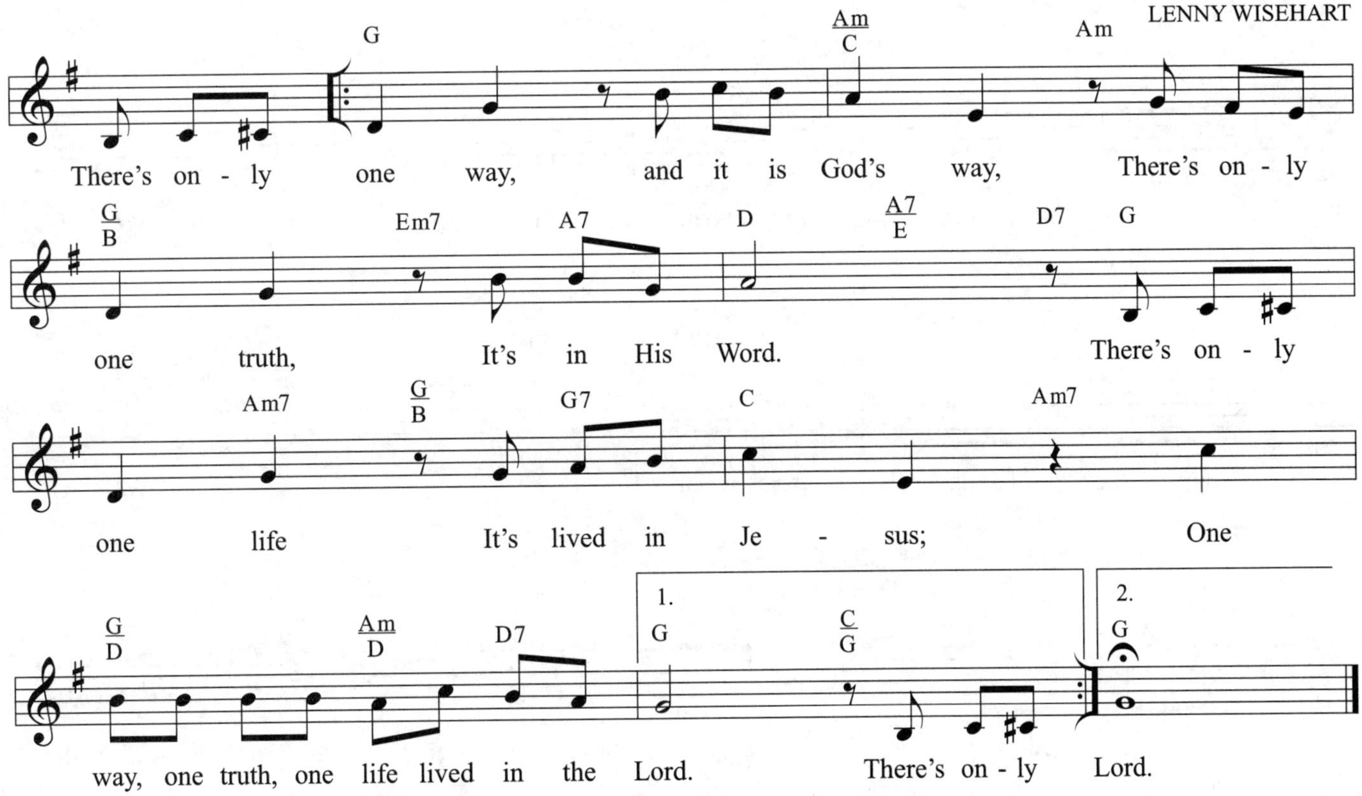

G Am/C Am

There's on - ly one way, and it is God's way, There's on - ly

G/B Em7 A7 D A7/E D7 G

one truth, It's in His Word. There's on - ly

Am7 G/B G7 C Am7

one life It's lived in Je - sus; One

G/D Am/D D7 | 1. G C/G | 2. G

way, one truth, one life lived in the Lord. There's on - ly Lord.

He'll Be Comin' in Clouds of Glory

(To the tune of She'll Be Comin' Around the Mountain)

Words and Music by
TRISH MENDOZA

Gm7 F
1. He'll be com - in' in clouds of glo - ry when He comes. He'll be
(2. We will) all go up to meet Him when He comes. We will
G7 C7 Gm7 C7 Dm7(4) C7/E
com - in' in clouds of glo - ry when He comes. He'll be
all go up to meet Him when He comes. We will
F Gm7(4) F/A B♭ G7
com - in' in clouds of glo - ry, He'll be com - in' in clouds of glo - ry, He'll be
all go up to meet Him, we will all go up to meet Him, we will
F/C Gm7 C7
com - in' in clouds of glo - ry when He comes.
all go up to meet Him when He
1. F B♭ F/A Gm7(4)
2. We will
2. F F/E♭ D♭7
comes. 3. We will
G♭
have the wed - ding sup - per when He comes. We will
G♭ A♭7 D♭7 A♭7 D♭7 E♭m7(4) D♭7/F
have the wed - ding sup - per when He comes. We will
G♭ A♭m7(4) G♭/B♭ C♭ A♭7
have the wed - ding sup - per, we will have the wed - ding sup - per, we will

Gb/Db
Abm7
Db7
Gb
Gb/Fb
D7
have the wed - ding sup - per when He comes.
4. We will
G
C
G/B
Am7
live with Him for - ev - er when He comes.
We will
G
Em7
A7
D
Am7
D
Em7(4)
D7/F#
live with Him for - ev - er when He comes.
We will
G
Am7(4)
G/B
C
A7
live with Him for - ev - er, we will live with Him for - ev - er, we will
G/D
Am7
D7
G
Em7
live with Him for - ev - er when He comes.
We will
G/D
C/D
live with Him for - ev - er when He
N.C.
Am7
D7
G
comes.

Hear Us Roar

Words and Music by
JANET MCMAHAN-WILSON
and GRETA GARNER-HART

Seriously (♩=104)

Cm
1. Hear us roar. (roar) Hear us roar. (roar) Hear us
(2.) hands. (clap, clap, clap) Clap your hands, (clap, clap, clap) as we
(3.) prayer. (A - men) Say a prayer, (A - men) as we

C7/E
Fm
tell - ing all the world we love the Lord. We will
spread the word of God a - cross the land. We will
thank Him for His nev - er - end - ing care. We will

D7(♭5)
G7
Cm
A♭
cry out and pro - claim His high and ho - ly name. Hear us
cry out and pro - claim His high and ho - ly name. Clap your
cry out and pro - claim His high and ho - ly name. Say a

G
roar. (roar) Hear us roar. (roar) Hear us
hands. (clap, clap, clap) Clap your hands. (clap, clap, clap) Clap your
prayer. (A - men) Say a prayer. (A - men) Say a

Cm
1.2.
G Cm
3.
roar.
hands.
prayer.
2. Clap your
3. Say a
(A - men!)

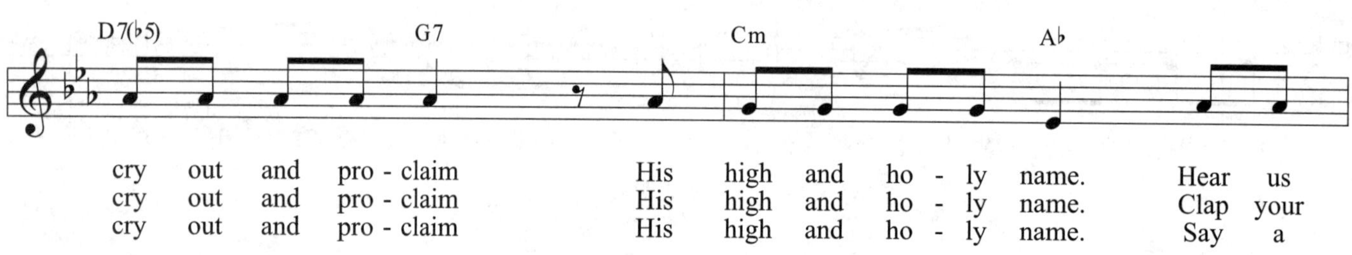

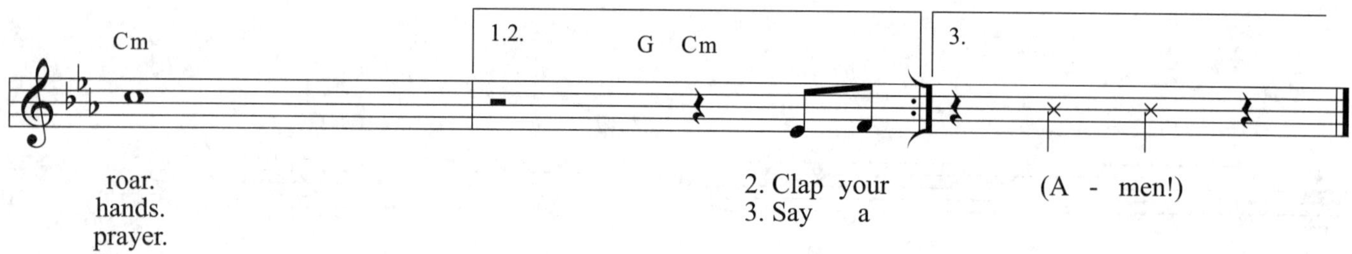

His Law Is My Delight

Words and Music by
JANET MCMAHAN-WILSON

Help Me to Grow

Words and Music by
HERB OWEN

Moderato, sweetly
As a new mem-ber of the fam - 'ly, I hard - ly know a
thing ex - cept that Je - sus loves me, and for
this His praise I sing. But I'm sure there must be
more that God wants me to know; so I
ask of you to help me, please, that I in the Lord might grow.
Help me to grow; teach me to live like Je - sus.
Teach me the truths of the Word of God, that I might live for
Him. Teach me to know ev - 'ry-thing He's
told us. Show me the way, teach me to pray,

G D/F♯ G F♯/A♯ Bm D7/A G D/F♯
help me to know how to live to - day; take the time to
Em7 A G D/F♯ Em7 A G D/F♯
help me to grow in the Lord. Take the time to
Em7 A7 2nd time to Coda D G D A7
help me to grow in the Lord. On the
F♯ Bm A
day I be-came a Chris - tian, I be-came a ba - by
D F♯ Bm D/A
boy who brought the Fa - ther hap - pi - ness and
E/G♯ D/E E7 A G A/G G
gave the an - gels joy! But I don't want to stay a
D/F♯ D F♯ Bm D7/A
ba - by, I want to be a man; so I'll
E/G♯ E D/F♯ E/G♯
grow in the Lord if you'll take the time to give me all the help you
A D.S. al Coda CODA D
can. Lord.

Help Me Walk in Your Way

Words and Music by
JANET MCMAHAN-WILSON and TED WILSON

Bright swing
C F G
Help me walk in Your way, oh Lord.
C F G
Help me walk in Your way.
C C7/B♭ F F♯°7
Reach me, teach me ev - 'ry day.
C/G G7 C F
Help me walk in Your way. (Help me walk.
C F C F
Help me walk. Help me walk in Your
A D
way - ay - ay - ay.) Help me talk in Your
G A D
way, oh Lord. Help me talk in Your
G A D D7/C G
way. Reach me, teach me ev -

G♯°7
D
A
A7
D
-
'ry
day.
Help
me
talk
in
Your
way.
G
D
G
(Help
me
talk.
Help
me
talk.
D
G
B
Help
me
talk
in
Your
way
-
ay
-
ay
-
ay.)
E
A
B
Help
me
live
in
Your
way,
oh
Lord.
E
A
B
Help
me
live
in
Your
way.
E
E7
D
A
A♯°7
Reach
me,
teach
me
ev
-
'ry
day.
E
B
B7
E
B
B7
Help
me
live
in
Your,
help
me
talk
in
Your,
E
B
B7
E
help
me
walk
in
Your
way.

Hey! I Need You!

Words and Music by
PAM ANDREWS and JOHNATHAN CRUMPTON

Cm
F/C
Would-n't it be sil - ly if the foot should say, "Hand, I don't need you an - y - more"?
ear
"Eye,
Would-n't it be sil - ly if the hand should say, "Ear, I don't need to hear an - y - more"?
eye
"Foot,
run
G7sus
G7
B♭/D
E♭
F
How would they sur - vive?
F7
How would they stay a - live?
G7(♯5♯9)
Hey! I need you! Hey! Hey! You need me! There are man - y, man - y parts, but just one bod - y.
F9
Hey! I need you! Hey! Hey! You need me! How good it is to dwell to-geth - er,
A♭maj9
so it is with Christ.
Cm7
1.

F G7(♯5♯9)
2. F/C Cm7
Would the
F7 Cm7
slide
bod - y sur - vive with just hands? No! No!
F/C Cm7 Cm7 F/C Cm7 F7
Would the bod - y sur - vive with just
Cm7 F/C Cm7 Cm7 F/C Cm7
slide
feet? No! No! Would the
F7 G7
bod - y sur - vive with just eyes and ears? It would not
G7(♯5♯9) Cm F/C Cm
be com - plete. Hey! I need you! Hey!
F/C Cm F7 F9
Hey! You need me! There are man - y, man - y parts,
G7 G7(♯5♯9) Cm F/C Cm
but just one bod - y. Hey! I need you! Hey!
F/C Cm F7 A♭maj9
Hey! You need me! How good it is to dwell to - geth - er,
G7(♯5♯9) Cm7 F/C Cm7 Cm B♭ Cm
so it is with Christ.

His Banner over Me Is Love

Traditional

E♭ B♭7
1. He brought me to His
(2.) lift - ed me up in - to
E♭ E♭/B♭ E♭ E♭/G B♭7 E♭/B♭ B♭7
ban - quet - ing ta - ble. His ban - ner o - ver me is love.
heav - en - ly plac - es. His ban - ner o - ver me is love.
B♭7/F B♭7 B♭7/F
He brought me to His
He lift - ed me up in - to
Fm7 B♭13 B♭7 E♭ E♭/B♭ E♭ Fm/B♭ E♭
ban - quet - ing ta - ble. His ban - ner o - ver me is love.
heav - en - ly plac - es. His ban - ner o - ver me is love.
E♭/B♭ E♭ E♭maj7/B♭
He brought me to His
He lift - ed me up in - to
E♭7 B♭m7 E♭7 A♭6 C7/G Fm
ban - quet - ing ta - ble. His ban - ner o - ver me is love.
heav - en - ly plac - es. His ban - ner o - ver me is love.
Fm7 Gm/B♭ B♭7 Fm7 Gm/B♭ B♭7 B♭13
His ban - ner o - ver me is
His ban - ner o - ver me is
B♭7/E♭ E♭ 1. A♭/B♭ 2. B♭/C C7
love.
love.
2. He

F F/E Dm C F Am7 A♭o
3. Jesus is the Rock of my salvation. His
C9/G C7 B♭/C Gm7 C7
banner over me is love.
Gm D Gm7 Am/C C7
Jesus is the Rock of my salvation. His
F Dm C F F/C
banner over me is love.
F F/C F Am7(♭5) D7(♯5) D7
Jesus is the Rock of my salvation. His
Gm/B♭ D7/A Gm Gm7(♭5)
banner over me is love. His
Am/C Gm/C Gm7 Am/C Gm/C C13
banner over me is
Gm/F F Dm Am/C Gm/C Gm7
love. His banner over
Am/C Gm/C C13 Gm/F F B♭/C F
me is love.

His Cheeseburger

Words and Music by
KURT HEINECKE and MICHAEL NAWROCKI

Steadily (♩=112)
1. He said to her, "I'd like a cheese - bur - ger, and I
(2. He) stayed at the drive - through 'til sun - rise– he
might like a milk - shake as well." She
may have dozed off once or twice– when he
said to him, "I can't give you ei - ther." And he said, "Is - n't this Bur - ger Bell?"
spot - ted a bill - board for Den - ny's: ba - con and eggs for half price!
She said, "Yes it is, but we're closed now, but we
How could he re - sist such an of - fer? He
o - pen to - mor - row at ten." He said, "I am ex - trem - e - ly hun -
real - ly need - ed some - thing to munch. Cheese - bur - ger, please do not get an -
- gry, but I guess I can wait un - til then."
- gry; he'll eat and be back here for lunch!
'Cause you're his cheese - bur - ger, his yum - my cheese - bur - ger! He'll wait for
'Cause you're his cheese - bur - ger! His pre - cious cheese - bur - ger! Be back for
you - oo, yeah! He'll wait for you - oo! Oh, you are his cheese - bur - ger, his tast - y
you - oo, he'll be back for you - oo! Won't be so long, cheese - bur - ger, oh, love - ly

F C B♭ 1. Dm/C C C4/2 C rit.
cheese - bur - ger! He'll wait for you-oo! Oh,___ he will wait for
cheese - bur - ger! Be back for you-oo, oh,___
F F4/2 F F4/2 F F4/2 B♭ C7 a tempo
you. 2. He
2. Dm/C C B♭/C C F A7sus A7
he'll be back for you. 'Cause he
Dm
loves you, cheese - bur - ger, with all his heart, and there ain't
Dm/C C accel.
noth - in' gon - na tear you two - oo a - part. And if the world sud - den - ly ran
F/C C A♭ G♭/A♭ E♭m/A♭
out of cheese, he would get down on his hands and knees to see if
E/A♭ A♭
some - one ac - ci - dent - 'ly dropped some cheese in the dirt. And he would
B♭ molto rit.
wash it off for you, wipe it off for you, clean that dirt - y cheese off just for
Slowly and freely N.C. E♭
you. You are his cheese - bur - ger.

How Did Moses Cross the Red Sea?

Words and Music by
HUGH MITCHELL

How did Mos - es cross the Red Sea? How did Mos - es cross the
Red Sea? How did Mos - es cross the Red Sea? How did he get a -
cross? Did he swim? No! No! Did he fly? No! No! Did he
sail? No! No! No! No! Did he run? No! No! Did he walk? No! No! How
did he get a - cross? God blew with His wind, puff,
puff, puff, puff. He blew just e - nough, nough, nough, nough, nough, and
through the sea He made a path. That's how he got a -
cross! how he got a - cross! And through the sea He
made a path. That's how he got a - cross!

I Am a "C"(H-R-I-S-T-I-A-N)

Traditional

I Can Do All Things Through Christ

Words and Music by
TROY NILSSON and GENIE NILSSON

Quickly, in two (𝅗𝅥=110)

D E/G♯

1. I can do___ all things through Christ who gives me
(2.)___ "Hey, moun - tain, jump in - to the
(4.)___ a touch - down in the Su - per

A E A D

2nd time (shout): Jump!

strength. I can do___ all things through
sea." I can be___ the per - son
Bowl. I can take___ the cake when

E/G♯ A E A

Christ who gives me strength. I can do an -
God wants me to be. I can heal___
I go for the goal. I can run___

D E/G♯ D/F♯ E/G♯

- y - thing,___ an - y - thing,___ an - y - thing___ in faith,___
___ the sick,___ raise the dead,___ make a blind___ man see,___
___ the race,___ win the game,___ and be a cham - pi - on___ of faith,___

A D E/G♯

___ 'cause I can do___ all things through Christ who gives me
___ 'cause I can do___ all things through Christ who strength - ens
___ 'cause I can do___ all things through Christ who gives me

1. A E A   2.3. A E A

strength. 2. I can say,___ me. Phil - ip - pi - ans four: thir - teen!
strength. Phil - ip - pi - ans four: thir - teen!

1st time: A°7
2nd time: Asus/D

1st time (spoken): Uh, does that mean that I can, like, jump tall buildings in a single bound?
2nd time (spoken): Uh, could I make a rock so big that I can't lift it?

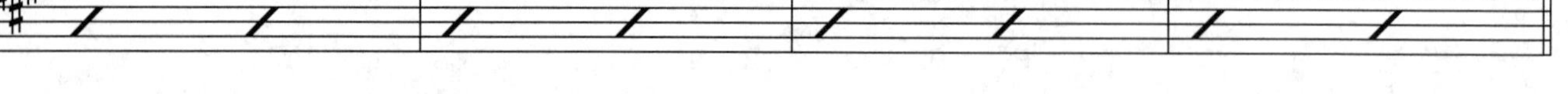

A D E D2
All things are pos - si - ble with God.
A D E
All things are pos - si - ble with God.
D2 slide! C F
All things are pos - si - ble with
G F2 C
God. All things are
F G F♯ F E
pos - si - ble with God.
3. I can play
5. With God's su -
D E/G♯ A E
a scream - in' gui - tar so - lo.
- per - hu - man pow - er, I can win.
A D E/G♯
I can play the drums so loud, you'll hold your nose,
I'll go a - gainst the world's flow, and I won't sin.
A E A D
or lay a groove down on my bass
Just think of all the nev -
E D/F♯ E/G♯ A
that puts a smile up - on your face, 'cause I can do
- er - end - ing pos - si - bi - li - ties, 'cause I can do

2nd time to Coda
D E/G♯ A E
— all things through Christ who gives me strength. Phil - ip - pi - ans
— all things through Christ who strength - ens
A F
four: thir - teen! I can do so much more — than
G Bm
I can ask or i - mag - ine by His pow'r
E D.S. al Coda
that's at work — in me. — 4. I can make —
CODA
A E A D
me. With all — His en - er - gy
E/G♯ D/F♯ E/G♯ A/C♯
— that works so pow - er - f'lly — in me, — I can do —
D E/G♯ A E
— all things through Christ who strength - ens me.
A D E
Yeah, ev - 'ry - thing — is pos - si - ble — for —
D/F♯ E/G♯ A D
— him who be - lieves, — and I can do — all things through
E/G♯ A E A
Christ who strength - ens me.

I Cry-yi-yi to My God Most High

Words and Music by
JANET MCMAHAN-WILSON

50's rock

I cry - yi - yi to my God most high.__
In His wings my heart can hide.__ I cry - yi - yi to my
God most high.__ He a - lone knows how to guide__ me.
When my feet__ start to fall,__ all I have to
do is call and cry - yi - yi - yi - yi__ to my God most high.

2nd time to Coda

If I lie__ in the li - on's lair__ in the
midst of my en - e - my,__ I just say__ a
sim - ple prayer__ and He'll come res - cue me. I

D.S. al Coda

CODA

high. Cry - yi - yi - yi - yi__
__ to my God most high.

I Have Decided

Traditional

Confidently (♩=116)
SOLO
D C
1. I have de - cid - ed to fol - low Je - sus. I have de -
(2.) with me, I still will fol - low. Though none go
(3.) with me and fol - low Je - sus? Won't you come
G C G
cid - ed to fol - low Je - sus. I have de -
with me, I still will fol - low. Though none go
with me and fol - low Je - sus? Won't you come
D G
cid - ed to fol - low Je - sus. No turn - ing back.
with me, I still will fol - low. No turn - ing back.
with me and fol - low Je - sus? No turn - ing back.
D CHOIR A SOLO D G D
(No, no, no, no.) No turn - ing back. Sing - ing,
(No, no, no, no.) No turn - ing back.
(No, no, no, no.) No turn - ing back.
D ALL C G
ha - la - la - la - la - la - la - la, ha - la - le - lu - jah. (Huh!) Sing - ing,
D C G
ha - la - la - la - la - la - la - la, ha - la - le - lu - jah. (Huh!)
D C G
Ha - la - la - la - la - la - la - la, ha - la - le - lu - jah.
C G/B Am7 G SOLO D CHOIR A SOLO
Last time to Coda
No turn - ing back. (No, no, no, no.) No turn - ing back.
1. D G D 2. D G D D
2. Though none go

C G D C G D.S. al Coda
3. Won't you come
CODA
D G D D C G
Sing-ing, ha-la-la - la-la - la-la-la, ha-la-le - lu - jah. (Huh!)
D C G
Ha-la - la - la - la - la - la-la, ha - la - le - lu - jah. (Huh!) Sing - ing,
D C G A
ha-la - la - la - la - la - la-la, ha-la-le - lu - jah.
E D A
Ha - la-la - la - la - la - la-la, ha - la - le - lu - jah. (Huh!) Sing - ing,
E D A
ha - la - la - la - la - la - la-la, ha - la - le - lu - jah. (Huh!) Sing - ing,
E D A
ha - la - la - la - la - la - la-la, ha - la - le - lu - jah.
D A/C# Bm7 A SOLO E CHOIR B SOLO
No turn - ing back. (No, no, no, no.) No turn - ing back.
E A E A E CHOIR B SOLO
No turn - ing back. (No, no, no, no.) No turn - ing back.
E A E A E CHOIR molto rit. B SOLO A7 (ad lib fill) E7
No turn - ing back. (No, no, no, no.) No turn - ing back.

I Have Decided to Follow Jesus

(Traditional)

Traditional

I Love My Duck

Words and Music by
PHIL VISCHER

Freely
D♭ G♭m E♭o D♭
Some kings love hors - es and some kings love cat - tle.
G♭m E♭o D♭
Some kings love lead - ing their troops in - to bat - tle. But
A(no3) B/A E D♭/F G♭m A♭ D♭
me, I'm not like that. I find that stuff yuck - y. I'd
E♭o B/D♯ E F♯m D♭/A♭ E♭/B♭ E♭ A♭
much rath - er stay in my tub with my duck - y.
In tempo (♩=140)
G♭ A♭ D♭
(Be - cause I love my duck.)
G♭ E♭m Funis G♭unis Gunis A♭unis G♭/B♭ A♭ D♭
Sir, if I could have a min - ute? (Love my duck.) There are some
E♭ E♭/G A♭ G♭ A♭ D♭
things we must dis - cuss. (I love my duck.) See,
G♭ E♭m Funis G♭unis Gunis A♭unis G♭ A♭ D♭
there's a war and, well, we're in it. (Love my duck.) Oh, I don't
Spoken: Then don't. Sing with me, Louis!
E♭ A♭
mean to make a fuss. (Be - cause he

loves his duck.) And that is why I can't be both - ered
(Loves his duck.) with the par - tic - u - lars of war. (He
loves his duck.) 'Cause, quite un - like my dear old fa - ther,
(Loves his duck) I find it all a bore. Now
freely
con - cen - trate, dear Lou - is, and I think you will a - gree the
most im - por - tant per - son in the whole wide world is me. So
please don't drag me down with all the peo - ple and their trou - bles. Go
run some wa - ter in my tub to fresh - en up my bub - bles.
a tempo
(Be - cause I love my duck.) I don't know why I e - ven both - er.

G♭ A♭ D♭ E♭ E♭/G A♭ G♭ A♭ D♭
(Love my duck.) You just can't rea - son with this guy. (Be - cause I love my duck.) It's
E♭ A♭
time to face the facts: I think we're all a lit - tle stuck. So let the
E♭ A♭ E♭ A♭
ar - my run a - muck. I fear the king - dom's out of luck. (Be - cause I
G♭ A♭ D♭ A♭/C
love my duck.) Yes, un - doubt - ed - ly we're stuck. So let the
B♭m A♭ G♭ D♭/F
ar - my run a - muck. Oh boy, we're real - ly out of luck. (Be - cause I
G♭ A♭ N.C. E♭ D♭ E♭ A♭
Slowly and freely
love my duck. Yes, I love my duck. You're
D♭ E♭ A♭ B♭m A♭/C D♭ E♭ A♭
al - ways there to make me smile. I love my duck. You're my
B♭ B♭7/D E♭ D♭ E♭ A♭ D♭ E♭ A♭
ver - y fa - v'rite toy. Hm, hm, hm, hm, hm, hm, hm, hm, hm, hm, hm,
B♭ B♭7/D E♭ D♭ E♭ A♭
hm, hm, hm, hm, hm. Be - cause I love my duck.

I Just Wanna Be a Sheep

Words and Music by
BRIAN HOWARD

(make animal noises ad lib)
D A G A D
Don't wan - na be a
Bm F#7
Phar - i - see. Don't wan - na be a Phar - i - see. 'Cause they're not
G A D
fair, you see. Don't wan - na be a Phar - i - see. I just wan - na be a
D A
sheep. Baa, baa, baa! I just wan - na be a sheep. Baa, baa, baa! I pray the
G A D
Lord my soul to keep. I just wan - na be a sheep. Baa, baa, baa! Don't wan - na be a
Bm F#7 G A
Sad-du-cee. Don't wan-na be a Sad-du-cee. 'Cause they're so sad, you see. Don't want to be a
D
Sad - du - cee. I just wan - na be a child of God. I just wan - na be a
A G A
child of God, walk - ing the same path He trod. I just wan - na be a
D
child of God. I just wan - na be a sheep. Baa, baa, baa! I just wan - na be a
A G A D C# D
sheep. Baa, baa, baa! I pray the Lord my soul to keep. I just wan-na be a sheep. Baa, baa, baa!

I Love to P-R-A-I-S-E My Lord

Words and Music by
JANET MCMAHAN-WILSON

March tempo
A♭
1st time: sing as written
On repeats: substitute a hand clap for each letter
I love to P - R - A - I - S - E my Lord.
E♭7
P - R - A - I - S - E all the time.
B♭m E♭ A♭ F
When I think a - bout Him, it makes me want to sing.
B♭ E♭
repeat 4 times
How I love to praise my Lord more than an - y - thing. I love to
A♭
P - R - A - I - S - E my Lord. P - R - A - I - S - E all the
D♭6 B♭7/D
time. He's the One that I o - bey. There
A♭/E♭ F B♭7
are so man - y, man - y ways to P - R - A - I -
E♭ A♭ E A♭
S - E my Lord.

I Want to Sing for My Lord

(To the tune of Billy Boy)

Words and Music by
JANET MCMAHAN-WILSON and TED WILSON

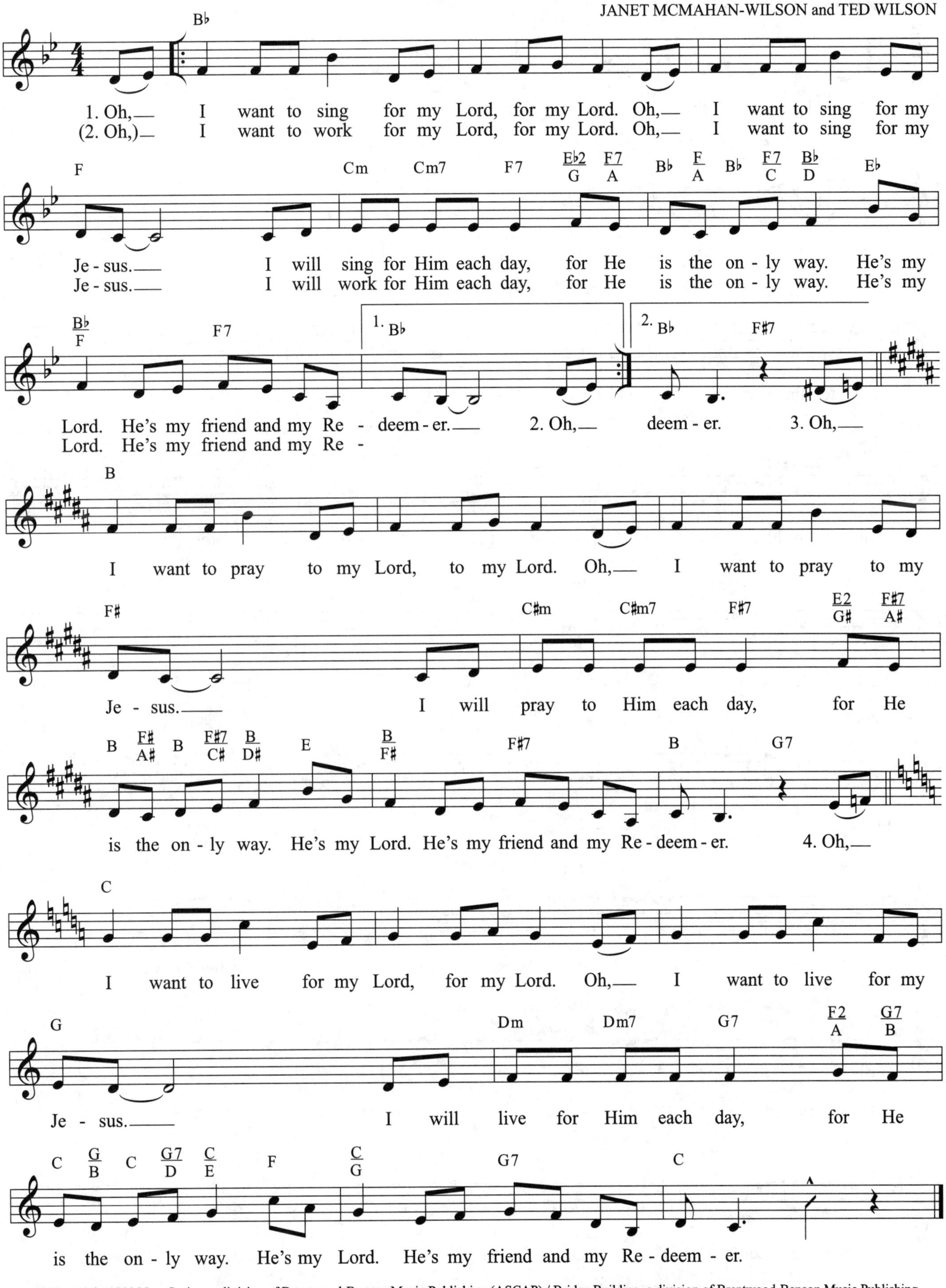
B♭
1. Oh, I want to sing for my Lord, for my Lord. Oh, I want to sing for my
(2. Oh,) I want to work for my Lord, for my Lord. Oh, I want to sing for my
F Cm Cm7 F7 E♭2/G F7/A B♭ F/A B♭ F7/C B♭/D E♭
Je - sus. I will sing for Him each day, for He is the on - ly way. He's my
Je - sus. I will work for Him each day, for He is the on - ly way. He's my
B♭/F F7 1. B♭ 2. B♭ F♯7
Lord. He's my friend and my Re - deem - er. 2. Oh, deem - er. 3. Oh,
Lord. He's my friend and my Re -
B
I want to pray to my Lord, to my Lord. Oh, I want to pray to my
F♯ C♯m C♯m7 F♯7 E2/G♯ F♯7/A♯
Je - sus. I will pray to Him each day, for He
B F♯/A♯ B F♯7/C♯ B/D♯ E B/F♯ F♯7 B G7
is the on - ly way. He's my Lord. He's my friend and my Re - deem - er. 4. Oh,
C
I want to live for my Lord, for my Lord. Oh, I want to live for my
G Dm Dm7 G7 F2/A G7/B
Je - sus. I will live for Him each day, for He
C G/B C G7/D C/E F C/G G7 C
is the on - ly way. He's my Lord. He's my friend and my Re - deem - er.

I Love to Sing, Sing, Sing

Words and Music by
JANET MCMAHAN-WILSON

Happily
F Bb F
I love to sing, sing, sing a song to the Lord,
Bb F/A Gm C F Bb
sing of His glo - ry for-ev - er - more. He loves to sing, sing, sing a song
F Gm C F
to the Lord and praise His ho - ly name. I'll
Bb F
clap my hands (Clap, clap, clap, clap) and shout for joy.
Bb
Hal - le - lu - jah! Sing and dance and
C Dm C/E D Em D/F#
make a joy - ful noise. Ev - 'ry-bod - y re-joice!
G C G
I love to sing, sing, sing a song to the Lord,
C G/B Am D G C
sing of His glo - ry for-ev - er - more. She loves to sing, sing, sing a song
G Am D G
to the Lord and praise His ho - ly name. I'll

C
clap my hands (Clap, clap, clap, clap) and
G C
shout for joy. Hal - le - lu - jah! Sing and dance
D Em D/F♯
and make a joy - ful noise.
E F♯m E/G♯
Ev - 'ry - bod - y re - joice! We love to
A D A D A/C♯ Bm
sing, sing, sing a song to the Lord, sing of His glo - ry for - ev -
E A D A
- er - more. We love to sing, sing, sing a song to the Lord and
Bm E A Bm E A
praise His ho - ly name. Let us all pro - claim
Bm Esus E/G♯
His high and ho - ly
A D A Bm E A
name.

I Think I'm Gonna Throw Up

Unknown

Moderately (♩=100)
C F C G
1. I think I'm gon - na throw — up... I think I'm gon - na throw — up... I
(2.) think I'm gon - na hurl... I think I'm gon - na hurl... I
C F C G C
think I'm gon - na throw — up my hands to the Lord. — I
think I'm gon - na hurl my sins out the door. — I
F C G
think I'm gon - na throw — up... I think I'm gon - na throw — up... I
think I'm gon - na hurl... I think I'm gon - na hurl... I
C F C G C
think I'm gon - na throw — up my hands to the Lord. —
think I'm gon - na hurl my sins out the door. —
C F C G C F
Throw up, throw up, throw up my
Hurl, hurl, hurl my
C G C F C G
hands to the Lord. — Throw up, throw up,
sins out the door. — Hurl, hurl,
C F C G C C F
throw up my hands to the Lord. —
hurl my sins out the door. —

C G C F 1. C G 2. C G
2. I I
D G D A
think I'm gon - na throw — up... I think I'm gon - na throw — up... I
D G D A D
think I'm gon - na throw — up my hands to the Lord. — I
G D A
think I'm gon - na throw — up... I think I'm gon - na throw — up... I
D G D A D Fine
think I'm gon - na throw — up my hands to the Lord. —
D G D A D G
Throw — up, throw — up, throw — up my
D A D G D A
hands to the Lord. — Throw — up, throw — up,
D G D A D D.S. al Fine
throw — up my hands to the Lord. — I

I Want to Be a Light Bulb

Words and Music by
GARY FORSYTHE

Jazz feel
Cm
I wan - na be a light bulb. I
G
wan - na be a light bulb. I
Cm
wan - na be a light bulb. Let the
G7
Lord's light shine on
1. Cm
through. I
2. Cm
through. 1. I
Cm
live each day in a dark, dark world,
(2.) read my Bi - ble ev - 'ry day to
F
fac - es sad and blue,
get my en - er - gy.
Cm
peo - ple search - ing
The words all jump right
in the night for a
off the page, start a
G
light they can turn to. Well,
fire in - side of me. Well, the
Cm
God is light and He lives in me and I
fire gives light and the light burns bright and there's
F
want to spread the news. I
no place for the blues. I

Cm
G
plug in - to the source. I turn a time or two.
plug in - to the word. I turn a page or two.
Je - sus hits my switch and His light shines through. Yes, I
Je - sus hits my switch and His light shines through.
Cm
G
wan - na be a light bulb. I wan - na be a light bulb.
Cm
I wan - na be a light bulb. Let the
G7
1. Cm
2. Cm
Lord's light shine on through. 2. I through. I
C♯m
wan - na be a light - bulb. I
G♯
wan - na be a light - bulb. I
C♯m
G♯7
wan - na be a light - bulb. Let the Lord's light shine on
C♯m
G♯7
C♯m G♯m C♯m
through. Let the Lord's light shine on through.

I Want to Be a Lighthouse for the Lord

Words and Music by
JAMES L.MCKEE

1. I like to go to Sun - day School and take my Bi - ble too. I like to learn of Je - sus, who cares for me and you. I learn how Je - sus shines His light so all the world can see and I can be a light - house if I let Him shine through me. I want to
(2.) Jo - nah spent three days and nights in - side that big old fish, to shed the light to Nin - e - veh be - came His great - est wish. I don't want things to get that dark be - fore I do what's right. I'll be a lit - tle light - house and shine out in - to the
2nd time to Coda
be a lit - tle light - house for the Lord. I want to be a lit - tle light - house for the Lord. I want to shine my light so oth - ers can see to climb on board. I want to be a lit - tle light - house for the Lord. 2. When
D.S. al Coda
CODA
night. 3. Poor Dan - iel was sup - posed to be the

G♭ D♭
li - on's meat one night, but God kept all their mouths shut so they
E♭7 A♭7 D♭
could - n't take a bite. I want to pray like Dan - iel did and
G♭ G°7 D♭/A♭ D♭ B♭m
please God ev - 'ry day and be a lit - tle light - house so my
E♭m A♭7 D♭
friends can see the way. I want to be a lit - tle
A♭7
light - house for the Lord. I want to be a lit - tle
D♭ D♭7
light - house for the Lord. I want to shine my light so oth - ers can
G♭ A°7 D♭/A♭ A♭7
see to climb on board. I want to be a lit - tle light - house for the
G° D♭/A♭ G♭/A♭
Lord. I want to be a lit - tle light - house,
D♭/A♭ G♭/A♭ D♭/A♭ A♭7 D♭
be a lit - tle light - house, be a lit - tle light - house for the Lord.

I Will Lift up My Voice

Words and Music by
JANET MCMAHAN-WILSON

Lively
B♭
I will lift up my voice to the Lord. Hal - le - lu - jah! I will
F
lift up my voice to the Lord. Hal - le - lu - jah! I
B♭ E♭7/A♭ E♭/G E♭m/G♭
know He loves me so and so the world will know. I will
B♭/F F B♭
lift up my voice to the Lord. Hal - le - lu - jah!
B A♯ B
I will
lift up my hands to the Lord. (clap, clap, clap) I will
F♯
lift up my hands to the Lord. (clap, clap, clap) I
B B7/A E/G♯ Em/G
know He loves me so and so the world will know. I will

B/F♯
F♯
B
lift up my hands to the Lord. (clap, clap, clap)
C
B
C
I will
lift up my prayers to the Lord. A - men! I will
G
lift up my prayers to the Lord. A - men! I
C
C7/B♭
F/A
Fm/A♭
know He loves me so and so the world will know. I will
C/G
lift up my prayers, I will lift up my hands, I will
lift up my voice, A - men! (clap, clap, clap) Hal - le -
G
C
lu - jah! to the Lord.

I Will Praise You with All My Heart

Words and Music by
JANET MCMAHAN-WILSON

Brightly
1.3. I will praise You with all my heart, oh Lord. I will
(2.) love You with all my heart, oh Lord. I will
praise You with all my heart. I will tell of the won - der of
love You with all my heart. I will tell of the won - der of
3rd time to Coda
who You are. I will praise You with all my heart.
who You are. I will love You with all my heart.
2. I will
For - ev - er and ev - er my heart will sing. For - ev - er and ev - er You are my King.
You are my for - tress and my strength, my re - fuge from the en - e - my.
D.S. al Coda
3. I will
CODA
I will love You with all my heart.
I will praise You with all my heart.

I Will Sing of the Mercies of the Lord

Words and Music by
J. H. FILLMORE

Happy!
C C/G C C/G F/G C
I will sing of the mer - cies of the Lord for - ev - er. I will
G7 Dm7 G7 C F/G G C Cmaj7/G
sing. I will sing. I will sing of the mer - cies of the
C6 Am7 Dm7 G7 C Dm7 D♯° C/E
Lord for - ev - er. I will sing of the mer - cies of the Lord. With my
F F/C F C G7
mouth will I make known Thy faith - ful - ness, Thy
F/C C F F/C F C
faith - ful - ness. With my mouth will I make known Thy
G/D D7 G7 F/G G C Cmaj7/G
faith - ful - ness to all gen - er - a - tions. I will sing of the mer - cies of the
C6 A7(♭9) Dm7 G7 1. C Dm7 D♯° C/E
Lord for - ev - er. I will sing of the mer - cies of the Lord. With my
2. C Am Dm7 G7 C
Lord. I will sing of the mer - cies of the Lord.

I'll Be a Sunbeam

Words and Music by
E. O. EXCELL

F
F/A
C7
Gm7
C7/E
C7
Je - sus wants me for a sun - beam to shine for Him each

F
F/C
F
F/A
Ab°
C7/G
C7
Gm7/C
day.
In ev - 'ry way try to please Him, at

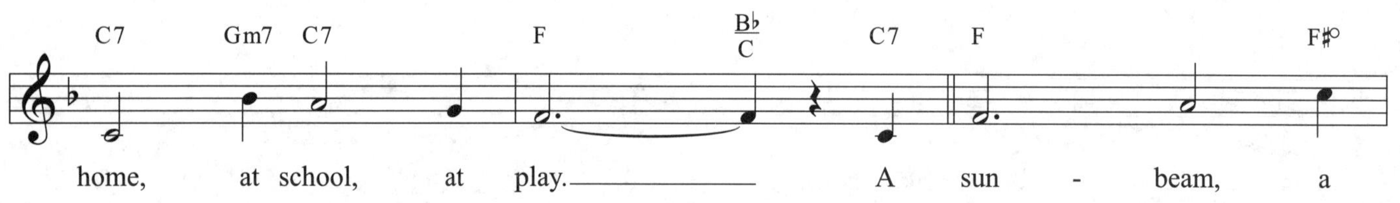
C7
Gm7
C7
F
Bb/C
C7
F
F#°
home, at school, at play.
A sun - beam, a

C7/G
Bb/F
C7/G
C7
Bb/F
F
sun - beam, Je - sus wants me for a sun - beam. A

F/C
F
F#°
C7/G
Bb/F
C7/G
C7
C
Gm7
C7
1.
F
C7
Bb/D
C7/E
sun - beam, a sun - beam, I'll be a sun - beam for Him.

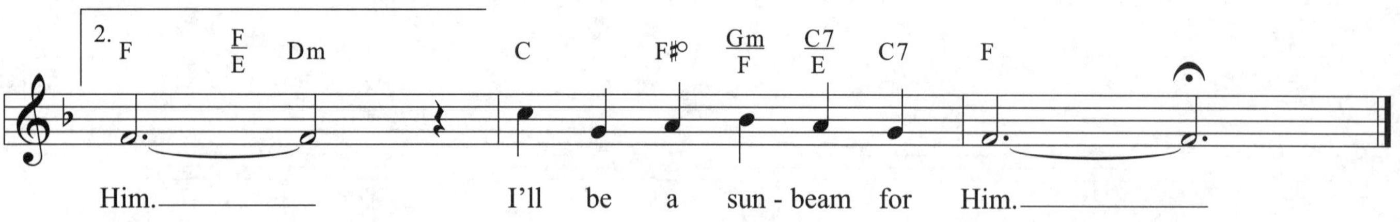
2.
F
F/E
Dm
C
F#°
Gm/F
C7/E
C7
F
Him. I'll be a sun - beam for Him.

I'm a Missionary's Helper

(To the tune of Did You Ever See a Lassie?)

Words and Music by
RUTH ELAINE SCHRAM

A D A7 D
I'm a mis - sion - ar - y's help - er, a help - er, a help - er. I'm a
D A7 D
mis - sion - ar - y's help - er. A help - er am I. 1. I
2. I
A7 D A7 D
pray ev - 'ry day for my friends far a - way. I'm a
tell ev - 'ry - one a - bout God's on - ly Son. I'm a
D A7
mis - sion - ar - y's help - er. A help - er am
mis - sion - ar - y's help - er. A help - er am
1. D 2. D B♭7 E♭
I. I'm a I. I'm a mis - sion - ar - y's help - er, a
B♭7 E♭
help - er, a help - er. I'm a mis - sion - ar - y's help - er. A
B♭7 E♭ B♭7 E♭
help - er am I. 3. I pray and I give so that
B♭7 E♭
oth - ers might live. I'm a mis - sion - ar - y's help - er. A
B♭7 E♭ Fm7 B♭ E♭
help - er am I.

I'll Surely Shine

Words and Music by
RUTH SCHRAM

N.C.
C
N.C.
D♭
G♭
C♭/G♭
G♭
3. I'll bright - ly beam. I'll bright - ly
B♭m
E♭m/B♭
B♭m
A♭m
beam. I'll bright - ly beam for my
D♭
G♭
C♭/G♭
G♭
Sav - ior. I'll bright - ly beam. I'll bright - ly
B♭m
E♭m/B♭
B♭m
C♭
beam. I'll bright - ly beam for my
A♭m
D♭
G♭
C♭/G♭
G♭
Lord. I will il - lu - mi - nate my lit - tle
B♭m
C♭
B♭m
A♭m
G♭
cor - ner in a world so dark and
D♭/F
E♭m
D♭
C♭
G♭
dim. I'll bright - ly beam. I'll bright - ly
B♭m
C♭
D♭
G♭
beam. I'll bright - ly beam for Him.

I'm Glad

Words and Music by
RUTH SCHRAM

E♭ Gm7 Cm7
1. I'm glad, I'm glad, I'm glad! I'm
(2.) glad, are you glad, are you glad? Are you
Fm7 B♭7 E♭ A♭/B♭ E♭ E♭maj7
glad He is my Sav - ior! I'm glad, I'm glad, I'm
glad He is your Sav - ior? Are you glad, are you glad, are you
Gm7 C7(♭9) Fm7 B♭7 E♭
glad! I'm glad He is my Lord! I'm
glad? Are you glad He is your Lord? Are you
A♭ Fm7 B♭ B♭7/D E♭ E♭maj7
glad! (clap clap) I'm glad! (clap clap) I'm glad! (clap clap) I'm
glad? (clap clap) Are you glad? (clap clap) Are you glad? (clap clap) Are you
A♭ A♭/B♭ E♭ B♭m6/D♭ C7
glad! (clap clap) I'm glad, I'm glad, I'm glad! I'm
glad? (clap clap) Are you glad, are you glad, are you glad? Are you
Fm7 B♭7 1. E♭ E♭/B♭ E♭ E♭/B♭
glad He is my Lord!
glad He is your
E♭ E♭/B♭ E♭ 2. E♭ E♭/B♭
2. Are you Lord?
E♭ E♭/B♭ E♭ E♭/D B♭/C B♭/D C7/E
1. I'm

F Am7 Dm7 Gm7 C7
glad, I'm___ glad, I'm___ glad! I'm___ glad I'll live in
(2.) glad, are you glad, are you glad? Are you glad you'll live in
F Bb/F C7 F Fmaj7 Am7 D7(b9)
heav - en! I'm___ glad, I'm___ glad, I'm___ glad! I'm___
heav - en? Are you glad, are you glad, are you glad? Are you
Gm7 C7 F Fsus/G F/A Bb Gm7
glad I'll live with Him! I'm___ glad! (clap clap) I'm___
glad you'll live with Him? Are you glad? (clap clap) Are you
C7 Gm7/D C7/E F Am7 Bb Bb/C
glad! (clap clap) I'm___ glad! (clap clap) I'm___ glad! (clap clap) I'm___
glad? (clap clap) Are you glad? (clap clap) Are you glad? (clap clap) Are you
F Am7 D7(b9) Gm7 C7
glad, I'm___ glad, I'm___ glad! I'm___ glad I'll live with
glad, are you glad, are you glad? Are you glad you'll live with
1. F F/C F 2. F F/A Bb Bb2/C
Him! 2. Are you Him! I'm
F F/E Cm6/Eb D7 Gm7 Am7 Bb6 Gm7
glad, I'm glad, I'm glad! I'm glad I'll
Bbmaj7/C C C7 F F/C F F/C F F/C F C7 F
live with Him!___

I'm Gonna Sing, Sing, Sing

Writer Unknown

Bluegrass (♩=120)
G(no3)
1.6. I'm gon - na sing, sing, sing. I'm gon - na shout, shout, shout. I'm gon - na
(2.) clap, clap, clap. I'm gon - na snap, snap, snap. I'm gon - na
(3.) stomp, stomp, stomp. I'm gon - na jump, jump, jump. I'm gon - na
(4.) twirl, twirl, twirl. I'm gon - na hurl, hurl, hurl. I'm gon - na
(5.) (whistle)
D
D/F♯
sing, I'm gon - na shout and praise the Lord.___ Oh, when those
clap, I'm gon - na snap and praise the Lord.___ Oh, when those
stomp, I'm gon - na jump and praise the Lord.___ Oh, when those
twirl, I'm gon - na hurl and praise the Lord.___ Oh, when those
G(no3)
G7
C
G(no3)
gates are o - pened wide, I'll___ be sit - tin' by Je - sus' side.___ I'm gon - na
gates are o - pened wide, I'll___ be sit - tin' by Je - sus' side.___ I'm gon - na
gates are o - pened wide, I'll___ be sit - tin' by Je - sus' side.___ I'm gon - na
gates are o - pened wide, I'll___ be sit - tin' by Je - sus' side.___ I'm gon - na
Em7
D
1.4.
G(no3)
sing, I'm gon - na shout and praise the Lord.___
clap, I'm gon - na snap and praise the Lord.___
stomp, I'm gon - na jump and praise the Lord.___
twirl, I'm gon - na hurl and praise the Lord.___
G(no3)/C
G(no3)
G(no3)/C
G(no3)
2.3.5.
G(no3)
2. I'm gon - na ___
5. (Whistle) ___
3. I'm gon - na
4. I'm gon - na
6. I'm gon - na
6.
G(no3)
D/F♯
Em
D
G(no3)
D/F♯
___ I'm gon - na sing, I'm gon - na shout and praise the Lord.___ I'm gon - na
Em
D
G(no3)
sing, I'm gon - na shout and praise the Lord.___

I'm in the Lord's Army

Traditional

Strict four
F F/E Dm C F F/C F F/A C7 C7/G C7
I may nev - er march in the in - fan-try, Ride in the cav - al-ry,
F F/C F B♭/C F F/E Dm C
shoot the ar - til - ler - y; I may nev - er
F A7/E Dm F7/C B♭6 Am/C C7
zoom o'er the en - e - my, But I'm in the Lord's ar -
F B♭/C F B♭ F F/C
my. I'm in the Lord's ar - my,
F F7 B♭/F C7/F F F/C F F/E Dm C
I'm in the Lord's ar - my. I may nev - er
F F/C F F/A B♭ C7 C7/G C7
march in the in - fan - try, Ride in the cav - al - ry,
F F/C F B♭/C F F/E Dm C
shoot the ar - til - ler - y; I may nev - er
A7 A7/C♯ Dm F7/C B♭6 Am/C C7 F
zoom o'er the en - e - my, But I'm in the Lord's ar - my.

I've Got Joy

Unknown

Simply (♩=72)

C G F G C
repeat as desired, faster and faster each time

I've got joy down in my heart, deep, deep down in my heart.

G F G C

J - O - Y down in my heart, deep, deep down in my heart.

F C Csus

Je - sus put it there, and noth - ing can de - stroy it, de - stroy it, de - stroy it, huh!

C G F G C

I've got joy down in my heart, deep, deep down in my heart.

Into My Heart

Words and Music by
HARRY D. CLARKE

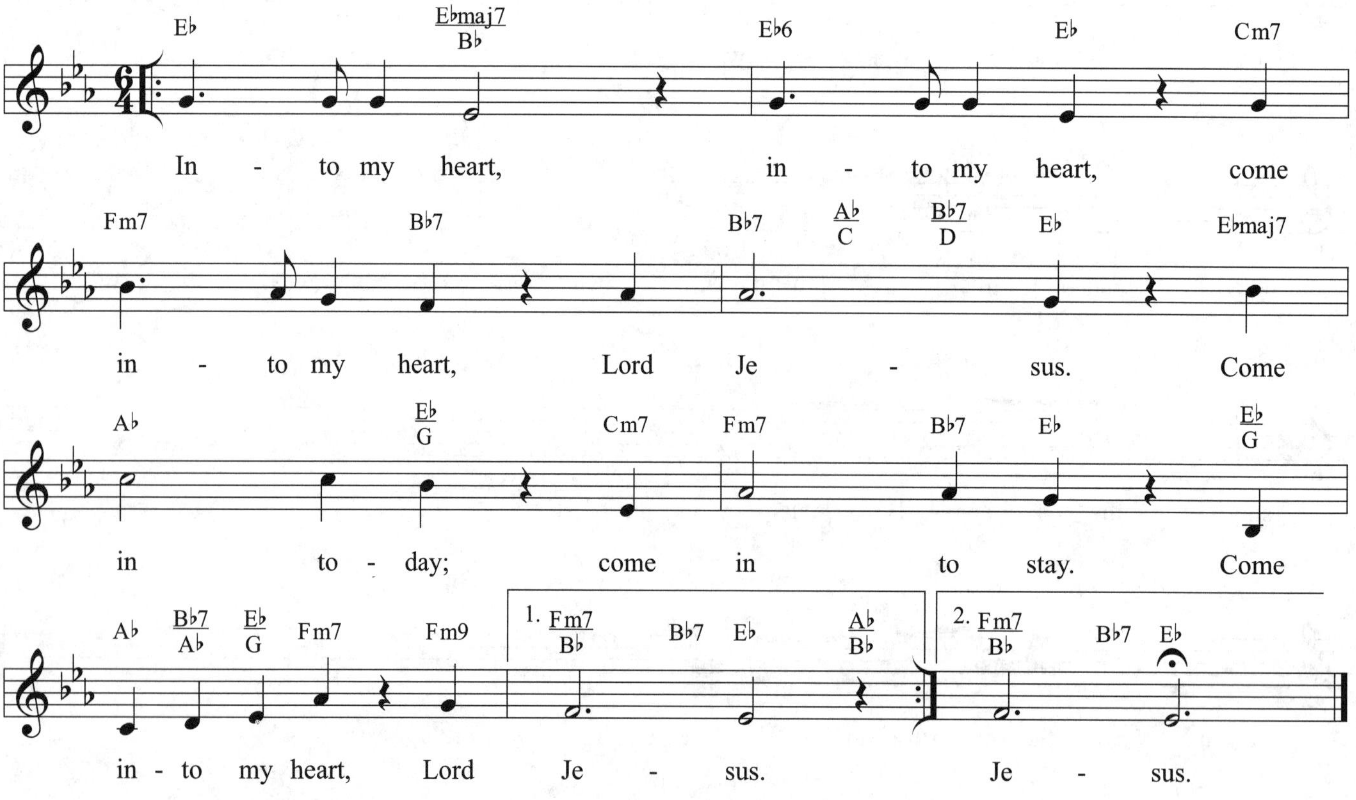

E♭ E♭maj7/B♭ E♭6 E♭ Cm7

In - to my heart, in - to my heart, come

Fm7 B♭7 B♭7 A♭/C B♭7/D E♭ E♭maj7

in - to my heart, Lord Je - sus. Come

A♭ E♭/G Cm7 Fm7 B♭7 E♭ E♭/G

in to - day; come in to stay. Come

A♭ B♭7/A♭ E♭/G Fm7 Fm9 1. Fm7/B♭ B♭7 E♭ A♭/B♭ 2. Fm7/B♭ B♭7 E♭

in - to my heart, Lord Je - sus. Je - sus.

I've Been Redeemed

Traditional

R & B (♩=182)
Eb Gm/Bb Cm7/Eb Gm/Bb Fm Bb Eb Eb/F Eb/G Ab Fm7 Gm Cm7 Fm7 Ab/Bb Eb
1. I've been re - deemed by the blood of the Lamb. I've been re - deemed by the blood of the Lamb. I've been re - deemed by the blood of the Lamb.
2. God sent His Son to die for me. God sent His Son to die for me. God sent His Son to die for me
3. You can talk a - bout me just all you please. You can talk a - bout me just all you please. You can talk a - bout me just all you please.
4. I'm on my way to Heav - en a - bove. I'm on my way to Heav - en a - bove. I'm on my way to Heav - en a - bove.
I'm go - in' to the Prom - ised Land.
so I could live e - ter - nal - ly.
I'll talk a - bout you when I'm on my knees.
I'm filled with God's fan - tas - tic love.
All my sins are washed a - way. I've been re - deemed.

I've Been Workin' for the Savior

(To the tune of I've Been Workin' on the Railroad)

Words and Music by
RUTH ELAINE SCHRAM

I've been work - in' for the Sav - ior, all the live - long day.

I've been work - in' for the Sav - ior, say - ing "Je - sus is the way."

Je - sus gave His life on Cal - v'ry, paid for all our sin.

Je - sus gave His life on Cal - v'ry, died and rose a - gain,

died and rose a - gain, died and rose a - gain. Je - sus died and rose a - gain,

died and rose a - gain, died and rose a - gain. Je - sus died and rose a - gain.

Go and tell the world a - bout Je - sus. Go and tell the world a - bout Him.

Go and tell the world a - bout Je - sus. He will take a - way their sin. So go and

tell the won - der - ful news. Tell the news a - bout Je - sus.

Tell the won - der - ful news. He will take a - way their sin.

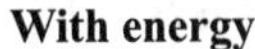

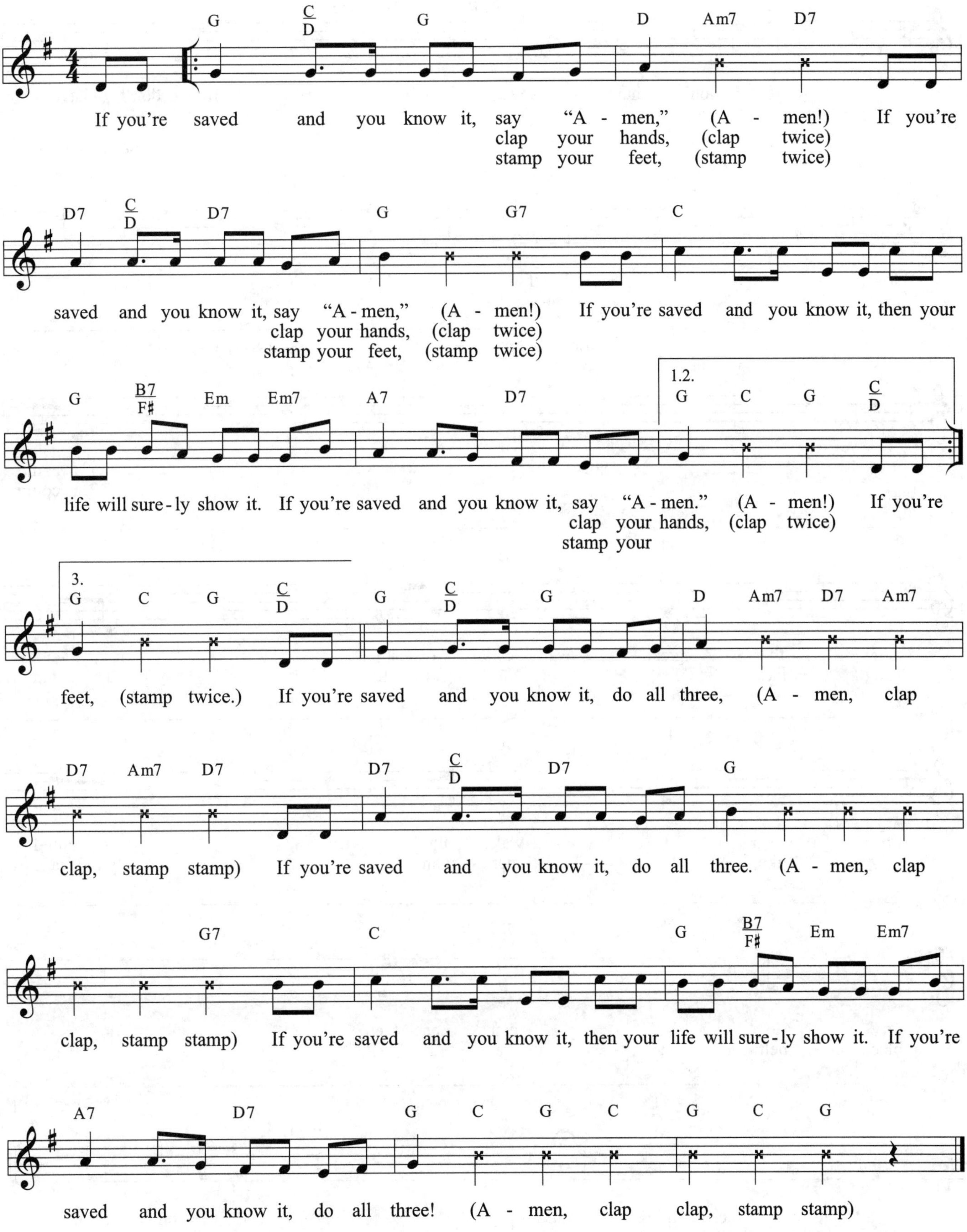

If You're Saved and You Know It

Words and Music by
ALFRED B. SMITH

With energy

G C/D G D Am7 D7
If you're saved and you know it, say "A - men," (A - men!) If you're
clap your hands, (clap twice)
stamp your feet, (stamp twice)
D7 C/D D7 G G7 C
saved and you know it, say "A - men," (A - men!) If you're saved and you know it, then your
clap your hands, (clap twice)
stamp your feet, (stamp twice)
G B7/F♯ Em Em7 A7 D7
1.2.
G C G C/D
life will sure - ly show it. If you're saved and you know it, say "A - men." (A - men!) If you're
clap your hands, (clap twice)
stamp your
3.
G C G C/D G C/D G D Am7 D7 Am7
feet, (stamp twice.) If you're saved and you know it, do all three, (A - men, clap
D7 Am7 D7 D7 C/D D7 G
clap, stamp stamp) If you're saved and you know it, do all three. (A - men, clap
G7 C G B7/F♯ Em Em7
clap, stamp stamp) If you're saved and you know it, then your life will sure - ly show it. If you're
A7 D7 G C G C G C G
saved and you know it, do all three! (A - men, clap clap, stamp stamp)

If I Don't Have Love

Words and Music by
ANDY GULLAHORN
and ANDREW PETERSON
Swing (♩=168)
(Opt.: Repeat Chorus on D.S.)
If I don't have love, if I don't have love, if I don't have love, I'm just mak - ing noise.
Last time to Coda
1.2.
Straight eighths (♩=110)
1. I could sing the great - est wor - ship, pray ten times when I wake up. I could try to be just per - fect, do all of these things, but...
2. I could sing like Pav - a - rot - ti. I could fly like Su - per - man, get a black belt in ka - ra - te, do all these things, but then...
rit.
Tempo I
If I don't have

3.
D
noise. Like the clang - ing of a
Bm
cym - bal, like the bang - ing of a
A
gong, like all the cra - zy
E7
3
peo - ple sing - ing this sil - ly wil - ly
A
D.S. al Coda
song. If I don't have
CODA
D/A A G
mak - ing, oh, I'm just
D/A A G
mak - ing, oh, I'm just
D/A A D G D G D7
mak - ing noise.

If You Want to Be Wise

Words and Music by
JANET MCMAHAN-WILSON

Brightly (♩=88)
E♭
If you want to be wise, (if you want to be
Fm7 B♭7
wise) then o - pen your eyes (then o - pen your eyes) and take a
Fm7 B♭7 E♭
look (take a look, take a look) in - to God's book. (Take a look in the
E♭7 A♭ D♭9
book.) And you must trust Him for His word is true.
E♭ C7 Fm Gm A♭ A
He'll show you just what to do to help you to be
B♭ B♭7 E♭ A♭7 E♭
wise if you'll o - pen your eyes. (O - pen your eyes.)
D E♭
If you want to un - der -
stand (if you want to un - der - stand) His per - fect
Fm7 B♭7 Fm7
plan, (His per - fect plan) then stay a - way (stay a - way, stay a -
B♭7 E♭ E♭7
way) from e - vil ways. (Stay a - way from e - vil ways.) And you must

A♭ D♭9 E♭
trust Him for His word is true.— He'll show you just
C7 Fm Gm A♭ A B♭ B♭7
what to do— to help you un - der - stand His per - fect
E♭ A♭7 E♭ D
plan. (per - fect plan)
E♭
If you want to do right, (if you want to do
Fm7
right) love the Lord with all your might (love the Lord with all your
B♭7 Fm7 B♭7
might) and fol - low Him (fol - low Him, fol - low Him) through thick and
E♭ E♭7 A♭
thin. (Fol - low Him through thick and thin.) And you must trust Him for His
D♭9 E♭ C7
word is true.— He'll show you just what to do— to
Fm Gm A♭ A B♭ B♭7
help you to do right. Love the Lord with all your
E♭ A♭7 E♭
might. (Love the Lord with all your might.)

In the Beginning

Words and Music by
TROY NILSSON and GENIE NILSSON

With energy (♩=109)
D
Gen - e - sis one: one, the fun's just be - gun in Gen - e - sis one: one.
Gen - e - sis one: one, the fun's just be - gun in
Gen - e - sis one: one.
D
In the be - gin - ning, God
G Asus D
cre - at - ed the heav - ens and the earth.
G Asus
In the be - gin - ning, God cre - at - ed the heav - ens and the earth.
D F
In the be - gin - ning, God cre - at - ed the
B♭ Csus F
heav - ens and the earth. In the be - gin - ning, God
B♭sus Csus 2nd time to Coda F
cre - at - ed the heav - ens and the earth. Day
N.C.
Spoken: Let there be light.
God made the sky.
one! Day two!

Plants, land, and sea.
Day three! Day
Sun, moon, and stars.
Fish and the birds.
four! Day five! Day
Animals and man.
six! Day sev - en was the
I did good. I'm taking a rest.
A7
D.S. al Coda
day He blessed. He said:
CODA
F D G A Bm7
It is good. Check it out;
G Asus A G A D
you're gon - na love it. It is good,
G2 A
so have fun and take care of it.
E
Gen - e - sis one: one, the fun's just be - gun in

Gen - e - sis one: one.
Gen - e - sis one: one, the fun's
just be - gun in Gen - e - sis one: one.
F
In the be - gin - ning, God cre - at - ed
Bb Csus
the heav - ens and the earth.
F
In the be - gin - ning, God cre - at - ed the
Bb Csus Dunis Eunis Funis F#unis
heav - ens and the earth.
G
In the be - gin - ning, God
C Dsus G
cre - at - ed the heav - ens and the earth.
In the be - gin - ning, God cre - at - ed
1.
C Dsus
the heav - ens and the earth.
G
2.
C Dsus G
heav - ens and the earth.

Is There Anything I Can Do for You?

Words and Music by
DAVID HUNTSINGER and DOTTIE RAMBO

1. Is there an - y - thing I can do for You? Is there
(2. Is there) an - y - where I can go for You? Is there
an - y - thing I can do? For
an - y - where I can go? For the
all the things You've done for me, is there
plac - es You have been for me, is there
an - y - thing I can do? I'm
an - y - where I can go?
will - ing to be used, dear Lord, what - e'er the price may
be. So if there's an - y - thing I can do for You, just
an - y - where I can go for You, just
make it known to me. 2. Is there
me. Just make it known to me.

Inside My Heart

Words and Music by
ANDY GULLAHORN

Shuffle sixteenths (♩=92)
G D/F♯ A Bm
1. Da - vid saw Go - li - ath, the big old ug - ly gi - ant.
2. Prayer was law - de - fy - in', but Dan - iel kept on try - ing, so they
G D/F♯ A
Da - vid was not fright - ened. He did not run a - way. He
threw him with the li - ons right a - bout their sup - per time. They were
G D/F♯ A Bm
walked in - to the bat - tle with a sling - shot and a peb - ble. He said, "I'll
close e - nough to eat him; he could smell their bad breath breath - ing. But he
G D/F♯ A
tell you some - thing deb - ble: Well, I am not a - fraid." My God is
sure sur - prised those hea - thens when he came out a - live.
G D A D D/F♯
big, big, big. His love is wide, wide, wide. And in my
G D A6 G6 D G/D D
heart, heart, heart, He lives in - side, side, side. He lives in -
G D A Bm
side my heart. He lives in - side my heart, deep in -
G D A6 G6 1. D G/D D
side my heart. He lives in - side, side, side.

2.
D
G/D D
G
D
A
Bm
G
D
A
G
D
G
D
When I'm feel - ing lone - ly,
A
D
G
when I'm feel - ing scared,
when I eat bo - lo - gna,
E7
A
I know God is there.
My God is
G
D
A
D
big, big, big. His love is wide, wide, wide. And in my
G
D
1.
A6
G6
D
heart, heart, heart, He lives in - side, side, side. My God is
2.
A6
G6
D
G/D D
G
D
side, side, side. He lives in - side my heart. He lives in -
A
Bm
Bm/F♯
G
D
side my heart, deep in - side my heart. He lives in -
A6
G6
1.
D
G/D D
2.
D
G/D D
side, side, side. He lives in

It's Wise

Words and Music by
JANET MCMAHAN-WILSON

50's rock

A

It's eas - y to stay in bed all day and

F♯m D

sleep the end - less hours a - way, but there's so much that you can do. A

E7 N.C.

great big world waits for you. It's

𝄋 A F♯m D

wi - yi - yi - yi - yi - yi - yise___ to o - pen (o - pen up) your

E A F♯m

sleep - y eyes.___ It's wi - yi - yi - yi - yi - yi - yise___ to

D E

get up (get up) when it's time to rise.___

F♯m
D
Go out and do the best you can,___ 'cause you

F♯m B A F♯m
nev - er know— what God has planned. So get up. Get up. Be
D Esus E A
2nd time to Coda
A7
wi - yi - yi - yi - yise.—
D A
Don't be a slob. (no, no, no) You've got a job.
D
(oh, oh, oh) Don't wait a - round. (so, so, so)
E E7 N.C.
D.S. al Coda
Get up and do it now - ow - ow - ow. It's
CODA
F♯m A F♯m D Esus E A
Get up, get up, be wi - yi - yi - yi - yise.—
1.
F♯m
2.

Isn't It Grand to Be a Christian

Words and Music by
CHARLOTTE MCCROSSAN and H. G. TOVEY

Jesus Bids Us Shine

Words and Music by
SUSAN WARNER and EDWIN O. EXCELL

F C7sus C7
1. Je - sus bids us shine, with a clear, pure light,
2. Je - sus bids us shine, first of all for Him,
F
Like a lit - tle can - dle burn - ing in the night;
Well He sees and knows it if our light is dim;
F/A B♭ F
In this world of dark - ness, we must shine,
He looks down from heav - en, sees us shine,
F/A B♭ 1. F/C C7 F B♭ C7
You in your small cor - ner and I in mine.
2. F C7 F D7 G D7sus D7
I in mine. 3. Je - sus bids us shine as we work for Him,
G
Bring - ing those that wan - der from the paths of sin;
G/B C G
He will ev - er help us if we shine,
G/B C G/D D7 G
You in your small cor - ner and I in mine!

Jesus in the Boat

Words and Music by
HERMAN VOSS

faster: both times
2nd time: omit words in parenthesis
1.
2.
G C2
With With in the you can in the (storm,)
D G C2
in the (storm,) in the (storm.) With in the you can in the (storm)
G D G D7
when you're sail - ing home. Sail - ing, sail - ing home,
G Am C
sail - ing, sail - ing home, with in the you can in the (storm)
G D7 G
accel.
1.
when you're sail - ing home. With
2.
faster: both times
2nd time: omit words in parenthesis
G C2 D
With in the you can in the in the
G C2 G D
in the with in the you can in the when you're
G D7
(home.) Hmm, hmm, hmm, hmm, home, hmm, hmm,
(2nd time) (hmm)
G Am C
1. G D7
hmm, hmm, home, with in the you can in the when you're
(2nd time) (hmm)
G
accel.
2. G D7 G
home. With when you're hmm, hmm.

Jesus in the Morning

Traditional

1. Je - sus, Je - sus, Je - sus in the morn - ing,
2. Love Him, love Him, Love Him in the morn - ing,
Je - sus at the noon - time. Je - sus, Je - sus,
love Him at the noon - time. Love Him, love Him,
Je - sus when the sun goes down. down.
Love Him when the sun goes
3. Serve Him, serve Him, Serve Him in the morn - ing,
4. Praise Him, praise Him, Praise Him in the morn - ing,
serve Him at the noon - time. Serve Him, serve Him,
praise Him at the noon - time. Praise Him, praise Him,
Serve Him when the sun goes down.
Praise Him when the sun goes
down,
Praise Him when the sun goes down.

Jesus Is the Son of God

(To the tune of Mary Had a Little Lamb)

Words and Music by
JANET MCMAHAN-WILSON
and TED WILSON

C Dm7 G C Dm7 G
1. Je - sus is the Son of God, Son of God, Son of God.
(2.) came to earth from heav'n a - bove, heav'n a - bove, heav'n a - bove,
C Gm6/B♭ A7 1. D G7 C
Je - sus is the Son of God. It says so in the Word. 2. He
came to earth from heav'n a - bove. It
2. D G7 C A♭7 D♭
says so in the Word. 3. He died to save us from our sins,
(4. He) rose to heav - en from the grave,
E♭m7 A♭7 D♭ E♭m7 A♭7 D♭ A♭m6/C♭ B♭7
from our sins, from our sins, died to save us from our sins. It
from the grave, from the grave, rose to heav - en from the grave. It
1. E♭7 A♭7 D♭ 2. E♭m7 A♭7 D♭ A7
says so in the Word. 4. He says so in the Word.
D Em7 A7 D Em7 A
5. He is com - ing back a - gain, back a - gain, back a - gain.
D Am6/C B7 Em7 A7 D B♭7
He is com - ing back a - gain. It says so in the Word.
E♭ Fm7 B♭7 E♭ Fm7(4) B♭7
6. He will take me home with Him, home with Him, home with Him.
E♭ Cm Fm B♭6 B♭7 E♭
rit.
He will take me home with Him. It says so in the Word.

Jesus Is a River of Love

Words and Music by
DALLAS HOLM

Fast swing (♩=192)
G
Well, my Je - sus is a riv - er of love
and He flows

C
from heav - en a - bove.
G
He'll take ev - 'ry sin that you

have and He'll wash it a - way.
D

You just jump
G
in the wa - ter to - day.

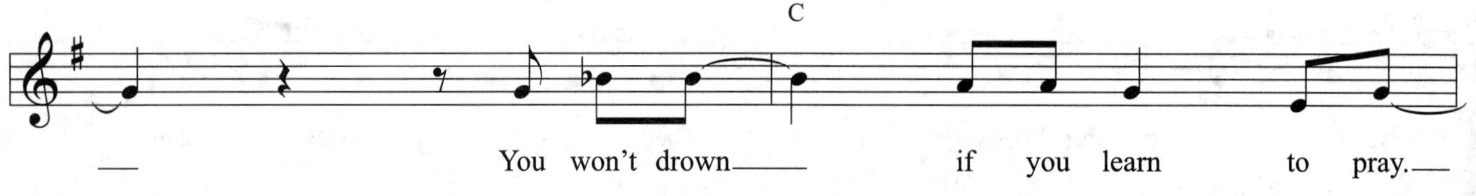
You won't drown
C
if you learn to pray.

Well, my Je
G
- sus is a riv - er of love

D
and He's flow - ing
G
your way.
Last time to Coda

G
C
1. There's a riv - er flow - ing out from heav - en's sea.
2. If you need a cleans - ing, chil - dren, don't de - lay.
G
There's a riv - er reach - ing out
There's a might - y riv - er flow -
A
D
for you and me,
in' here to - day.
G
streams of Liv - ing Wa - ter
It can wash and make you
C
A
G
C
clear as they can be. So come on in; the
clean as you can be.
G
D
G
D.S. (twice) al Coda
wa - ter's fine, and it will set you free. Well, my Je -
CODA
Well, my Je - sus is a riv - er of love
D
rit.
C7
G
and He's flow - ing your way.

Jesus Loves Even Me

(I Am So Glad)

P. P. BLISS

Jazz waltz
F Fmaj7/C F7 B♭ Gm7 C7sus C7
I am so glad that Je - sus loves me, Je - sus loves me,
F C7/F F Fmaj7/C F7 B♭ Gm7
Je - sus loves me. I am so glad that Je - sus loves me,
2nd time to Coda
C7 Gm7 C13 F Am Gm7 C7
Je - sus loves e - ven me.
F Fmaj7/C F6 Dm Dm7 Gm Gm7
I am so glad that my Fa - ther in heav'n Tells of His love in the
Am/C C7 F F/C F C7/G F/A F C/E D7(♭9)
Book He has giv'n; Won - der - ful things in the Bi - ble I see,
D.C. al Coda
G13 G7 B♭m6 Am/C C7 F F/C
This is the dear - est– that Je - sus loves me.
CODA
F Dm Gm7(4) Gm7/C C13 F
me, Je - sus loves e - ven me.

Jesus Loves Me
(Traditional)

Words and Music by
WILLIAM B. BRADBURY and ANNA B. WARNER

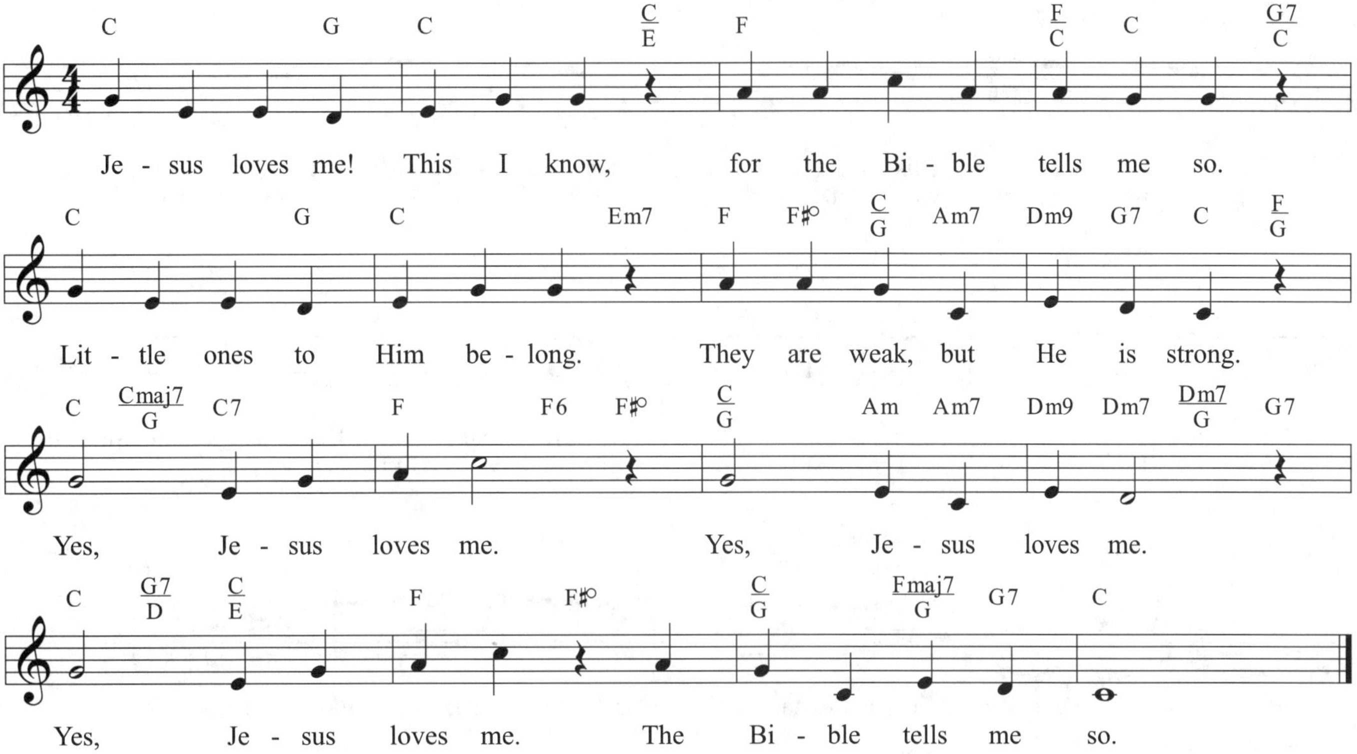
C G C C/E F F/C C G7/C
Je - sus loves me! This I know, for the Bi - ble tells me so.
C G C Em7 F F#° C/G Am7 Dm9 G7 C F/G
Lit - tle ones to Him be - long. They are weak, but He is strong.
C Cmaj7/G C7 F F6 F#° C/G Am Am7 Dm9 Dm7 Dm7/G G7
Yes, Je - sus loves me. Yes, Je - sus loves me.
C G7/D C/E F F#° C/G Fmaj7/G G7 C
Yes, Je - sus loves me. The Bi - ble tells me so.

Jesus Loves the Little Children

Words and Music by
G. F. ROOT

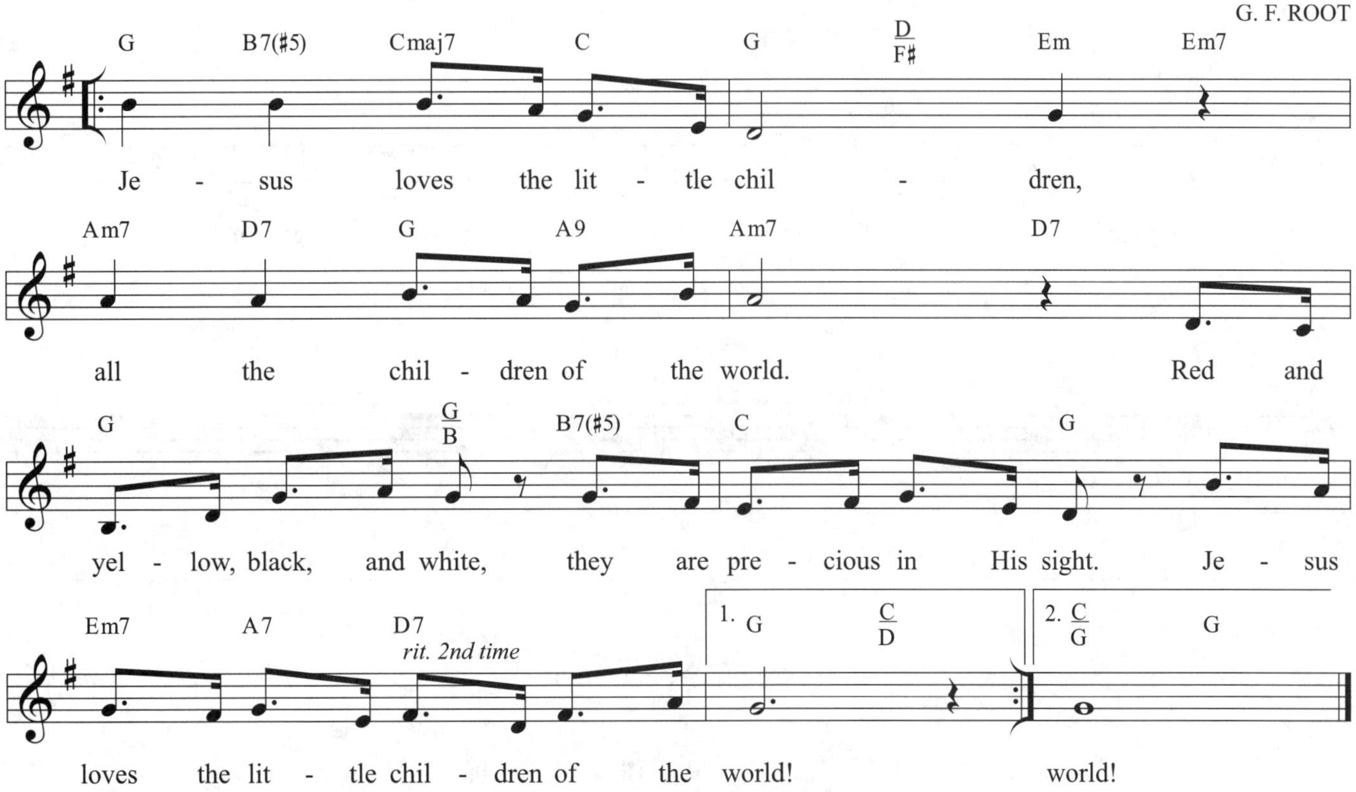
G B7(#5) Cmaj7 C G D/F# Em Em7
Je - sus loves the lit - tle chil - dren,
Am7 D7 G A9 Am7 D7
all the chil - dren of the world. Red and
G G/B B7(#5) C G
yel - low, black, and white, they are pre - cious in His sight. Je - sus
Em7 A7 D7
rit. 2nd time
1. G C/D
2. C/G G
loves the lit - tle chil - dren of the world! world!

Jesus Loves Me

Words and Music by
WILLIAM B. BRADBURY and ANNA B. WARNER

Moderately (♩=88)

C

1. Je - sus loves me! This I know, for the Bi - ble tells me so.
2. Je - sus loves me when I'm good, when I do the things I should.

G C

Lit - tle ones to Him be - long; they are weak, but He is strong. Sing - ing
Je - sus loves me when I'm bad, though it makes Him ver - y sad.

F C G C

na na na— na na— na na na. Na na na— na na— na na na.

F C G C

Na na na— na na— na na na. Na na na— na na— na na na.

F C G

Yes, Je - sus loves me! Yes, Je - sus loves me!

C F 1. C G C

Yes, Je - sus loves me! The Bi - ble tells me so.

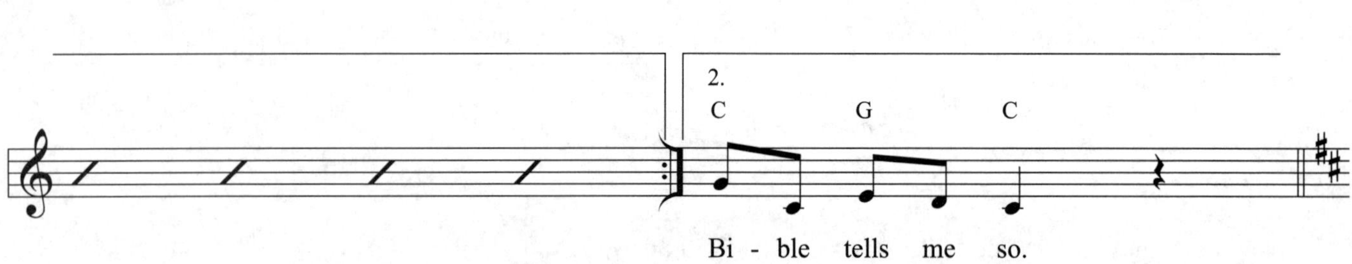
2.
C G C
Bi - ble tells me so.

D
Sing a - bout His love, a - bout His love, sing a - bout.
A D
Sing a - bout His love, a - bout His love, sing.
Sing a - bout His love, a - bout His love, sing a - bout.
A D
Sing a - bout His love, a - bout His love, sing.
G D A D
Na na na na na na na na. Na na na na na na na na.
G D A D
Na na na na na na na na. Na na na na na na na na.
D G D A
Yes, Je - sus loves me! Yes, Je - sus loves me!
1. 2.
D G D A D D A D
Yes, Je - sus loves me! The Bi - ble tells me so. Bi - ble tells me so.

Jesus, Born in Bethlehem

Words and Music by
ED KEE

E♭ B♭/D A♭/C E♭/B♭ A♭ E♭/G
Je - sus, born in Beth - le - hem, born a babe in a
Fm7 B♭7sus B♭ E♭ B♭/D A♭/C E♭/B♭
cat - tle stall. Je - sus, born in Beth - le - hem,
A♭ E♭/G Cm Fm7 A♭/B♭ E♭
born in Beth - le - hem, Lord of all.
B♭/A♭ E♭/G
Hear the An - gels sing,
B♭/A♭ E♭/G B♭/A♭
"Glo - ry to the King." See the wise men
E♭/G B♭/F E♭ D♭2 D♭ B♭7sus B♭7
wor - ship Him with gifts they bring.
E♭ B♭/D A♭/C E♭/B♭ A♭ E♭/G
Je - sus, born in Beth - le - hem in a man - ger up -
Fm7 B♭7sus B♭7 E♭ B♭/D A♭/C E♭/B♭
on the hay. Je - sus, born in Beth - le - hem,
A♭ E♭/G Cm Fm7 A♭/B♭ E♭
born in Beth - le - hem on Christ - mas Day.

C7sus C7 F C/E B♭/D F/C
Je - sus, born in Beth - le - hem,
B♭ F/A Gm7 C7sus C7 F C/E
born to bring hope to ev - 'ry - one. Je - sus,
B♭/D F/C B♭ F/A Gm7 B♭/C
born in Beth - le - hem, born in Beth - le - hem, God's on - ly
F C/B♭ F2/A F/A
Son. All the world should know
C/B♭ F2/A F/A C/B♭
Je - sus loves them so. That is why He
F/A C/G F E♭2 E♭ C7sus C7
came to earth so long a - go.
F C/E B♭/D F/C B♭ F/A
Je - sus, born in Beth - le - hem, born a babe in a
Gm7 C7sus C7 F C/E B♭/D F/C
cat - tle stall. Je - sus, born in Beth - le - hem,
B♭ F/A Dm Gm7 B♭/C F
born in Beth - le - hem, Lord of all.

Jesus, God's Son
(To the tune of Camptown Races)

Words and Music by
JIMBO STEVENS

B♭
F
1. Who was born in Beth - le - hem?
2. Who died on the cross for me?
Je - sus, Je - sus,
B♭
F
B♭
born to save the lost from sin, Je - sus, God's Son.
died that He might set me free, Je - sus, God's Son.
B♭
N.C. B♭ Cm7(4) B♭/D
B♭
B♭
Je - sus, God's Son, Je - sus, God's Son,
B♭
F
B♭
He was born in Beth - le - hem, Je - sus, God's Son.
He died on the cross for me, Je - sus, God's Son.
B♭
G Am7(4) G/B
C
3. Who has ris - en from the grave?
G
C
Je - sus, Je - sus, rose a - gain my soul to save,
G
C
C
N.C. C Dm7(4) C/E
Je - sus, God's Son. Je - sus, God's Son,
F
C
Je - sus, God's Son, He has ris - en
C
G
C
rit.
from the grave, Je - sus, God's Son.

Jesus, My Savior
(To the tune of Go Tell Aunt Rhodie)

Words and Music by
RUTH ELAINE SCHRAM

C Dm7 G7 C
1. Je - sus, my Sav - ior, Je - sus, my Sav - ior,
2. Wom - en were weep - ing. Wom - en were weep - ing.
C 1. Dm7 G7 C 2. Dm7 G7 C A♭7
Je - sus, my Sav - ior, my Lord, was cru - ci - fied. day that Je - sus died.
Wom - en were weep - ing the
D♭ E♭m7 A♭7 D♭
3. On Eas - ter morn - ing, on Eas - ter morn - ing, on Eas - ter morn - ing, Lord
E♭m7 A♭7 D♭ A9 D Em7 D/F♯
Je - sus rose a - gain. 4. An - gel said to Mar - y,
5. Tell His dis - ci - ples.
G6 A7 D G/A D Em9 D/F♯
an - gel said to Mar - y, an - gel said to Mar - y, "Lord
Tell His dis - ci - ples. Tell His dis - ci - ples Lord
1. G6 A7 D 2. G6 A7 D D/C B♭7 E♭ Fm7(4) E♭/G G♭°
Je - sus rose a - gain." Je - sus rose a - gain. 6. We have a Sav - ior.
Fm7 B♭7 E♭ A♭/B♭ E♭ B♭7/D B♭m6/D♭ C7 Fm7 B♭ E♭sus E♭
We have a Sav - ior. We have a Sav - ior who died and rose a - gain.

John 3:16

Words and Music by
TROY NILSSON and GENIE NILSSON

Quickly (♩=186)

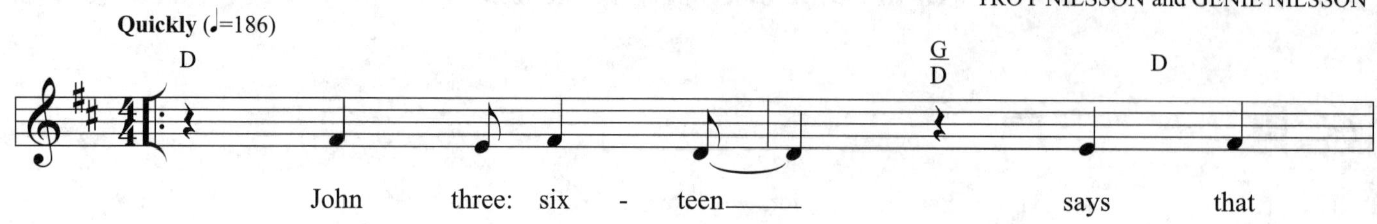
D
G/D
D
John three: six - teen
says that

G
A
God so loved the world,
He gave His

D
G/D
D
on - ly be - got - ten Son,
that who -

G
A
ev - er be - lieves in Him
will nev - er die,

Bm7
A/C#
D
but have e - ter - nal life.

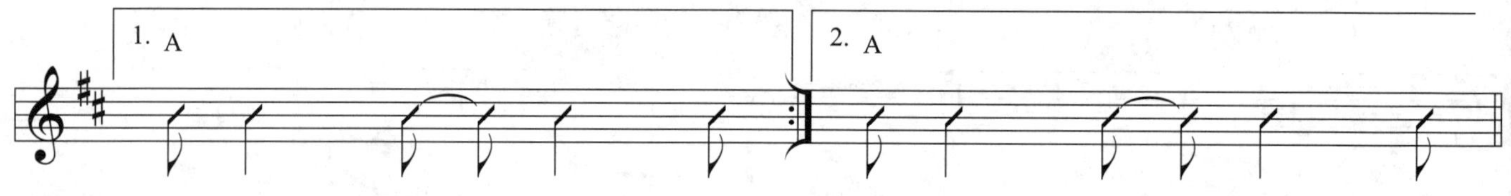
1. A
2. A

D/F#
He is the Way.
He is the Truth.

G2
G
F♯
He is the Life, so put your faith
Em
D
in Je - sus Christ and your
2nd time to Coda
C
Asus
A
soul will nev - er die, will nev - er
D
G2
Asus
A
die, will nev - er
D
G2
Asus
A
D.C. al Coda
die.
CODA
Asus
A
D
G2
Asus
will nev - er die,
A
D
G2
Asus
will nev - er die.
1. A
2. A
D
Will nev - er

Joy from Head to Toe

Words and Music by
JANET MCMAHAN-WILSON

Brightly
E♭ A♭ E♭/G E♭ F
He gives me joy, joy, joy from my head to my toes. I
B♭ E♭ Fm7 B♭
know, I know, I know He gives me joy that o - ver - flows with - in me.
E♭ A♭
My heart can't keep from prais - ing God for all this most a - maz - ing
B♭ B♭° B♭ E♭
joy, joy, joy from head to toe, head to toe! He gives me
A♭ E♭/G E♭ F
love, love, love from my head to my toes. I
B♭ E♭ Fm7 B♭
know, I know, I know He gives me love that o - ver - flows with - in me.
E♭ A♭
My heart can't keep from prais - ing God for all this most a - maz - ing
B♭ B♭° B♭ B♭° B♭ E♭
love, love, love, and joy, joy, joy from head to toe, head to toe! He gives me
A♭ E♭/G E♭ F
hope, hope, hope from my head to my toes. I

B♭ E♭ Fm7 B♭
know, I know, I know He gives me hope that o - ver - flows with - in me.
E♭ A♭
My heart can't keep from prais - ing God for all this most a - maz - ing
B♭ B♭° B♭ B♭° B♭
hope, hope, hope, and love, love, love, and
B♭° B♭ E♭
joy, joy, joy from head to toe, head to toe! He gives me
A♭ E♭/G E♭ F
peace, peace, peace from my head to my toes. I
B♭ E♭ Fm7 B♭
know, I know, I know He gives me peace that o - ver - flows with - in me.
E♭ A♭
My heart can't keep from prais - ing God for all this most a - maz - ing
B♭ B♭° B♭ B♭° B♭ B♭° B♭
peace, peace, peace and hope, hope, hope, and love, love, love, and
B♭° B♭ E♭ Fm B♭ E♭
joy, joy, joy from head to toe, head to toe!

Joshua Fought the Battle of Jericho

Spiritual

Cm Gm7 Cm
Josh - ua fought the bat - tle of Jer - i - cho,
G7 Cm Cm/G
Jer - i - cho, Jer - i - cho.
Cm Cm/B♭ A♭ Gm7 Cm Fm7
Josh - ua fought the bat - tle of Jer - i - cho, and the
2nd time to Coda
Cm/G Fm6/A♭ Cm6/A G7/B Cm Cm/G
walls came tum - bl - in' down! Now you may
Cm Cm6/G Dm7(4) G7
talk a - bout your men of Gid - e - on, you may
Cm Cm Gm/B♭ A♭maj7 G7 Cm G7/D
talk a - bout your men of Saul; but there's none like good ol'
D.C. al Coda
Cm/E♭ Fm9 Cm/G Fm6/A♭ Cm/A G7/B Cm Gm7
Josh - u - a at the bat - tle of Jer - i - cho!
CODA
Cm Cm/E♭ Fm7 Cm/G Fm6/A♭ Cm6/A G7/B Cm Fm7
down! And the walls came tum - bl - in' down! And the
Cm/G B♭/G A♭/G G7 Cm Cm/G Cm6
walls came tum - bl - in' down!

Keep Cool

Words and Music by
JANET MCMAHAN-WILSON

Calypso (♩=132)
B♭ E♭
When you're get - tin' hot un - der the col - lar and you
B♭ F B♭
feel so mad that you wan - na hol - ler, stop your stew - in' be -
E♭ F
fore you start spew - in' out words you're gon - na re -
B♭ F B♭ B♭7/A♭ E♭/G B♭7/F
gret. Try this in - stead:
E♭ B♭ F
Keep cool when you wan - na shout. Keep cool and
B♭ B♭7 E♭
talk it out. Keep cool. It's the
B♭ F
wis - est way. As long as you keep cool, you'll be O.
B♭ 1. B♭7/A♭ E♭/G B♭7/F 2.
K. As
F B♭6
long as you keep cool, you'll be O. K.

Ketchup on My Apples

Words and Music by
MATT GLASS and DAVE HUNT

Laid back (♩=96)
D
G
1. It's o - kay if I___ like ketch - up on my
(2.) kay if I___ like syr - up on my
(3.) kay if I___ like mayon - naise in my
(4.) kay if I___ like mus - tard on my

D
ap - ples. It's o - kay if I___ like ketch - up on my
ba - con. It's o - kay if I___ like syr - up on my
chil - i. It's o - kay if I___ like mayon - naise in my
o - kra. It's o - kay if I___ like mus - tard on my

A
D/F♯
G
ap - ples. 'Cause ketch - up on my ap - ples
ba - con. 'Cause syr - up on my ba - con might just
chil - i. 'Cause mayon - naise in my chil - i
o - kra. 'Cause mus - tard on my o - kra beats

Bm
G
A
makes the whole___ world daz - zle. It's o - kay if I___ like ketch - up on my
calm my tum - my ach - in'. It's o - kay if I___ like syr - up on my
gets me feel - ing sil - ly. It's o - kay if I___ like mayon - naise in my
mus - tard in___ my so - da. It's o - kay if I___ like mus - tard on my

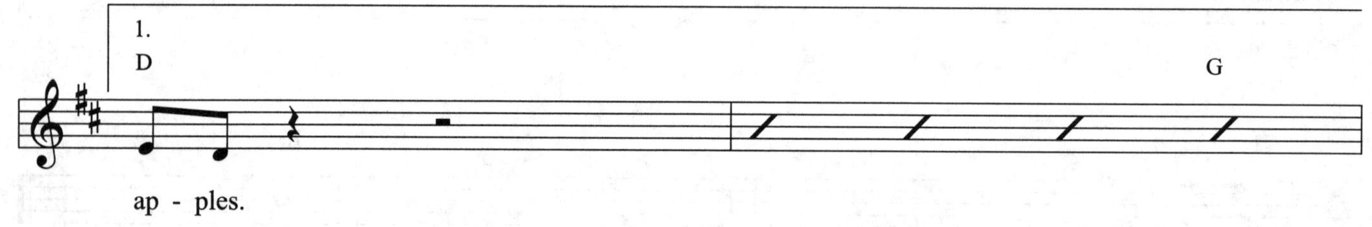
1.
D
G
ap - ples.

D
G
2. It's o -
2.3.4.
D
D/F♯
G
A
ba - con. 'Cause God has made me who I am.
chil - i.
o - kra.
D
D/F♯
G
A
He loves me just the way I am.
D
D/F♯
G
A
And I know that when He looks at me, it's not the cra -
D
A/C♯
Bm
G
A
- zy things He sees. He loves me just the way I
D
G
am.
Last time to Coda
D
G
D.S. (twice) al Coda
3. It's o -
4. It's o -
CODA
G
D

Kum Ba Yah

African Folk Song

Bossa
1. Kum ba yah, my Lord, kum ba yah! Kum ba
(2.) pray - ing, Lord, kum ba yah! Some - one's
yah, my Lord, kum ba yah! Kum ba
pray - ing, Lord, kum ba yah! Some - one's
yah, my Lord, kum ba yah! O
pray - ing, Lord, kum ba yah! O
Lord, kum ba yah! 2. Some - one's yah! 3. Some - one's
Lord, kum ba
sing - ing, Lord, kum ba yah! Some - one's
sing - ing, Lord, kum ba yah! Some - one's
sing - ing, Lord, kum ba yah! O
Lord, kum ba yah! O
Lord, kum ba yah!

Let the Lord Lead Your Way

Words and Music by
JANET MCMAHAN-WILSON

Tenderly (♩=80)
B♭ B♭/D E♭
Let the Lord lead your way.
Cm7 E♭ F
Let the Lord lead your way
F/A B♭ F/E♭ E♭ B♭/D
and He will guide you ev - 'ry
E♭ B♭/D B♭ F B♭
2nd time to Coda
day. Let the Lord lead your way.
B♭/D Cm F7 B♭
Fol - low where He leads
Cm7 B♭/D E♭ E°
and He will sup - ply your ev - 'ry
Fsus F F6
D.S. al Coda
need.
Let the
CODA E♭ B♭/F Fsus
Let the Lord lead your
B♭ B♭/D B♭
way.

Larry Boy
(Theme Song)

Words and Music by
DAVID MULLEN and PHIL VISCHER

Funky groove (♩=96)

E♭7(♯9)

Lar - ry Boy! Lar - ry Boy!

A♭7 B♭7 E♭7(♯9)

Lean and mean green ma - chine, Lar - ry Boy!

A♭7 B♭7

Lar - ry Boy! Out - ta sight veg - gie might,

E♭7(♯9) E♭7(♯9)

Lar - ry Boy! Lar - ry Boy!

A♭7 B♭7

Lar - ry Boy! Lean and mean green ma - chine,

E♭7(♯9)

Lar - ry Boy! Lar - ry Boy!

A♭7 B♭7 E♭7(♯9) *3rd time to Coda* 𝄌

Out - ta sight veg - gie might, Lar - ry Boy!

E♭

1. Who do they call when Bum - bly - burg's in trou - ble?
2. Where do you turn when this world needs a he - ro?

Who's got the suit with su - per suc - tion ears? There's
A man with style and plung - ers on his head? It's
A♭
no need to pan - ic 'cause this guy is man - ic, and you
ea - sy to prove he's just one of the groov - i - est
A♭7
B♭m/A♭
A♭7
E♭
know that he'll save the day. You need a hand, he's
cats that you'll ev - er know. It's plain to see in
right there on the dou - ble.
fash - ion he's no ze - ro.
1. B♭7
Hey, hey, he's on the way.
B7 C7 D♭7 D7
Pur-ple and yel-low, he's one su-per fel-low.
2.
At the wheel of the Lar-ry mo-bile.
D.C. al Coda
B7 C7 D♭7 D7
Pur - ple and yel - low, he's one su - per fel - low.
CODA
E♭7(♯9)
Lar - ry Boy!
E♭7(♯9)
Lar - ry Boy!
Dy - no - mite!

Let Life Live

Words and Music by
TROY NILSSON and GENIE NILSSON

Brightly (♩=134)
C
C/E
F
C/E
Dm
C
G7/B
Am
G7
Love life and let life live. Life is God's to
take and give. Love life and let life live
all o - ver God's green earth.
G
N.C.
God breathed His life in - to us all; God breathed His life in you.
Life is a pre - cious gift from God, He num - bers all our days;
And on - ly God is to de - cide when each life is
And if you take an - oth - er's life you throw that gift a -
1. C
through.
2. C
way.
Love life and let life live. Life is God's to take and give.

C C/E F C/E Dm C G7/B G7
Love life and let life live all o - ver God's green
N.C. A♭7 D♭ D♭/F G♭ D♭/F E♭m D♭
earth. Love life and let life live.
A♭7/C B♭m A♭7 D♭ A♭ D♭ D♭/F
Life is God's to take and give. Love life and
G♭ D♭/F E♭m D♭ A♭7/C A♭7 N.C. A7
let life live all o - ver God's green earth.
D D/F♯ G D/F♯ Em D
Love life and let life live.
A7/C♯ Bm A7 D A D D/F♯
Life is God's to take and give. Love life and
G D/F♯ Em D A7/C♯ A7 N.C.
let life live all o - ver God's green earth.

Light

Words and Music by
HERB OWEN

Country, in 2
B♭ E♭ F
I was lost in dark - ness, could - n't find my
B♭ E♭ F
way; trip - pin', fall - in' in - to sin, un - til that glo - rious
B♭ E♭ F F7
day when the sun came out from be - hind the cloud, then the
B♭ Gm Cm7
dark - ness was all gone. When the light poured down on my
F Cm7 F6 F B♭ Cm7(4) B♭/D
long - ing heart, 'twas the res - ur - rec - tion morn. And then said
E♭ F E♭/B♭ B♭
Je - sus, "My friend, I want to know you,
Cm7 B♭/D E♭ F
and shine a lit - tle light in the cor - ner of your
B♭ F/A Gm
heart." And then His love flood - ed in my soul
Dm E♭ F B♭ Gm
and my heart - ache rolled a - way, when

Bb/F Cm7 F Bb Eb Bb/D Cm7
Je - sus made my dark - ness de - part.
Bb Eb F
Je - sus is the Son of God, I learned that glo - rious
Bb Eb Cm7
day. He died and shed His pre - cious blood to
F Bb Bb7 Eb
take my sins a - way. When I trust - ed Him, He
F Bb Gm
came and turned my dark - ness in - to light; He
Cm7 F6 F Eb F
took a - way my blind - ness, and in its place He gave me
Bb G F2/A G/B C
sight. I am like a
F/C G/C C F/C
lit - tle tree, I'm grow - in' all the time. I
C F G C C7
can't be - lieve the change in me since I made Je - sus mine! And

F G C
since I'm grow - in' big - ger, I'm work - in' with all my
Am Dm7 G7
might to find some peo - ple lost in dark - ness and lead them
F G C Dm7(4) C/E
out in - to the light. For when my
F G F/C C
Je - sus said, "Friend, I want to know you,
Dm7(4) C/E F G
and shine a lit - tle light in the cor - ner of your
C Em/B Am
heart," well, then His love flood - ed in my
Em F G C Am
soul and my heart - ache rolled a - way, when
C/G Am Dm7 G Am Am/G F F♯m7(♭5)
Je - sus made my dark - ness de - part, when
C/G G7 C
Je - sus made my dark - ness de - part!

Little David

(Play on Your Harp)

Spiritual

Lit-tle Da-vid, play on your harp. Hal-le-lu, Hal-le-lu! Lit-tle Da-vid,
Last time to Coda
play on your harp. Hal-le-lu! Lit-tle Da-vid,
lu! Lit-tle Da-vid was a shep-herd boy. He
D.S. al Coda
killed Go-li-ath and he shout-ed for joy! Lit-tle Da-vid,
CODA
lu! Lit-tle Da-vid, play on your harp. Hal-le-
lu, Hal-le-lu! Lit-tle Da-vid, play on your harp. Hal-le-
lu! Lit-tle Da-vid, play on your harp. Hal-le-
lu, Hal-le-lu! Lit-tle Da-vid, play on your harp.
Hal-le-lu!

Like a Lamp

Words and Music by
GARY FORSYTHE

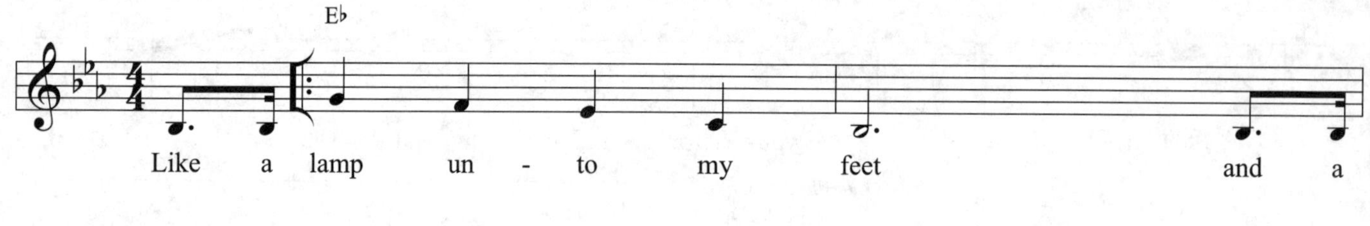
E♭
Like a lamp un - to my feet and a

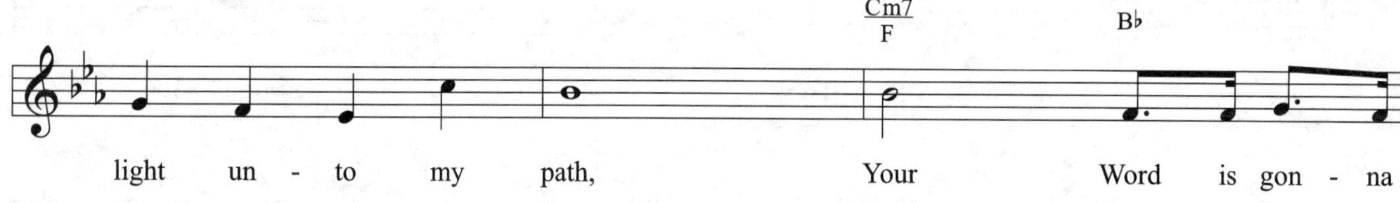
Cm7/F
B♭
light un - to my path, Your Word is gon - na

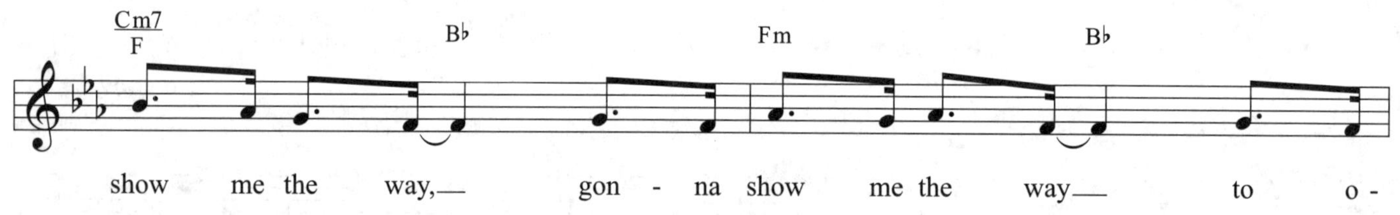
Cm7/F
B♭
Fm
B♭
show me the way, gon - na show me the way to o -

Cm7/F
B♭
E♭
bey ev - 'ry day. Like a lamp un - to my

feet and a light un - to my path,

Cm7/F
B♭
Cm7/F
B♭
Your Word, I'm gon - na hide it a - way, gon - na

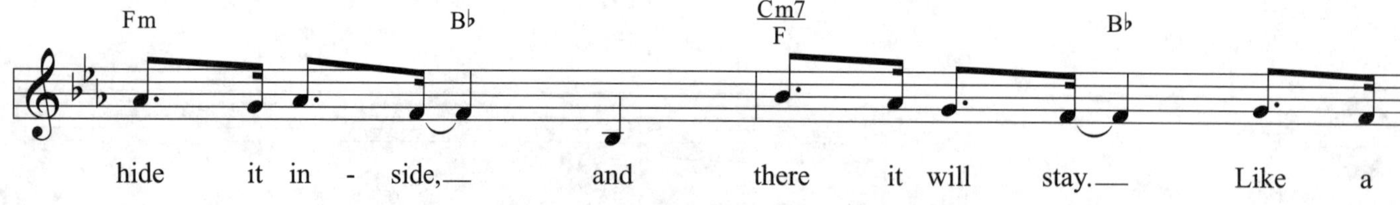
Fm
B♭
Cm7/F
B♭
hide it in - side, and there it will stay. Like a

Cm
C♭
lamp, like a light, like a
E♭/B♭
F7/A
lan - tern in the night, oh Lord, oh
E♭/B♭
Cm7
E♭/F
E♭/A♭
E♭/B♭
B♭
Lord, how I love to learn Your
1. E♭
Word. Like a
2. E♭/G
Cm7
E♭/F
E♭/A♭
E♭/B♭
B♭
E♭/B♭
Cm7
Word. Oh Lord,
E♭/F
E♭/B♭
B♭
E♭/G
Cm7
how I love to learn Your Word.
E♭/F
E♭/A♭
E♭/B♭
B♭
E♭
How I love to learn Your Word.

Lock on Your Lips

Words and Music by
JANET MCMAHAN-WILSON

Bright shuffle
B♭ Gm7 Cm F
If you can't say an - y - thing nice, you
Cm E♭/F B♭ E♭ C/E
bet - ter just not say an - y - thing. Put a lock on your lips be - fore they
B♭/F G Cm F
have a chance to slip. Throw the key a - way un - til you
B♭ G Cm
find some - thing kind to say. It's bet - ter to nev - er say a sin - gle word than to
E♭/F F7 B♭ G C/D G
say things that should - n't be heard. If you
C Am7 Dm G Dm F/G
can't say an - y - thing nice, you bet - ter just not say
C F D/F♯
an - y - thing. Put a lock on your lips be - fore they
C/G A Dm G
have a chance to slip. Throw the key a - way un - til you
C A Dm
find some - thing kind to say. It's bet - ter to nev - er say a sin - gle
F/G G7 C
word than to say things that should - n't be heard.

Lord, Help Me to Be Kind

Words and Music by
JANET MCMAHAN-WILSON

With sincerity (♩=96)

F Dm7 Gm7 C
1. Lord, help me to be kind. Lord,

Gm7 C F F9 B♭ F/A
help me to be kind. Ev - 'ry day, in

A/E A7 Dm C6 B♭ C6 C Fmaj7
all I say, Lord, help me to be kind.

Gm7/F Fmaj7 Gm7/F
2. Lord,

F Dm7 Gm7 C Gm7 C
help me to be pa - tient. Lord, help me to be
(3.) help me to be lov - ing. Lord, help me to be

F F9 B♭ F/A A/E A7 Dm C6
pa - tient. Ev - 'ry day, in all I say, Lord,
lov - ing. Ev - 'ry day, in all I say, Lord,

B♭ C6 C 1. Fmaj7 Gm7/F B♭ B♭maj7
help me to be pa - tient.
help me to be

B♭/C C 2. F Dm B♭ C6 C F Dm
3. Lord, lov - ing. Lord, help me to be pa - tient. Lord

B♭ C6 C7 Fmaj7 B♭/F Fmaj7 F
help me to be kind.

Lord, Let Me Dwell

Words and Music by
JANET MCMAHAN-WILSON

Two-beat feel

A D A
Lord, let me dwell in your tent for - ev - er. Keep me

F♯m Bm E
safe in the shel - ter of your wings.

A D A
Lord, let me dwell in your tent for - ev - er, for

E *2nd time to Coda* A
you a - lone are Lord of ev - 'ry - thing.

Dm A
You are my ref - uge and my rock, a

Dm A Dm
strong and might - y tow'r. You've o - ver - come the

A Dm Bm7(♭5) E *D.C. al Coda*
e - vil one by Your might - y pow'r.

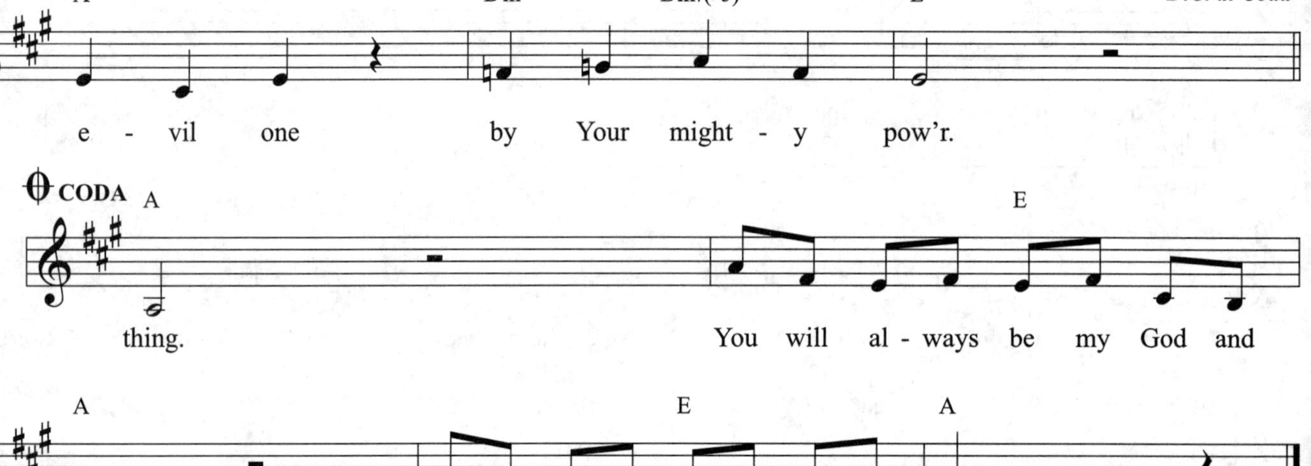
CODA
A
thing.
E
You will al - ways be my God and
A
King.
E
A
You are Lord, are Lord of ev - 'ry - thing.

Love Is

Words and Music by
DOTTIE RAMBO

C
G/B
Am
Am7
Dm
G
Love is a ver - y spe - cial thing, A

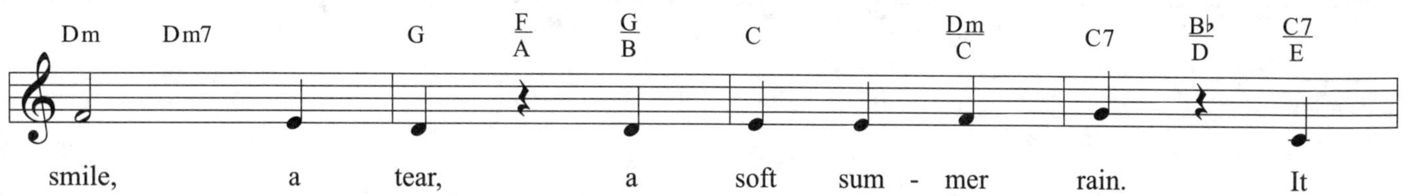
Dm
Dm7
G
F/A
G/B
C
Dm/C
C7
B♭/D
C7/E
smile, a tear, a soft sum - mer rain. It

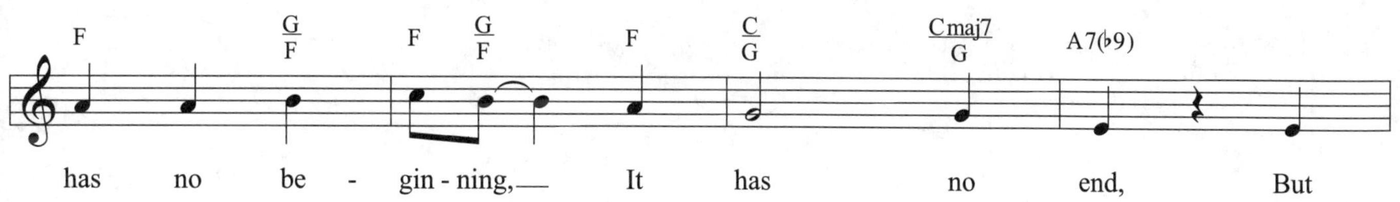
F
G/F
F
G/F
F
C/G
Cmaj7/G
A7(♭9)
has no be - gin - ning, It has no end, But

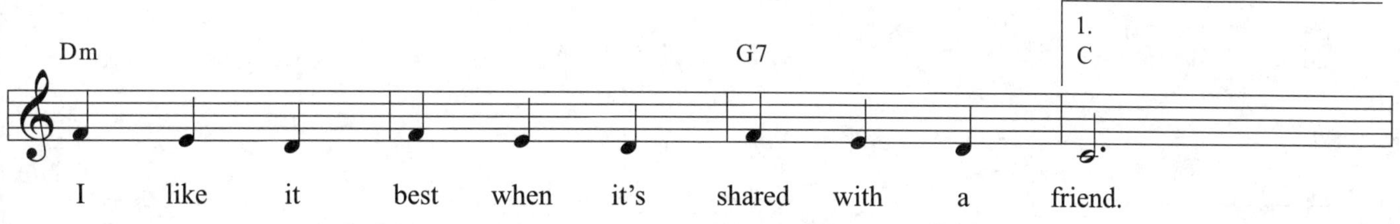
Dm
G7
1.
C
I like it best when it's shared with a friend.

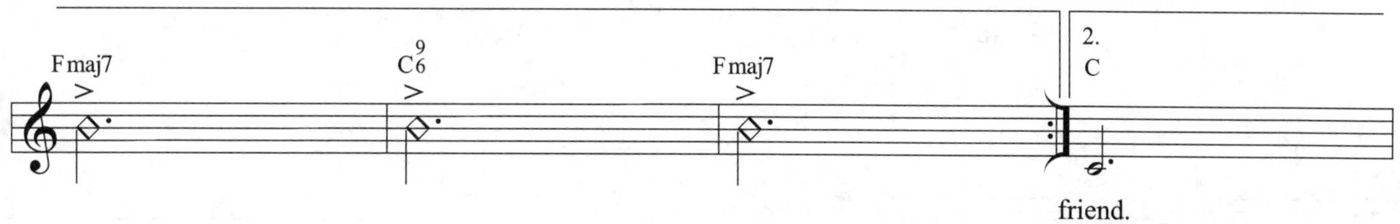
Fmaj7
C6/9
Fmaj7
2.
C
friend.

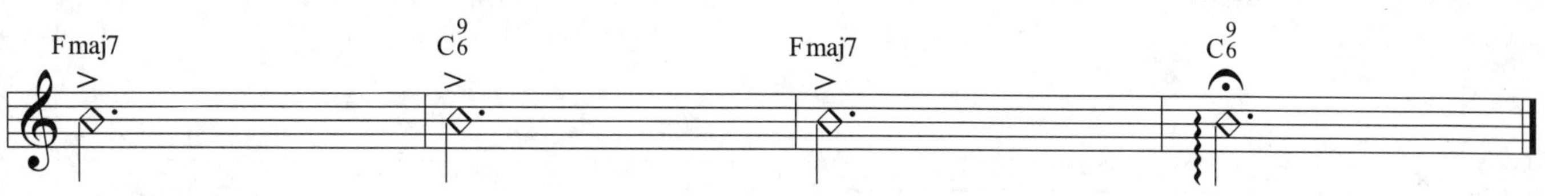
Fmaj7
C6/9
Fmaj7
C6/9

Love Light

Words and Music by
GARY FORSYTHE

C G F C/G C F C/E
1. I've got the love light in my heart. Je - sus lives in me.
2. Love light lives in - side my heart; He's for - ev - er mine.
G C G F G C
It glows like sun - shine in the dark for
Yet for those still in the dark,
F C/E G F G
all the world to see. It ra - di - ates the
I will let Him shine. In ev - 'ry - thing I
C F G C F
Fa - ther's love, beams like dia - monds in the sun,
do and say, I will give my life a - way.
G C F
mak - ing known what God has done
When I walk in love light's way,
G C
deep in - side of me. Shines
He comes shin - ing through.
G F C/G G
bright like a big flash - light. Shines

F G C
bright like the moon at night. Shines
G F G C F C/E
bright so the world can see that God is love and His
3rd time to Coda
Dm G7 1. C F G
love light lives in me.
2. C D.S. al Coda
me. Shines
CODA
C F G F C/E
me. God is love and His
Dm G7 C/G C
love light lives in me.
F G C F G
Shines bright. Shines
C F G C
bright. Shines bright.

Love Me

Words and Music by
BEN RYAN

Ballad (♩=92)
D Em A
1. Hear me. Hear what I say.
2. See me. See what I do.
3. Love me. Love who I am.
D Em A
Hear me. I've some - thing to say.
See me. Watch what I can do.
Love me and all that I am. Though
G D/F♯ Em D
Show me you un - der - stand what I mean
Watch me and show that you real - ly care
what I can do and say may be small
G D/F♯ Em A7
when I say words, and you look at me.
as I pre - tend I can fly in the air.
and I may not change the world o - ver - all, still
3rd time to Coda
G A B♭° Bm A
Let me see in your eyes that you re - al -
Let me see in your eyes that you re - al -
all that I am is here in your gen - tle
G D/F♯ Em
ize my words are me. Hear me.
ize what I do is me. See me.
1. D Em A
2. D Em B♭°

Bm
A/C♯
D
I thank the Lord each day for
Am7(♭5)
C
Bm7
G
B
par - ents who teach and guide me,
Em7(♭5)
D
A
show - ing me both in word and deed that
A♭m7(♭5)
A
G
A
D
A
A
D.C. al Coda
Je - sus is the way.
CODA
G
D
F♯
G
hands. This is me en - joy - ing your com -
D
F♯
Em7
D
F♯
- pa - ny, so glad we're a fam - i - ly
G
rit.
A
D
a tempo
Em
A
and that you love me.
D
Em
A
C♯
D2

Love Your Neighbor
Words and Music by
PHIL VISCHER
Waltz (♩=176)
He has a shoe and I have a pot, but when we look
deep - er, there's more that we've got. God made us spe - cial, and
now I can see if you're spe - cial to Him, then you're spe - cial to me.
Love your neigh - bor. When some - one
helps you, then you'll un - der - stand. When you love your
2nd time to Coda
neigh - bor, lov - ing means lend - ing a hand.
rit.
faster
If you see some - one who's hurt or in
need, may - be it's time to per - form a good deed.
And when you've fin - ished, you'll find that it's true: When you make them feel
D.S. al Coda
bet - ter, you'll feel bet - ter, too.
CODA
hand.

Monkey See

Words and Music by
STEVE KELLER

Blues rock (♩=106)
1. Mon - keys in the jun - gle have a game they like to play. They
(2.) care - ful who you fol - low; be care - ful what you do. Be
im - i - tate each oth - er, mon - key - ing a - round all day. While
care - ful that your friends don't make a mon - key out of you. And
this is fine for mon - keys, there's some - thing you should know: It's not
if you have a ques - tion, if you have a doubt, don't mon -
al - ways wise to fol - low where all the oth - er mon - keys go. Mon - key see,
key a - round; just stop and think. It's best to check it out.
mon - key do. Just be - cause some - one can do some - thing does - n't
mean that you should, too. Mon - key see, mon - key do. Don't
let an - oth - er mon - key make a mon - key out of you.
2. So be mon - key out of you.
N.C.
1.
2.

Made to Praise the Lord

Words and Music by
JANET MCMAHAN-WILSON and TED WILSON

Brightly
G
A
1. Ev - 'ry lit - tle bit - ty crit - ter in the big wide world, the
(2.) squirm - y lit - tle worm - y in the mess - y mud, the
(3.) swish - y lit - tle fish - y in the deep blue sea, the
Am
G
big wide world, the big wide world, ev - 'ry lit - tle bit - ty crit - ter in the
mess - y mud, the mess - y mud, ev - 'ry squirm - y lit - tle worm - y in the
deep blue sea, the deep blue sea, ev - 'ry swish - y lit - tle fish - y in the
A
Am
big wide world was made to praise the
mess - y mud was made to praise the
deep blue sea was made to praise the
1. Cm
D
2.3. G
Lord. 2. Ev - 'ry Lord. Ev - 'ry
Lord.
C
D
G
bee that ev - er buzzed, ev - 'ry
C
D
G
C
B
crea - ture cov - ered with fuzz, ev - 'ry fur - ry, feath - er - y,
Em
A°/E♭
G/D
A
D
A/C♯
slick, or leath - er - y an - i - mal that ev - er was was
2nd time to Coda
D
A/C♯
D
A/C♯
D
A/C♯
D
A/C♯
made to praise in some most a - maz - ing

D
Cm
D
D.S. al Coda
ways.
3. Ev - 'ry
CODA
D
Cm
D
ways.
Ev - ry
G
lit - tle bit - ty crit - ter, ev - 'ry squirm - y lit - tle worm - y, ev - 'ry
A
swish - y lit - tle fish - y in the big wide world, the
Am
G
big wide world, the big wide world, ev - 'ry lit - tle bit - ty crit - ter, ev - 'ry
squirm - y lit - tle worm - y, ev - 'ry swish - y lit - tle fish - y in the
A
Am
G
big wide world was made to praise the Lord. They were
Am
D
Cm
G
made to praise the Lord.

Make a Big Splash

Words and Music by
TOM STEINMAN and JAY TYLER

Moderate rock (♩.=78)

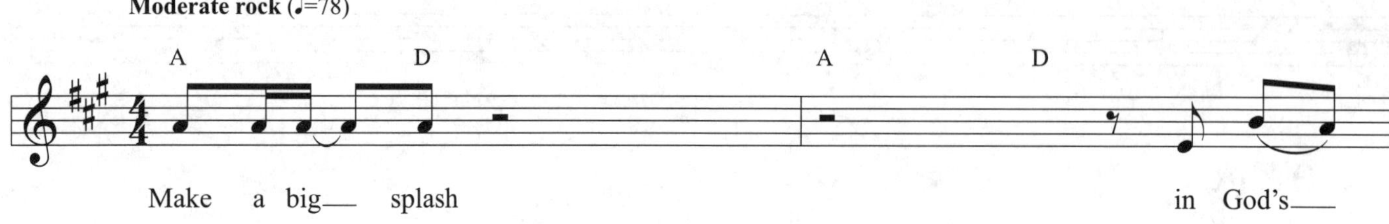
A
D
A
D
Make a big splash
in God's

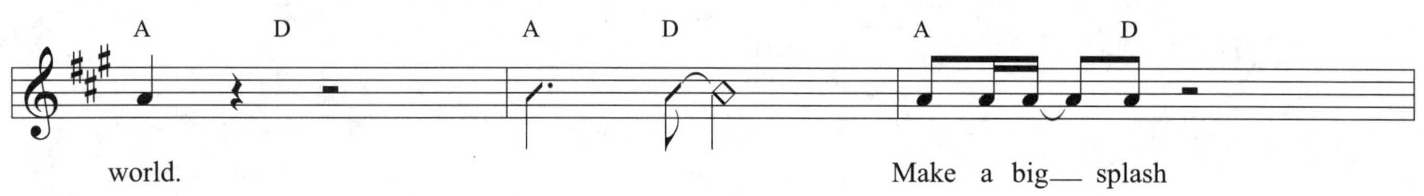
A
D
A
D
A
D
world.
Make a big splash

A
D
A
D
A
D
in God's world.

A
D
F♯m7
E
1. Ev - 'ry ot - ter got - ta splash in the wa - ter. Ev - 'ry ot - ter ought - ta slide down the riv - er - side.

A
D
F♯m7
E
God makes the rain, the rain makes the riv - er. The riv - er makes ev - 'ry ot - ter wan - na make a big

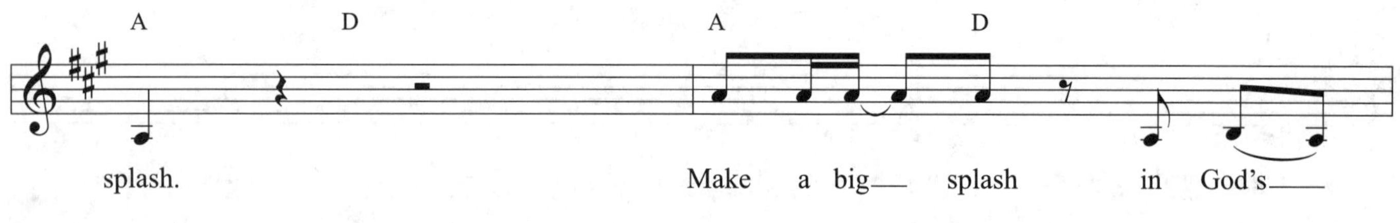
A
D
A
D
splash.
Make a big splash in God's

A
D
A
D
world.
Make a big splash.

A D F♯m7 E
2. Got-ta love God's world. Ev-'ry ot-ter ought-ta soak up the sun-shine, slip__ in the wa-ter.
3. Got-ta love God's world. Got-ta love the wa-ter. Find a new friend and play__ like an ot-ter.
A D F♯m7 E
Got-ta love God's world. Ev-'ry ot-ter knows it; the big-ger the splash, the more__ an ot-ter shows it.
Got-ta love God's world. Got-ta love the Giv-er.__ Ev-'ry-bod-y shows it down by__ the riv-er.
D A F♯m7 E
Ev-'ry an-i-mal does__ what it ought-ta, swim-min', div-in', splash-in' in the wa-ter.
Ev-'ry-bod-y does__ what they ought-ta, swim-min', div-in', splash-in' in the wa-ter.
D A F♯m7 E
God makes the rain; the rain__ makes the riv-er. The riv-er makes an-i-mals wan-na make a big
A D A D A D
splash. Make a big__ splash in God's__ world.
1. A D
Make a big__ splash.
2. A D
Make a big__ splash in God's__
A D A/C♯ Bm7 A D
world. Make a big__ splash
A D A D A/C♯ Bm7
Repeat and fade
in God's__ world.

Mister Noah

(To the tune of Old MacDonald)

Words and Music by
TRISH MENDOZA

F F/A B♭ F G9 C7 F
1. Mis - ter No - ah built an ark, splish, splash, splish, splash, splish! And
2. Mis - ter No - ah built an ark, splish, splash, splish, splash, splish! And
F F/A B♭ F G9 C7 F
on this ark he had a duck, splish, splash, splish, splash, splish! With a
on this ark he had a cow, splish, splash, splish, splash, splish! With a
(Repeat 2nd time only)
F Gm7(4) F/A Gm7(4) F Gm7(4) F/A Gm7(4)
quack, quack here and a quack, quack there, here a quack, there a quack, ev - 'ry - where a quack, quack.
moo, moo here and a moo, moo there, here a moo, there a moo, ev - 'ry - where a moo, moo.
F F/A B♭ F 1. G9 C7 F
Mis - ter No - ah built an ark, splish, splash, splish, splash, splish!
2. G9 C7 F D♭7 G♭ G♭/B♭ C♭ G♭
splish, splash, splish, splash, splish! Mis - ter No - ah built an ark,
A♭9 D♭7 G♭ G♭ G♭/B♭ C♭ G♭
splish, splash, splish, splash, splish! And on this ark he had a sheep,
A♭9 D♭7 G♭ G♭ A♭m7(4) G♭/B♭ A♭m7(4)
splish, splash, splish, splash, splish! With a baa, baa here and a baa, baa there,
G♭ A♭m7(4) G♭ A♭m7(4) G♭ A♭m7(4) G♭/B♭ A♭m7(4)
here a baa, there a baa, ev - 'ry - where a baa, baa; a moo, moo here and a moo, moo there,
quack, quack here and a quack, quack there,
G♭ A♭m7(4) G♭/B♭ A♭m7(4) G♭ G♭/B♭ C♭ G♭
here a moo, there a moo, ev - 'ry - where a moo, moo; a Mis - ter No - ah built an ark,
here a quack, there a quack, ev - 'ry - where a quack, quack.

splish, splash, splish, splash, splish! Mis-ter No-ah built an ark, splish, splash, splish, splash, splish! And
on this ark he had a dog, splish, splash, splish, splash, splish! With a
(play four times)
woof, woof here and a woof, woof there, here a woof, there a woof, ev-'ry-where a woof, woof; a
baa, baa here and a baa, baa there, here a baa, there a baa, ev-'ry-where a baa, baa; a
moo, moo, here and a moo, moo there, here a moo, there a moo, ev-'ry-where a moo, moo; a
quack, quack here and a quack, quack there, here a quack, there a quack, ev-'ry-where a quack, quack.
Mis-ter No-ah built an ark, splish, splash, splish, splash, splish!
Mis-ter No-ah built an ark, splish, splash, splish, splash, splish! And
on this ark he had a bird, splish, splash, splish, splash, splish! With a
chirp, chirp here and a chirp, chirp there, here a chirp, there a chirp, ev-'ry-where a chirp, chirp; a
woof, woof here and a woof, woof there, here a woof, there a woof, ev-'ry-where a woof, woof; a
baa, baa here and a baa, baa there, here a baa, there a baa, ev-'ry-where a baa, baa; a
moo, moo here and a moo, moo there, here a moo, there a moo, ev-'ry-where a moo, moo; a
quack, quack here and a quack, quack there, here a quack, there a quack, ev-'ry-where a quack, quack.
Mis-ter No-ah built an ark, splish, splash, splish, splash, splish!

My Brother, My Friend

Words and Music by
TONY CONGI and BILL MCCOY

With excitement (♩=116)
G7 C7
You're my broth - er, You're my friend. You're my be -
G7 C7 G D/F♯ Em
gin - ning and my end. You're all a - round me when the world
Am/C D
just turns and walks a - way. You're my sun -
G7 C7 G7
- shine on a cloud - y day. You're the rain that washed my blues a - way.
C7 G D/F♯ Em
And I can al - ways count on You, 'cause You're my
Am/C D 1. G7
broth - er, and You're my friend.
C7 G7 C7
Well, You're my
2. G7 C7 G7 C7

G7 C7 G7 C7
A7 D7
Well, You're my brother, You're my friend. You're my be-
A7 D7 A E/G♯ F♯m
ginning and my end. You're all around me when the world
Bm/D E
just turns and walks away. You're my sun-
A7 D7 A7
shine on a cloudy day. You're the rain that washed my blues away.
D7 A E/G♯ F♯m
And I can always count on You, 'cause You're my
Bm/D E A7 D7
brother, and You're my friend.
A7 D7
Well, You're my friend. 'Cause You're my friend.
A7 D7 A7
You're my friend.

My Father's Hands Are Busy

Words and Music by
MARY JORDAN, TOM MCBRYDE
and JANET MCMAHAN-WILSON

Moderate four
My Fa - ther's hands are bus - y. They shape my life each day. He is the Pot - ter,
I am the clay. When my heart's in trou - ble I know that I can turn to my
Fa - ther who will teach me just what I need to learn. My
Fa - ther's hands are bus - y. They col - or me with love beau - ti - ful as rain - bows that
fill the sky a - bove. My heart is the can - vas and with the Mas - ter's touch I'll be -
come a work of art all be - cause He cares so much. My
Fa - ther's hands are bus - y. They hold me near His heart. Ten - der - ly He shows me that
I'm a spec - ial part of His mar - vel - ous cre - a - tion de - signed in ev - 'ry way to re -
veal His per - fect love in the won - ders on dis - play.

My Heart Is Steadfast

Words and Music by
BRIAN CARR and ED KEE

Driving Rock
My heart is stead - fast. What He does in me will last.
My heart is stead - fast. I will not be moved.
My heart is stead - fast. What He does in me will last. My heart is
stead - fast. I will not be moved.
1.
2.
moved.
My heart is stead - fast.
What He does in me will last. My heart is stead - fast.
I will not be moved. My heart is stead - fast.
What He does in me will last. My heart is stead - fast.
I will not be moved. I will not be
moved.

My God Is So Big

Writer Unknown
With confidence (♩.=72)
D(no3)
A
My God is so big, so strong and so might - y, there's noth - ing my God can - not
D(no3)
do. My God is so big, so strong and so might - y, there's
A
D(no3)
G(no3)
noth - ing my God can - not do. And the moun - tains are His. The
D
A
D
val - leys are His. The stars are His hand - i - work too. My
D(no3)
A
God is so big, so strong and so might - y, there's noth - ing my God can - not
1. D(no3)
2. D(no3)
D(no3)
do. My do. My God is so big, so strong and so might - y, there's
Asus
D(no3)
noth - ing my God can - not do. My God is so big, so
Asus
D(no3)
strong and so might - y, there's noth - ing my God can - not do. The
G(no3)
D
A(no3)
moun - tains are His. The val - leys are His. The stars are His hand - i - work

D(no3)
too. My God is so big, so strong and so might - y, there's
Asus
1. D(no3)
2. D(no3)
noth - ing my God can - not do. My do. My
E(no3)
B
God is so big, so strong and so might - y, there's noth - ing my God can - not
E(no3)
do. My God is so big, so strong and so might - y, there's
B
E(no3)
A(no3)
noth - ing my God can - not do. The moun - tains are His. The
E
B
E
val - leys are His. The stars are His hand - i - work too. My
E(no3)
B
God is so big, so strong and so might - y, there's noth - ing my God can - not
1. E(no3)
2. E(no3)
B
do. The do, well, there's noth - ing my God can - not
E(no3)
B
E(no3)
do, there's noth - ing my God can - not do.

Never Too Late

Words and Music by
KAREN DEAN

D
Dmaj7
A
D6
D#°
Nev - er too late, when you step toward Je - sus, you're
Em
B7(#5)
Em7
A7
start - ing life o - ver a - gain.
Nev - er too late, for Je - sus is wait - ing for
D
Em
Em7
A7
D
Dmaj7
D7
C
E
D7
F#
you to come to Him. To -
G
G#°
day is your day. When you hear Him call - ing, there's
D
A
Bb°
Bm
Bm7
E9
no need to hes - i - tate; for His voice is
say - ing, "I knew you'd be com - ing, and you know it's
1.
2.
G
B
A7
C#
nev - er too late." late."

Noah's Boat
(To the tune of London Bridge Is Falling Down)

Words and Music by
DAVITA HUNGATE,
JANET MCMAHAN-WILSON
and TED WILSON

1. God said, "No - ah, build a boat, build a boat, build a boat."
2. "Make it out of go - pher wood, go - pher wood, go - pher wood.
God said, "No - ah, build a boat. Rain is com - ing."
Make it out of go - pher wood. Rain is com - ing."
3. "Call the crit - ters two by two, two by two, two by two. Call the crit - ters two by two. Rain is com - ing."
4. Soon the rain came pour - ing down, pour - ing down, pour - ing down. Soon the rain came pour - ing down.
5. No - ah float - ed for - ty days, for - ty days, for - ty days. No - ah float - ed for - ty days.
Earth was flood - ed.
Earth was flood - ed. 6. He
parked the ark at Ar - a - rat, Ar - a - rat, Ar - a - rat. He parked the ark at Ar - a - rat. Earth was flood - ed.
7. Ev - 'ry - one was safe and sound, safe and sound, safe and sound. Ev - 'ry - one was safe and sound.
8. Soon a rain - bow filled the sky, filled the sky, filled the sky. Soon a rain - bow filled the sky.
1. God had spo - ken.
2. God had spo - ken. 9. "I'll nev - er flood the earth a - gain, earth a - gain, earth a - gain. I'll nev - er flood the earth a - gain." God had spo - ken.

Noah
(Arky, Arky)

Traditional

Fun!
C Cmaj7/G Am/C C/G
1. The Lord said to No - ah, "There's gon - na be a flood - y, flood - y,"
(2.) No - ah, he build - ed, he build - ed an ark - y, ark - y,
C Cmaj7/G Am/C Dm7 G7
Lord said to No - ah, "There's gon - na be a flood - y, flood - y,
No - ah, he build - ed, he build - ed an ark - y, ark - y,
C Dm7 C/E C+/E F C
Get those chil - dren out of the mud - dy, mud - dy,"
Called his chil - dren in - to the ark - y, ark - y,
C Am7 Dm7 G7 1. C G9sus 2. C E♭m7/A♭
chil - dren of the Lord! 2. Old Lord! 3. It
D♭ D♭maj7/A♭ E♭m7 E♭m7/A♭
Rained and it poured for for - ty long days - ey, days - ey,
D♭ B♭7(♭9) E♭m7 E♭m7/A♭
Rained and it poured for for - ty long days - ey, days - ey,

D♭ F7(♯5) G♭ G° D♭/A♭
Near - ly drove those (clap) an - i - mals cra - zy, cra - zy,
D♭maj7/A♭ B♭7(♭9) E♭m7 A♭7 D♭ Em7/A
chil - dren of the Lord! 4. Then
D Gmaj9 F♯m7 Bm7 Em7 Em7/A
No - ah, he build - ed, he build - ed an al - tar, al - tar,
D Gmaj9 F♯m7 B7(♭9) Em7 Em7/A
No - ah, he build - ed, he build - ed an al - tar, al - tar,
D F♯7(♯5) G G/A A7
Thanked God with his (clap) sons and daugh - ters, daugh - ters,
D G6 A7 Bm Bm/G♯ D/A Dmaj7/A Em7 A7
chil - dren of the Lord, chil - dren of the
Bm Bm/G♯ D/A Dmaj7/A Em7 A7 D
Lord, chil - dren of the Lord!

Nothing but the Truth

Words and Music by
JANET MCMAHAN-WILSON and GRETA GARNER-HART

Country feel (♩=126)
D D7 G
Noth - ing but the truth, noth - ing else will do. There's
D Bm 1. Em A
some - thing to be said for say - ing noth - ing but the truth.
2.3. Em A D 2nd time to Coda G
noth - ing but the truth. It's nev - er ev - er
D G
right to tell a lie. That's a truth that
D D7 G
no one can de - ny. So if you've got a
E7/G♯ D/A B7 E
doubt a - bout it, don't let it out. If it's not the
Asus A Asus A D.C. al Coda
truth it's some - thing we'll do with - out.
CODA D Bm Em
There's some - thing to be said for say - ing noth - ing
A D G/D D A D
but the truth.

O How I Love Jesus

Traditional

O how I love Je - sus. O how I love
Je - sus. O how I love Je - sus, be -
2nd time to Coda
cause He first loved me. There
is a name I love to hear, I love to sing its
worth. It sounds like mu - sic
in my ear, the sweet - est name on earth.
D.C. al Coda
CODA
me, be - cause He first loved me.

Oh, How Happy We'll Be

Words and Music by
JANET MCMAHAN-WILSON and JAN ESTERLINE

E A E

Oh, how hap-py we'll be when we live to-geth-er in har - mo-ny. Oh, how

A B E A

hap-py we'll be when we live to-geth-er in love. Oh, how hap-py we'll be when all God's chil-dren

E B E

start to see things are bet-ter when we live to-geth-er in har-mo-ny.

A E A B

Oh, how hap - py we will be when we live in love, love, love,

E A E B

when God's chil - dren start to see it's bet-ter when we live to-geth-er in har-mo-

E F/C C F B♭

ny. Oh, how hap-py we'll be when we live to-geth-er in

F B♭

har - mo-ny. Oh, how hap-py we'll be when we live to - geth-er in

C F B♭

love. Oh, how hap-py we'll be when all God's chil - dren

F C F B♭

start to see things are bet-ter when we live to-geth-er in har-mo - ny. Things are

F C F B♭ F

bet-ter when we live to-geth-er in har-mo - ny, har-mo - ny.

Oh! Hosanna

(To the tune of Oh, Susanna)

Words and Music by
DAVITA HUNGATE, TRISH MENDOZA,
DOUG SARRETT and JANET MCMAHAN-WILSON

D D E7
1. Well, I'm go - in' through this big wide world, my Bi - ble on my
(2. He's) giv - en me a brand new life, a heart that's free from
A D E7/B D/A A D D/F♯
knee, and I want to tell the folks I meet how Je - sus set me free.
sin, 'cause Je - sus lives with - in me since I asked Him to come in.
G D A D
Oh, Ho - san - na! The Chris - tian life's for me. So I'm go - in' through this
E7/B D/A A7 1. D 2. D B♭7
big wide world, my Bi - ble on my knee. 2. He's knee 3. Well, I
E♭ F7/C B♭
love the Lord with all my heart. I'll serve Him ev - 'ry day. And
E♭ F7/C E♭/B♭ B♭ E♭ E♭/G
now I want the lost to know that Je - sus is the way.
A♭ E♭
Oh, Ho - san - na! The Chris - tian life's for
B♭ E♭ F7/C
me. And I'm go - in' through this big wide world, my
E♭/B♭ B♭ E♭ B♭ E♭
Bi - ble on my knee.

On a Day Like This

Writer Unknown

Hoedown (♩=120)
E
(clap)
(clap)
On a day like this, on a day like this, on a
A
E/B B E E2/B
(clap)
day like this, oh, I___ need the Lord to help me.
E A E B E E2/B E
(clap) (stomp)
On a day like this, on a
(clap) (stomp) (clap) (stomp)
A
day like this, on a day like this, oh, I___
E/B B E E2/B E A E B E E2/B
need the Lord to help me. On a
E
(clap) (stomp)
day like this, nee-ner, nee-ner, on a
(clap) (stomp)
day like this, nee-ner, nee-ner, on a
(clap) (stomp)
A
day like this, nee-ner, oh, I___

E/B B E E2/B E A E B E E2/B
need the Lord to help me. On a
E
(clap) (stomp)
day like this, nee - ner, nee - ner, wa - ka wa - ka, on a
(clap) (stomp)
day like this, nee - ner, nee - ner, wa - ka wa - ka, on a
(clap) (stomp)
A
day like this, nee - ner, wa - ka, oh, I
E/B B E E2/B E A E B E E2/B
need the Lord to help me. On a
E
(clap) (stomp)
day like this, nee - ner, nee - ner, wa - ka wa - ka, funk - y chick - en, on a
(clap) (stomp)
day like this, nee - ner, nee - ner, wa - ka wa - ka, funk - y chick - en, on a
(clap) (stomp)
A
day like this, nee - ner, wa - ka, funk - y, oh, I
E/B B E E2/B E A E/B B E
need the Lord to help me. Oh, I need the Lord to help me.

One Door and Only One

Traditional

1. One door, and on - ly one, and yet its sides are two,
2. One way, and on - ly one, a way that's right and true.
"in - side" and "out - side." On which side are you? One door, and on - ly one, and
God's way or man's way, on which side are you? One way, and on - ly one, a
yet its sides are two. I'm on the in - side. On which side are
way that's right and true. God's way is my way. On which side are
you?
you?
One door, and on - ly one, and yet its sides are two, "in - side" and "out - side." On
which side are you? One door, and on - ly one, and yet its sides are two.
I'm on the in - side. On which side are you? I'm on the in - side. On
which side are you?

Only a Boy Named David

Traditional

On - ly a boy named Dav - id, on - ly a lit - tle sling,
On - ly a boy named Dav - id, but he could pray and sing. On - ly a boy named Dav - id,
on - ly a rip - pling brook, On - ly a boy named Dav - id, but
five lit - tle stones he took. And one lit - tle stone went in - to the sling, and the
2.
sling went 'round and 'round. And one lit - tle stone went in - to the sling, and the
sling went 'round and 'round, And 'round and 'round and 'round and 'round and
'round and 'round and 'round; And one lit - tle stone went up in the air–
And the giant came tum - bling down!

Open Up

Words and Music by
JANET MCMAHAN-WILSON
Strong rhythmic feel (♩=126)
1. You've got to o - pen up and give all you've got.
(2.) o - pen up and share ev - 'ry day.
O - pen up and give all you've got.
O - pen up and share ev - 'ry day.
Wheth - er it's a lit - tle or wheth - er it's a lot, you've got to
There's some - one who needs you to help them find their way. You've got to
o - pen up and give what you've got.
o - pen up and share ev - 'ry
2. You've got to
day.
3. You've got to o - pen up and help some - one else.
O - pen up and help some - one else.
When you're help - in' some - one you're help - in' out your - self. You've got to
o - pen up and help some - one else.
O - pen up and share ev - 'ry day.
O - pen up and give all you've got.

Perfectly Placed There by God

Words and Music by
JANET MCMAHAN-WILSON

Waltz
1.3. Ev-'ry lit-tle crea-ture that crawls,
2. Ev-'ry lit-tle fish in the sea,
ev-'ry lit-tle snow-flake that falls,
ev-'ry lit-tle leaf on the tree,
3rd time to Coda
ev-'ry-thing is per-fect-ly put in its place, per-fect-ly
ev-'ry-thing is per-fect-ly put in its place, per-fect-ly
placed there by God.
placed there by God.
All of cre-a-tion is quite a sen-sa-tion. It's part of His pow-er-ful plan.
Ex-tra-or-d'nar-i-ly, He holds it care-ful-ly all in the palm of His hand.
D.C. al Coda
CODA
per-fect-ly placed there by God,
per-fect-ly placed there by God.

Peace Like a River

Traditional

Motown feel (♩=118)
E♭ Fm7 E♭ Fm7
1. I've got peace like a riv - er. I've got
(2.) love like an o - cean. I've got
E♭ Fm7 E♭ Fm7 Cm7
peace like a riv - er. I've got peace like a
love like an o - cean. I've got love like an
Gm7 A♭6 B♭
riv - er in my soul. I've got
o - cean in my soul. I've got
E♭ Fm7 E♭ Fm7 Cm7 Gm7
peace like a riv - er. I've got peace like a
love like an o - cean. I've got love like an
A♭ Gm7 Fm7 Gm7 A♭ B♭
riv - er. I've got peace like a riv - er in my
o - cean. I've got love like an o - cean in my
E♭ Fm7 1. E♭ Fm7 E♭ Fm7
soul.
soul.
E♭ Fm7 2. Fm7 Gm A♭ F Gm/F F
2. I've got

Gm/F F Gm/F F Gm/F F
3. I've got
F Gm7 F Gm7 F Gm7
joy like a foun - tain. I've got joy like a
F Gm7 Dm7 Am7
foun - tain. I've got joy like a foun - tain in my
B♭6 C F Gm7
soul. I've got joy like a
F Gm7 Dm7 Am7 B♭ Am7
foun - tain. I've got joy like a foun - tain. I've got
Gm7 Am7 B♭ C F Gm7
joy like a foun - tain in my soul.
F Gm7 F Gm7 F Gm7
I've got
Repeat and fade
F Gm7 F Gm7 F Gm7 F Gm7
peace.
love.
joy.
I've got
I've got

Philippians 1:6

Writer Unknown

Latin feel (♩=98)
D G A D
G A D
I am
D G A D
con - fi - dent in this ver - y thing, that He who be - gan a good work in you will per -
D G A D
fect it un - til the day of Christ Je - sus. (Cha - cha - cha!) I am
D G A D
con - fi - dent in this ver - y thing, that He who be - gan a good work in you will per -
D G A D 3rd time to Coda
fect it un - til the day of Christ Je - sus. (Cha - cha - cha!)
G A D
I am con - fi - dent. I am con - fi - dent.
D/F♯ G A D
I am con - fi - dent in Je - sus. (Cha - cha - cha!)

G A D
I am con - fi - dent. I am con - fi - dent.
D/F♯ G A D
D.C. al Coda
I am con - fi - dent in Je - sus. (Cha - cha - cha!)
CODA
I am con - fi - dent. I am con - fi - dent.
I am con - fi - dent in Je - sus.
D G A D D/F♯ G
I am con - fi - dent. I am con - fi - dent. I am con - fi - dent in
1. A D
Je - sus. (Cha - cha - cha!)
2. A D
Je - sus. (Cha - cha - cha!)
SOLO (ad lib)
G A D
La la la la la la la. La la la la la la la la la.
D/F♯ G A D
La la la la la la la la la la la la.

Praise God

Words and Music by
JANET MCMAHAN-WILSON

1. When I see a squirm - y worm dig - gin' 'round in the ground or watch a
(2.) see a ba - by bird hatch - ing out of its egg or watch a
sleep - y ole pos - sum hang - in' up - side down,
pink fla - min - go stand - in' on one leg,
see an ar - my of ants bus - y build - in' a hill or a par -
see a lit - ter of pups slow - ly o - p'nin their eyes or a
tic - u - lar pel - i - can with a fish in his bill,
buzz - in' bee col - o - ny mak - in' hon - ey all the time,
I want to
praise God for His cre - a - tion, praise God for crea - tures
great and small. Praise God, He is Cre - a - tor and
Mak - er of us all; Praise God! Praise
God! Praise God! 2. When I
Praise God!

Praise Him, Praise Him

Traditional

C F C Am Dm G7
1. Praise Him, praise Him, All ye lit - tle chil - dren, God is love,
2. Love Him, love Him, All ye lit - tle chil - dren, God is love,
C Em7/B D9/A G7sus G7 C C/E F C
God is love; Praise Him, praise Him, All ye lit - tle chil - dren,
God is love; Love Him, love Him, All ye lit - tle chil - dren,
Am Dm7 1. G7sus G7 F/G C F/G 2. G7sus G7 F/G C A♭7
God is love, God is love. God is love.
God is love,
D♭ E♭m7 D♭/F D♭ G♭ D♭/F D♭ B♭m E♭m7 A♭7
3. Thank Him, thank Him, All ye lit - tle chil - dren, God is love,
4. Serve Him, serve Him, All ye lit - tle chil - dren, God is love,
D♭ A♭/C B♭m6 A♭7sus A♭7 D♭ E♭m7 D♭/F D♭ G♭ D♭/F D♭
God is love; Thank Him, thank Him, All ye lit - tle chil - dren,
God is love; Serve Him, serve Him, All ye lit - tle chil - dren,
B♭m E♭m7 1. A♭7sus A♭7 G♭/A♭ D♭ G♭/A♭ 2. A♭7sus A♭7 G♭/A♭ D♭
God is love, God is love. God is love.
God is love,

Praise Him, All Ye People

Words and Music by
JANET MCMAHAN-WILSON and TED WILSON

Joyfully
C C#º Dsus Dm G
1. Praise Him, all ye peo - ple.
2. Praise Him, all ye peo - ple.
C C#º Dsus G
Lift your voice and sing.
Shout for joy and dance.
C F F#º
Hal - le - lu - jah! Je -
Hal - le - lu - jah! Come
C/G G C
ho - vah is our King. Cre -
on and clap your hands.
A♭ A♭7
a - tion cries, the earth ap - plauds,
C A♭ G C
"Glo - ry to our God." The
A♭ A♭7 G A♭
riv - ers roar, the seas pro - claim, "High and might - y

G
2nd time to Coda
D.C. al Coda
is His name."
CODA
A
D
D♯°
Esus
Praise Him, all
Em A D D♯° Esus A
ye peo - ple. Lift your voice and sing.
D G G♯° D/A A D
Hal - le - lu - jah! Je - ho - vah is our King,
D/A A D
Lord of ev - 'ry - thing. Je -
D D/C G/B Gm/B♭ D
ho - vah is our King.
G/B Gm/B♭ A D
Praise to the King!

Praise, Praise, Praise

Words and Music by
JANET MCMAHAN-WILSON

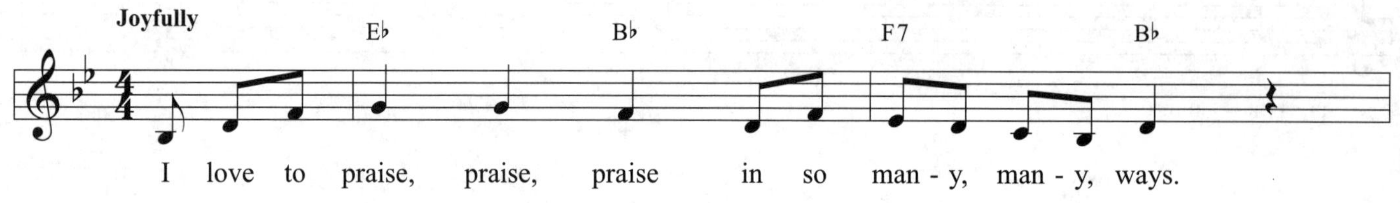
Joyfully
E♭ B♭ F7 B♭
I love to praise, praise, praise in so man - y, man - y, ways.

E♭ B♭ Fsus F B♭
Praise, praise, praise Him day and night. I love to

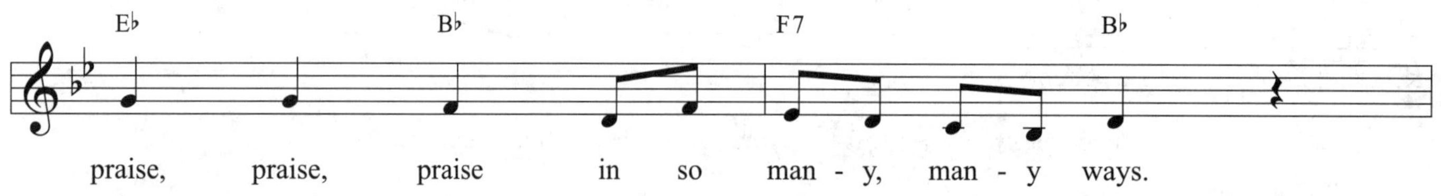
E♭ B♭ F7 B♭
praise, praise, praise in so man - y, man - y ways.

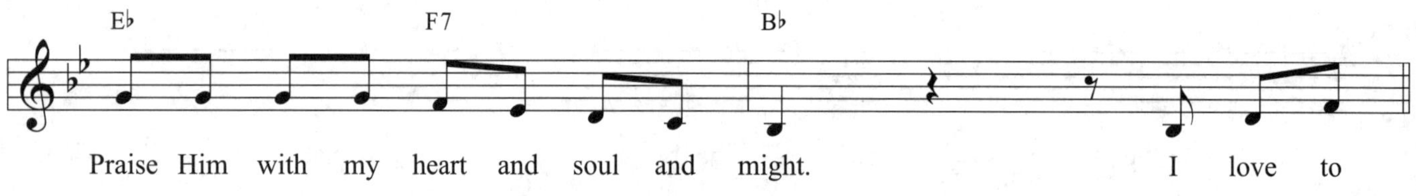
E♭ F7 B♭
Praise Him with my heart and soul and might. I love to

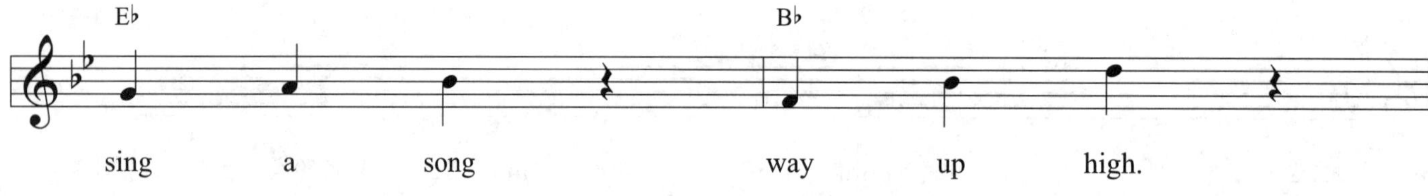
E♭ B♭
sing a song way up high.

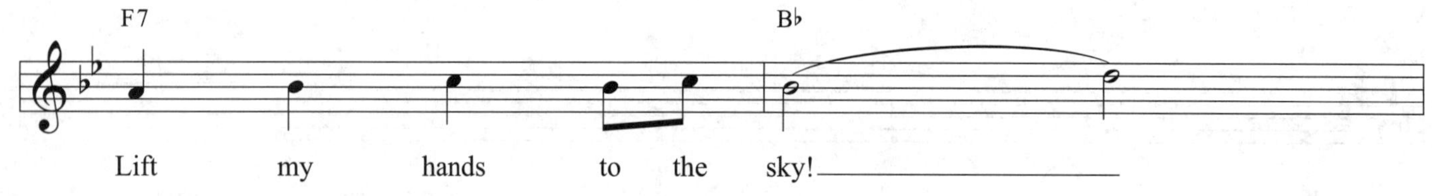
F7 B♭
Lift my hands to the sky!

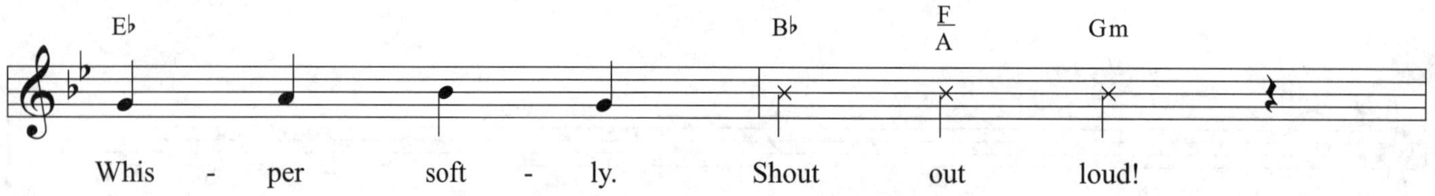
E♭ B♭ F/A Gm
Whis - per soft - ly. Shout out loud!

C
(whistle)
Whis - tle a mel - o - dy.
F
Hum a tune hap - pi - ly! (hm, hm, hm, hm, hm)
G
G°7 A♯
G B
G°7 C♯
G7
C
I love to
F C G7 C
praise, praise, praise in so man - y, man - y, ways.
F C Gsus G C
Praise, praise, praise Him day and night. I love to
F C G7 C
praise, praise, praise in so man - y, man - y ways.
F G7 C
Praise Him with my heart and soul and might.
F G C
Praise Him with my heart and soul and might.

Pure Delight Is in the Law of the Lord

Words and Music by
JANET MCMAHAN-WILSON

Calypso feel
A D A
Do not walk__ in the wick - ed way.__ Pure de - light__ is in the
E A D A
law of the Lord. Do not stand__ for what the dev - il say.__
E A D
Pure de - light__ is in the law of the Lord. Oh, how hap - py you__
A
__ will be,__ like a firm - ly plant - ed tree,__
D Bm
bear - ing fruit__ so boun - ti - f'ly.__ You'll nev - er with - er, what -
E
ev - er the weath - er. Ev - 'ry - bod - y now, say it to - geth - er.
A spoken D A
Do not walk__ in the wick - ed way.__
E A
Pure de - light__ is in the law of the Lord. Do not stand__ for what the
D A E A
dev - il say.__ Pure de - light__ is in the law of the Lord.

D
A
Oh, how hap - py you will be, like a firm - ly plant -
D
- ed tree, bear - ing fruit so boun - ti - f'ly.
Bm
E
You'll nev - er with - er, what - ev - er the weath - er. Ev - 'ry - bod - y now,
A
sing it to - geth - er. Ha - la - la - la - la - la -
D A E A
le - lu - jah! Pure de - light is in the law of the Lord.
D A
Ha - la - la - la - la - la - le - lu - jah! Pure de - light is in the
E A E A
law of the Lord. Pure de - light is in the law of the Lord.
E A D/E
Pure de - light is in the law of the Lord.
A D/E A D/E A

Praise Ye the Lord

Words and Music by
JANET MCMAHAN-WILSON
and TED WILSON

With energy
C F C F G
Praise ye— the Lord. Praise— Him all ye peo - ple.
C F Dm7 Gsus G
Praise ye— the Lord. Lift His prais - es high.—
G/A Am F C F
Sun and— moon— and stars of— light,—
C G C G/A Am F
praise Je - ho - vah in the heights. Birds and— beasts— and
C F C G C
creep - ing— things,— praise Je - ho - vah. He is King.
D G D G A
Praise ye— the Lord. Praise— Him all ye peo - ple.
D G Em7 D
Praise ye— the Lord. Lift His prais - es high.
E A E A B
Praise ye— the Lord. Praise— Him all ye peo - ple.
E A F♯m7 E B E
Praise ye— the Lord. Lift His prais - es high. Praise ye— the Lord!

R-E-J-O-I-C-I-N-G

Words and Music by
JANET MCMAHAN-WILSON

Happily!
I will re - joice in my Lord. I'll
R - E - J - O - I - C - E be - cause He's been so good to me.
I know I'll for - ev - er be prais - ing Him so joy - ful - ly,
2nd time to Coda
R - E - J - O - I - C - I - N - G! I will
clap my hands (clap, clap, clap) and I will sing al - le - lu - ia.
Al - le - lu - ia! He's my God and King,
D.S. al Coda
Lord of ev - 'ry - thing. I can't keep from sing - ing. I will re -
CODA
G!
He gives me such joy when I am R - E - J - O - I - C - I - N - G!

Read, Read, Read the Word

(To the tune of Row, Row, Row Your Boat)

Words and Music by
ED KEE, DALE MATHEWS
and TRISH MENDOZA

C
C
1. Read, read, read the word. Read it ev - 'ry day. Read the word and hide it down in -
2. Read, read, read the word. Read it and re - ceive. Noth - ing is im - pos - si - ble to

1. G7 C 2. G7 C A♭7

side your heart to stay. those who will be - lieve.

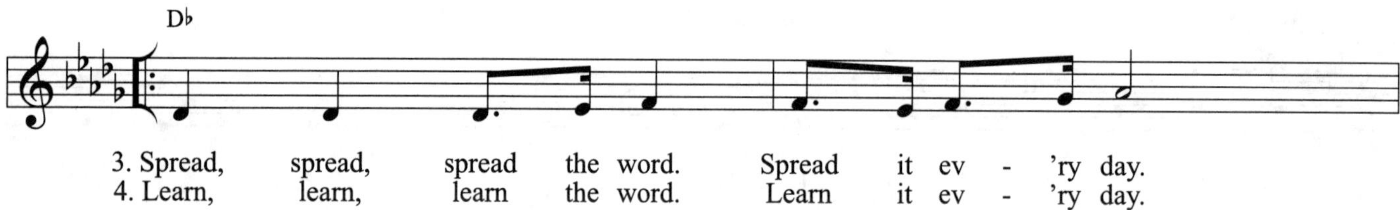
D♭
3. Spread, spread, spread the word. Spread it ev - 'ry day.
4. Learn, learn, learn the word. Learn it ev - 'ry day.

D♭
1. A♭7 D♭
Tell the peo - ple ev - 'ry - where that Je - sus is the way.
In my youth I'll learn the truth to

2.
A♭7 D♭ A7
(Round)
I D
II
keep the sin a - way. 5. Read, read, read the word. Read it ev - 'ry day.

III D
1.2.3.
4.
A7 D
Read the word and hide it down in - side your heart to stay. side your heart to stay.

Rejoice in the Lord Always

Traditional

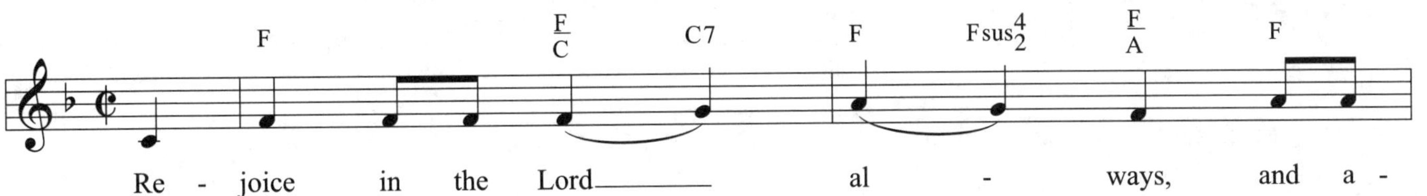
F
F/C
C7
F
Fsus4/2
F/A
F
Re - joice in the Lord al - ways, and a -

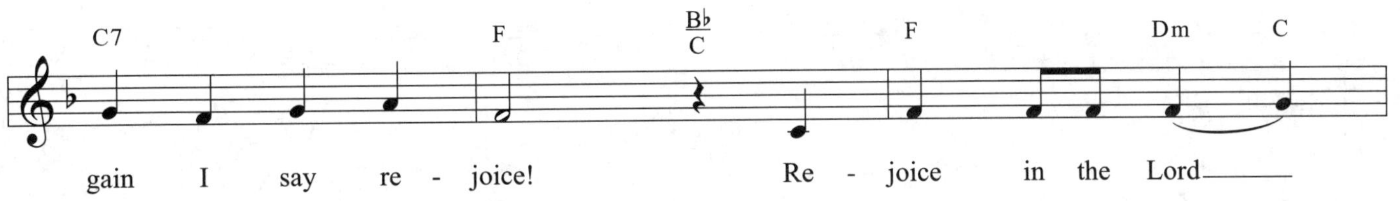
C7
F
B♭/C
F
Dm
C
gain I say re - joice! Re - joice in the Lord

F
A7/E
Dm
F7/C
B♭
C7
F
F/C
al - ways, and a - gain I say re - joice! Re -

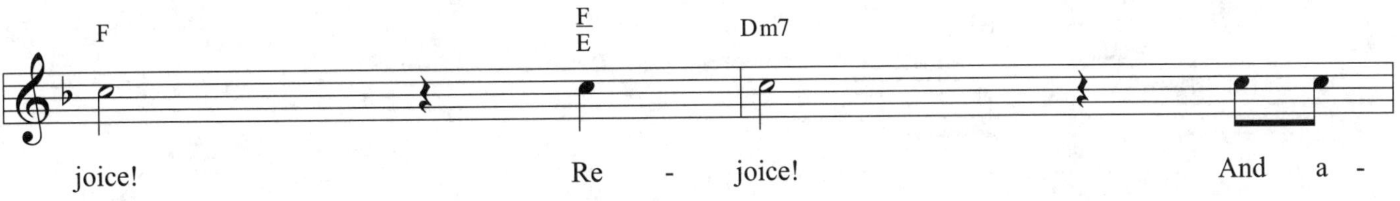
F
F/E
Dm7
joice! Re - joice! And a -

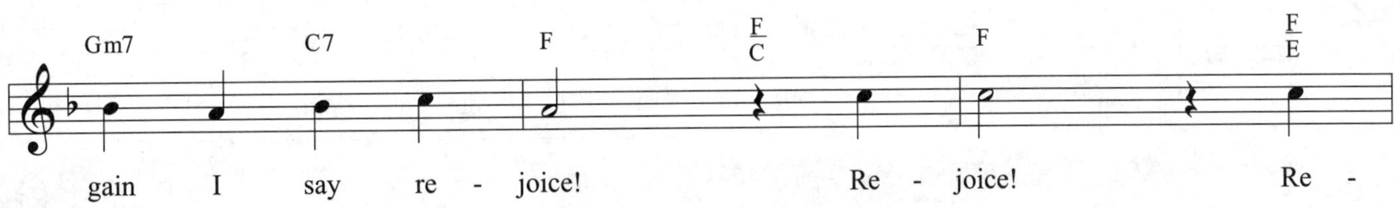
Gm7
C7
F
F/C
F
F/E
gain I say re - joice! Re - joice! Re -

Dm7
D7(♭9)
Gm7
C7
F
joice! And a - gain I say re - joice!

Ring the Bells

Words and Music by
HERB OWEN

On Christ-mas a long time a-go the Son of God came down. He
stepped from His gold-en throne to a small Ju-de-an town. The
por-tals of heav'n were filled with heav-en-ly an-gels who were
lin-ing the steps of the gold-en gates to see God's prom-is-es all come true.
Ring the bells, shout the news, and let the whole world know!
Tell the peo-ple ev-'ry-where what the pro-phet said is so.
God the Son is come to earth to save us from our sin. He'll
teach and preach and love and live and die and rise a-gain.
die and rise a-gain. He'll teach and preach and love and live and die and rise a-gain.

Rolled Away

Traditional

Rolled a - way, rolled a - way, rolled a - way, Ev - 'ry
bur - den of my heart rolled a - way! Rolled a - way, rolled a - way, rolled a -
way, ev - 'ry bur - den of my heart rolled a - way! Ev - 'ry
sin had to go 'neath the crim - son
flow, hal - le - lu - jah! Rolled a - way, rolled a - way, rolled a -
way. Ev - 'ry bur - den of my heart rolled a -
way! Ev - 'ry bur - den of my heart rolled a -
way. Ev - 'ry bur - den of my heart rolled a - way.

Romans 16:19

Words and Music by
GRAHAM BURT, JOHN CHILDERS,
DALE GARRETT and RAMON PINK

Raucous! (♩=122)
E D A G E
Ro - mans (yeah) six - teen (yeah) nine - teen_ says,_ (uh huh)
E D A G E
Ro - mans (yeah) six - teen (yeah) nine - teen_ says,_ (uh huh)
E D A G E
Ro - mans (yeah) six - teen (yeah) nine - teen_ says,_ (uh huh)
E D A G E
Ro - mans (yeah) six - teen (yeah) nine - teen_ says,_ (uh huh) Be
E A E C♯m
ex - cel - lent_ at what is good; be in - no - cent of
A E A E
e - vil. Be ex - cel - lent_ at what is good;_ be
C♯m 1. A 2.3. A
in - no - cent of e - vil. e - vil. And the

E D A E D
God of peace will soon crush Sa - tan, and God will crush him
A G E D
un - der - neath your feet. (huh) And the God of peace will
A E D A G E
soon crush Sa - tan, and God will crush him un - der - neath your feet. (huh) And the
God of peace will soon crush Sa - tan un - der - neath your feet. And the
building
God of peace will soon crush Sa - tan un - der - neath your feet. And the
2nd time to Coda
God of peace will soon crush Sa - tan un - der - neath your feet. And the
D.C. al Coda
God of peace will soon crush Sa - tan un - der - neath your feet. Let me hear you say
CODA
God of peace will soon crush Sa - tan un - der - neath your feet!

Satan, Don't Bother Me

Simple Gifts

Shaker Hymn

F
'Tis a gift to be sim - ple, 'tis a gift to be free, 'Tis a

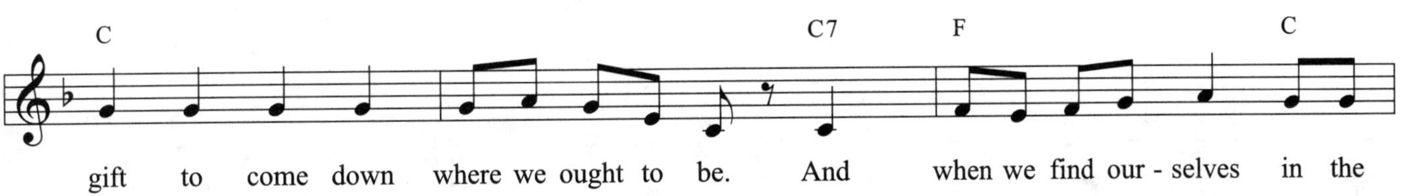
C C7 F C
gift to come down where we ought to be. And when we find our - selves in the

F Fsus F C F/C C7 F/A C7/G F F/C
place just right, 'Twill be in the val - ley of love and de - light.

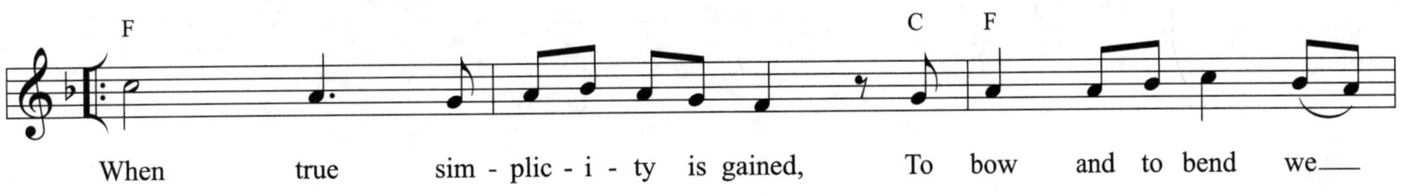
F C F
When true sim - plic - i - ty is gained, To bow and to bend we

C F
shan't be a - shamed. To turn, turn, will be our de - light, 'Til by

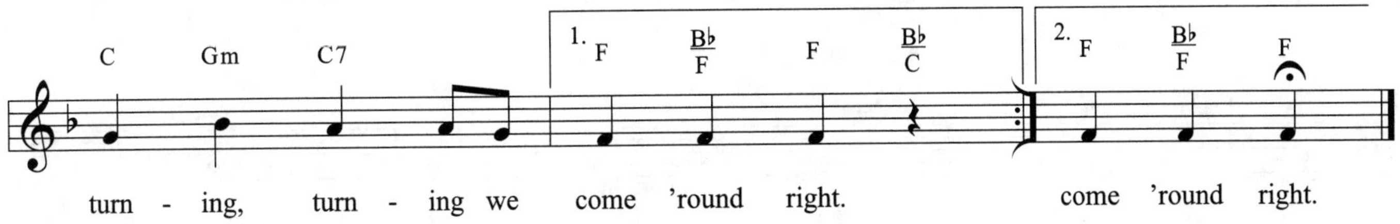
C Gm C7 1. F B♭/F F B♭/C 2. F B♭/F F
turn - ing, turn - ing we come 'round right. come 'round right.

See the Work of the Lord

Words and Music by
STEVE GROSSMAN, JILL GROSSMAN,
RICKY BLAIR and TRISHA BLAIR

G7 C F C G G7
The sun comes up in the morn - ing time. See the work of the
C2 C C/E C F C Am
Lord. Just the way that God de - signed.
Dm F/G G7 C C
See the work of the Lord. God com - mand - ed the
F C G G7 C2 C Cmaj7/G C/G
world to be. See the work of the Lord.
C G7/D C/E C F Em7 Am Dm F/G G7 C
Fish and birds, sand and sea, see the work of the Lord.
F C Am Dm7 Em/G G7 C Dm/C C C/E
Sun - light, moon - bright, all things for His de - light,
2nd time to Coda
F Em7 A7(♭9) Dm7 G9 G7
God made the whole world. See the work of the
C Dm7 G7sus G7 C
Lord. Da - vid killed him a

F C Dm7 G7 C Am7 Dm7 G7
gi - ant man. See the work of the Lord. When
C C/E C F/A F C Dm7 F/G G7
oth - er men doubt, Da - vid knows God can. See the work of the
C F/C G/C C F C/E C
Lord. Dan - iel put in the li - on's den.
G G7 C C#°7 Dm7 G7 C7
See the work of the Lord. When morn - ing come, old
F Em7 A7 Dm7 F/G G7 C
D.S. al Coda
Dan - iel, he grin. See the work of the Lord.
CODA
C Dm7 C/E F G9/F G7/F Em7 Am Am7
Lord. Oh, sun - light, moon - bright,
Dm7 Em/G G7 C G7/D C/E C F G9/F
all things for His de - light, God made the
Em7(♭5) A7 Dm7 F/G G7 C Am Am7
whole world. See the work of the Lord.
Dm7 G9 G7 C A7(♭9) Dm7 F/G G7 C
See the work of the Lord. See the work of the Lord.

Shake, Shake, Shake, Hallelujah

Words and Music by
BEN RYAN

With energy (♩=106)
C
G
Shake, shake, shake,— hal - le - lu - jah! Ev - 'ry - bod - y shake.—

C
Shake, shake, shake,— hal - le - lu - jah! Serve the Lord with grace.—

G
Shake, shake, shake,— hal - le - lu - jah! Ev - 'ry - bod - y shout.— Hey! When

3rd time to Coda
C
love finds you, what can— you do— but shake, shake, hal - le - lu - jah!
1. When
2. When

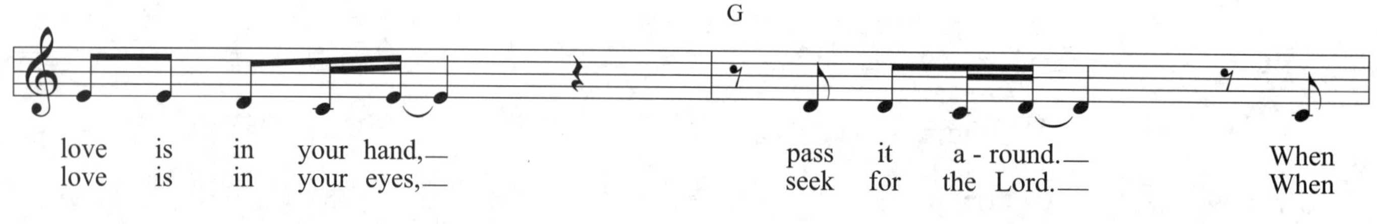
G
love is in your hand,— pass it a - round.— When
love is in your eyes,— seek for the Lord.— When

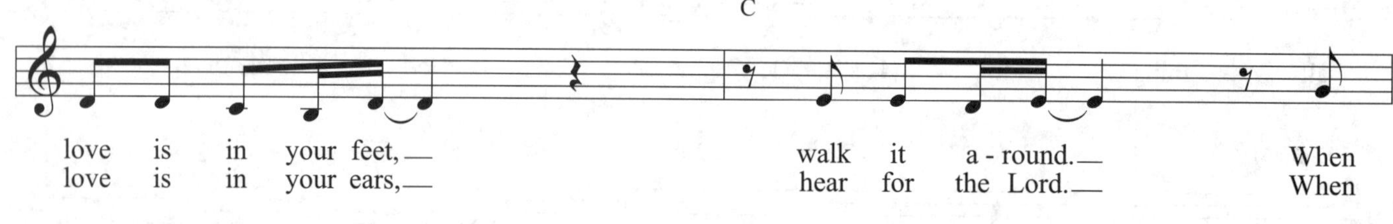
C
love is in your feet,— walk it a - round.— When
love is in your ears,— hear for the Lord.— When

G
love is in your voice,— sing it out.— When
love is in your voice,— sing it out.— When

D.C. (twice) al Coda
C
love is in your heart,— you've got to shake it all a - bout.— Oh,
love is in your heart,— you've got to shake it all a - bout.— Oh,
CODA
C
shake, shake, hal - le - lu - jah!
G
Shake, shake, shake,— hal - le - lu - jah! Ev - 'ry - bod - y shake.—
C
Shake, shake, shake,— hal - le - lu - jah! Serve the Lord with grace.—
G
Shake, shake, shake,— hal - le - lu - jah! Ev - 'ry - bod - y shout.— Hey! When
C
love finds you, what can— you do— but shake, shake, hal - le - lu - jah! When
G
C
love finds you, what can— you do— but shake, shake, hal - le - lu - jah! When
G N.C. G N.C. G C
love finds you, what can— you do— but shake, shake, hal - le - lu - jah!

Shine on

Words and Music by
GARY FORSYTHE

C Am Dm G
Light of the world, liv - ing in me,
C Am Dm
shine through the dark - ness for all to
G Am Em
see. Light of the world,
F A7 Dm
light - ing the way, shine on,
G7 C F/G G7
Je - sus, I pray.
C Am7 Dm
Shine on, Je - sus. Shine through me, I
G Dm G7
pray. Shine on, Je - sus.
C C7 F
Shine through me each day. In all that I

C/E
Dm
A7
do, in all that I say,
Dm
G7
C
G♭/A♭
A♭7
shine on, Je - sus, I pray.
D♭m
B♭m
E♭m
Shine on, Je - sus. Shine through me, I
A♭
E♭m
A♭7
pray. Shine on, Je - sus.
D♭
D♭7
G♭
Shine through me each day. In all that I
D♭/F
E♭m
B♭7
do, in all that I say,
E♭m
A♭7
B♭m
E♭7/G
shine on, Je - sus, I pray.
E♭m
A♭7
D♭
Shine on, Je - sus, I pray.

Sing a Sweet Tune
(About the Bible)
Words and Music by
HERB OWEN
With a country feel, in two
B♭
1. Think a - bout what He has taught us, fill your
(2.) hard ev - 'ry verse and ev - 'ry
F Cm7
mind with the things of God. Med - i - tate on the Ho - ly
chap - ter in the book; if you have lots of
F F7 E♭/G F7/A B♭
Scrip - tures as you learn a - bout the Word. Clean a -
ques - tions, o - pen up and take a look. Read the
F7/C B♭7/D
way all those cob - webs of un - be - lief and doubt and
truth the a - pos - tles taught us, learn each doc - trine care - ful -
E♭ B♭/F Gm
fear, as you let what's in the Bi - ble bring you
ly, for the ser - mons that they preached were meant for
2nd time to Coda
Cm7 F7 B♭ N.C.
truth and bring you cheer. Sing a sweet
you and were meant for
F B♭
tune a - bout the Bi - ble, for it tells us what is
F F7 B♭ E♭
so, gives us pow - er to live for Him be - cause of what we

B♭
F7
B♭
Cm7(4)
B♭/D
know. Sing it a - gain un - til they un - der - stand the
E♭
F
love of God on high, that Je - sus is my
D.S. al Coda
B♭
Gm
Cm7
F7
B♭
B♭/F
E♭/G
F/A
Sav - ior and it was for me He died. 2. Stud - y
CODA
B♭
Dm7
G7
F2/A
G/B
me.
3. There is
C
wis - dom in the Bi - ble to change our mind and to change our
G
Dm7
G
heart, as we un - der - stand the prov - erbs to be
G7
F/A
G7/B
C
wise and pure and smart. In the psalms we sing the prais - es of the
G7/D
C7/E
F
Lord in heav - en a - bove; with thanks - giv - ing we bow be -

C/G
Am
Dm7
G7
C
N.C.
fore Him as we sing a - bout His love.
Sing a sweet
G
C
tune a - bout the Bi - ble, for it tells us what is
G
G7
so, gives us pow - er to live for Him be -
C
F
C
cause of what we know.
Sing it a - gain un - til they
Dm7(4)
C/E
F
un - der - stand the love of God on high,
that
G
C
Am
1.
Dm7
G7
Je - sus is my Sav - ior and it was for me He
C
died.
Sing a sweet
2.
Dm7
was for
F/G
G
C
me He died!

Sing a Song of Jesus

(To the tune of Sing a Song of Sixpence)

Words and Music by
JANET MCMAHAN-WILSON
and TED WILSON

1. Sing a song of Je - sus. Sing a song of love.
2. Sing a - bout the ba - by born in Beth - le - hem.
Sing of how He left His Fa - ther's home a - bove.
Sing a - bout the wise men bow - ing down to Him.
Sing of how He saved us and how He set us free.
Sing of how He saved us and how He set us free.
Sing a song of Je - sus and His love for you and me!
Sing a song of Je - sus and His love for you and me!
3. Sing a - bout His love and how He said to give,
how He gave His life so all of us might live.
Sing of how He saved us and how He set us free.
Sing a song of Je - sus and His love for you and me!

Soldier in the Light Brigade

Words and Music by
GARY FORSYTHE

March
F
C
I'm a sol - dier in the Light Bri - gade. I'm a
Gm7
C7
F
sol - dier in the Light Bri - gade. I've got my
B♭
Gm
F
F/C
A7/C♯
Dm7
ar - mor and my sword, and I'm march - ing for the Lord. I'm a
Gm
C7
2nd time to Coda
F
sol - dier in the Light Bri - gade.
I've got my shield of faith and my
sword of the Spir - it. I'm read - y for the Lord's com -
C
mand. I've got my shield of faith and my
sword of the Spir - it. I'm read - y for the Lord's com -
F
mand. With Je - sus, my cap - tain, Sa - tan, the en - e - my, the

F7
Gm7
F7/A
B♭
bat - tle rag - ing close at hand. I am
F
Dm7
not a-fraid to fight, 'cause I'm a sol - dier of the Light, and I
G
C
B♭/D
Am/E
D.S. al Coda
know who wins the war in the end. I'm a
CODA
F
E♭
D
gade. I'm a
G
D
sol - dier in the Light Bri - gade. I'm a
Am7
D7
G
sol - dier in the Light Bri - gade. I've got my
C
Am
G
G/D
B7/D♯
Em7
ar - mor and my sword, and I'm march - ing for the Lord. I'm a
Am
D7
G
sol - dier in the Light Bri - gade. I'm a
sol - dier in the Light Bri - gade.

Solomon

Words and Music by
HERB OWEN

Sol - o - mon, who lived so long a - go,
asked the Lord if wis - dom He'd be - stow.
God was pleased to hon - or his re - quest, and
he be - came on earth his roy - al best.
Help me grow to be like Sol - o - mon, that
of Your serv - ants I might be the one
that grows tall to please You ev - 'ry day. I
want to fol - low in Your way. way.

Someone Around You

Writer Unknown

Sshh!

Words and Music by
JANET MCMAHAN-WILSON

Solemn (♩=126)
Cm
Don't say some - thing that is - n't nice.
N.C.
Bet - ter lis - ten to this ad - vice.
Cm
Fm
When your mouth is mak - ing fun you can real - ly hurt some - one. So
2nd time to Coda
Gsus
G7
Cm
keep your lips to - geth - er and sshh! If you
Fm
Cm
G7/D
Cm/E♭
can't say some - thing that's good and true, there's
D7
G
on - ly one thing you should do.
D.C. al Coda
CODA
Cm
Sshh! Sshh! Sshh! Sshh!

Stand Up for Jesus

Words and Music by
JAN ESTERLINE, JANET MCMAHAN WILSON
and TED WILSON

Stand up for Je - sus. Praise Him with a shout,
"Hey!" Ev - 'ry - bod - y, now sing glo - ry hal - le - lu - jah!
For He will be your ev - er - last - ing Friend
2nd time to Coda
when you ask Him in your heart.
Lift your voic - es to the sky yi! For He is for - ev - er - more the
Lord most high! Clap your hands; re - joice and sing, for
we be - long to the King! Stand
D.S. al Coda
CODA
heart. Ev - 'ry - bod - y
stand up for Je - sus!

Stand Up and Be Glad You're a Christian

(To the tune of My Bonnie Lies over the Ocean)

Words and Music by
RHETT PARRISH

In two
Stand up and be glad you're a Chris - tian. Stand up and be glad to o -
bey. Stand up and be glad you're a Chris - tian. Oh,
stand up for Je - sus to - day. Stand up. Stand up. Oh,
stand up for Je - sus and shout, "Hoo - ray!" Stand up.
Stand up. Oh, stand up for Je - sus to - day. Shake
hands with your neigh - bor be - side you. Shake hands with your neigh - bor and
say, "Stand up and be glad you're a Chris - tian." Oh,
stand up for Je - sus to - day. Stand up. Stand up. Oh,
stand up for Je - sus and shout, "Hoo - ray!" Stand up.

C♭ A♭/C D♭7 G♭ D7
Stand up. Oh, stand up for Je - sus to - day. Kneel
G C G A7
down and re - mem - ber He loves you. Kneel down and re - mem - ber to
D7 G C G A7 D7
pray. Stand up and be glad you're a Chris - tian. Oh, stand up for Je - sus to -
G D Em7(4) D/F♯ G Am7(4) G/B C A/C♯ D7
day. Stand up. Stand up. Oh, stand up for Je - sus and
G D G Am7(4) G/B C A/C♯ D7
shout, "Hoo - ray!" Stand up. Stand up. Oh, stand up for Je - sus to -
G E♭7 A♭ D♭ A♭
day. Sit down and get read - y to praise Him. Sit
A♭ B♭7 E♭7 A♭ D♭ A♭
down and get read - y to say, "Stand up and be glad you're a Chris - tian." Oh,
B♭7 E♭7 A♭ E♭ Fm7(4) E♭/G A♭ B♭m7(4) A♭/C
stand up for Je - sus to - day. Stand up.
D♭ B♭ Cm7(4) B♭7/D E♭7 A♭ E♭ A♭
Stand up. Oh, stand up for Je - sus and shout, "Hoo - ray!"
A♭ B♭m7(4) A♭/C D♭ B♭ Cm7(4) B♭7/D E♭7 A♭
Stand up. Stand up. Oh, stand up for Je - sus to - day.

Standin' in the Need of Prayer

Spiritual

F F Fsus4/2 F F/E
It's me, it's me, O Lord,
Dm C F F/D F/E F
Stand - in' in the need of prayer. It's me, it's
F A7/E Dm F7/C B♭ B♭/C C7 F B♭/C
2nd time to Coda
me, O Lord, Stand - in' in the need of prayer. Not my
F Fsus4/2 F F/E
fa - ther, not my moth - er, But it's me, O Lord,
Dm C F B♭/C C7
Stand - in' in the need of prayer. Not my
F A7/E Dm F7/C
sis - ter, not my broth - er, But it's me, O Lord,
B♭ F/A Gm7 F B♭/C
D.S. al Coda
Stand - in' in the need of prayer. It's
CODA
Dm F/C B♭/C C7 F
prayer. Stand - in' in the need of prayer.

Step into the Sunshine

Words and Music by
CLARK GASSMAN and MOLLY A. LEIKIN

D♭maj7 D♭m(maj7) D♭m6 Cm7 B°
Step in - to the sun - shine.__ Get out__ of the shade.

B♭m7 B♭m7/E♭ E♭7 E♭9 A♭ A♭7
This is the one__ time that you've got it made.__ And you can

D♭maj7 D♭m(maj7) D♭m6 Cm7 B°
feel____ your-self smil - in'__ way down__ to your shoes.

2nd time to Coda 𝄌

B♭m7 B♭m7/E♭ E♭7 B♭m7 E♭7 A♭ D♭ A♭/C A♭7
Step in - to the sun-shine, get the great good news!__ Come on and

D♭maj7 D♭m(maj7) D♭m6 Cm7 B°
step in - to the sun - shine.__ Get out__ of the shade.

B♭m7 B♭m7/E♭ E♭7 E♭9 A♭ A♭7
This is the one__ time that you've got it made.__ And you can

D♭maj7 D♭m(maj7) D♭m6 Cm7 B°
feel____ your-self smil - in'__ way down__ to your shoes.

D.C. al Coda

B♭m7 B♭m7/E♭ E♭7 B♭m7 E♭ A♭ D♭ A♭/C A♭7
Step in - to the sun-shine, get the great good news!__ Come on and

𝄌 **CODA** A♭ A♭/E♭ D♭6/A♭ D♭6/F A♭
great, good news!

Take a Step of Faith

Words and Music by
KATHIE HILL

No mat-ter how tight the spot you're in, here's what you should do:
Put your best foot for-ward, and God will see you through.
Take a step of faith. Take a step of faith. When you
can't see your hand in front of your face, take a step of
faith. With no star to guide your way,
God's still be-side you say-ing, "Take a step of
faith, just take a step of faith."
take a step of faith. Take a step of faith, just
take a step of faith."

Thank You, Lord

Traditional

Sweetly
F
F+
B♭
Thank you, Lord, for sav - ing my

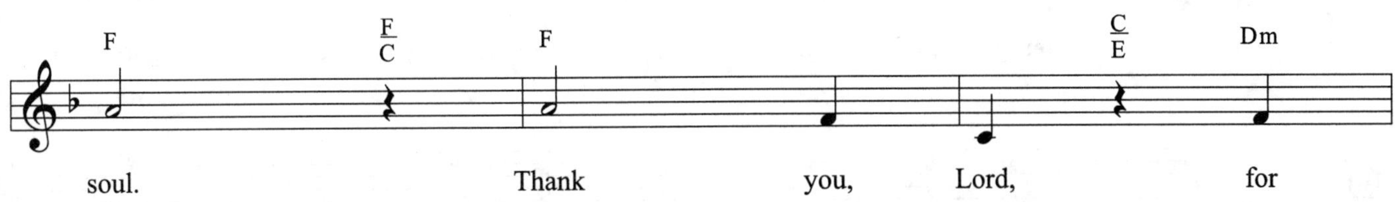
F
F/C
F
C/E
Dm
soul. Thank you, Lord, for

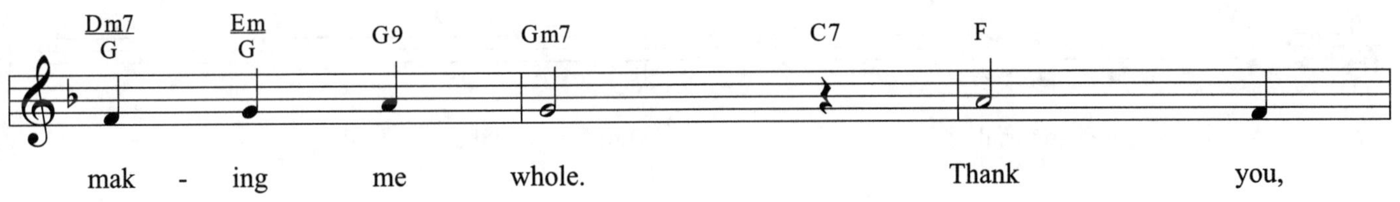
Dm7/G
Em/G
G9
Gm7
C7
F
mak - ing me whole. Thank you,

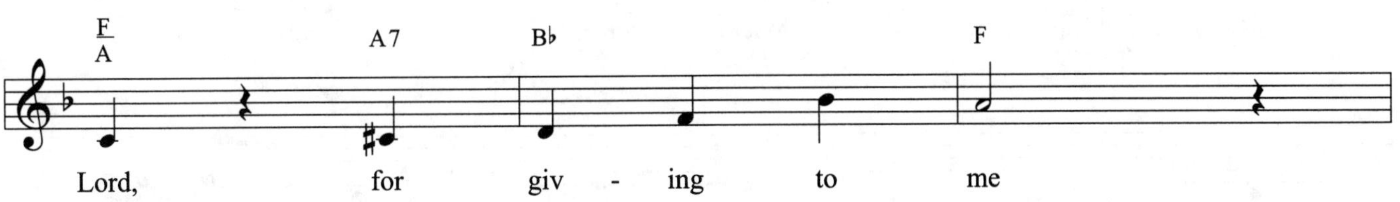
F/A
A7
B♭
F
Lord, for giv - ing to me

F
Fmaj7
F7
Gm/B♭
D7/A
Gm7(♭5)
Thy great sal - va - tion, so

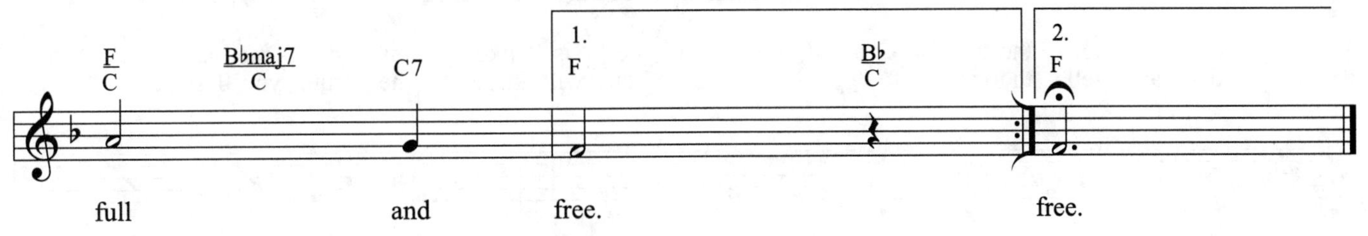
F/C
B♭maj7/C
C7
1.
F
B♭/C
2.
F
full and free. free.

Tell the Truth!

Words and Music by
TROY NILSSON and GENIE NILSSON

Fast driving 2 (𝅗𝅥=109)
C(no3)
You got to, you got to, you got to, you got to, you got to, you got to,
you got to, you got to, you got to, you got to, you got to, you got to,
you got to, you got to, you got to, you got to tell the truth.
Al - ways tell the truth. Tell the truth.
Al - ways tell the truth. Don't be tell - in'
lie - ee - i - ee - ies.
1. Truth is not a rub - ber - band;
2. Don't tell lies a - bout your friends;
it won't stretch and it won't bend, so tell the truth.
it'll just hurt them in the end, so tell the truth.
Al - ways tell the truth. A lie is like a boo - mer - ang;
Al - ways tell the truth. You will know the truth, you'll see,
it - 'll come back and bonk your brain, so tell the truth.
and the truth will set you free, so tell the truth.

A♭
Al - ways tell the truth. Some day you'll be think - ing,
E♭ E♭sus E♭ Fm
may - be just day - dream - ing a lit - tle bit - ty schem - ing
C A♭
lie, but you know de - ceiv - ing
E♭ E♭sus E♭ Fm C(no3)
on - ly ends up bring - ing trou - ble heaped up to the sky.
So tell the truth. Al - ways tell the truth.
Tell the truth. Al - ways tell the truth.
Don't be tell - in' lie - ee - i - ee - ies.
You got to, you got to, you got to, you got to, you got to, you got to,
you got to, you got to, you got to, you got to, you got to, you got to,
you got to, you got to, you got to, you got to tell the truth!

That Is the Reason

Words and Music by
HERB OWEN

1. Sav - ing me, set - ting me free,
2. Point - ing the way, fill - ing my day with
mak - ing me just what He wants me to be, let - ting me
lots of re - mind - ers, He hears when I pray, mak - ing me
know He's help - ing me grow: That is the
new so His work I can do: That is the
rea - son why I love Him so. true.
rea - son why I will be
3. Keep - ing me pure, mak - ing me sure that
all He has giv - en will ev - er en - dure,
stay - ing so near that I know He is here:
That is the rea - son why I will not fear.
That is the rea - son why I will not fear.

The B-I-B-L-E

Traditional

Lightly
B♭
B♭maj7/F
B♭7
A♭/C
B♭7/D
The B - I - B - L - E, yes,

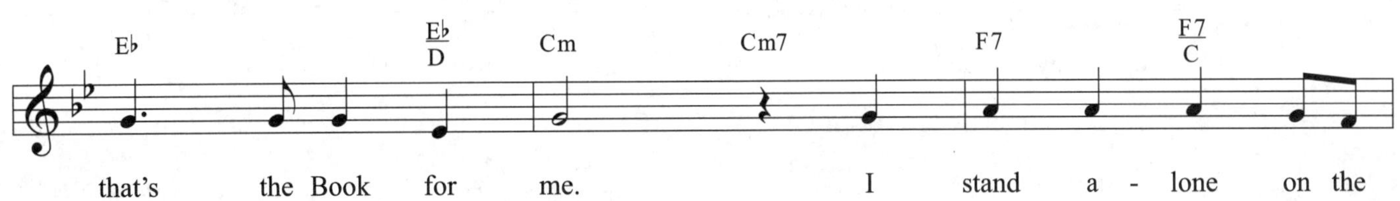
E♭
E♭/D
Cm
Cm7
F7
F7/C
that's the Book for me. I stand a - lone on the

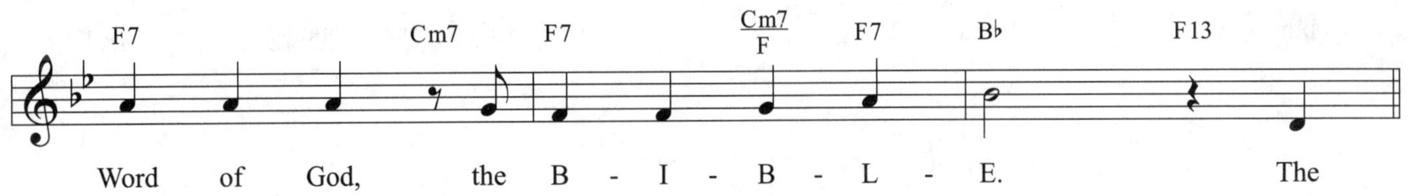
F7
Cm7
F7
Cm7/F
F7
B♭
F13
Word of God, the B - I - B - L - E. The

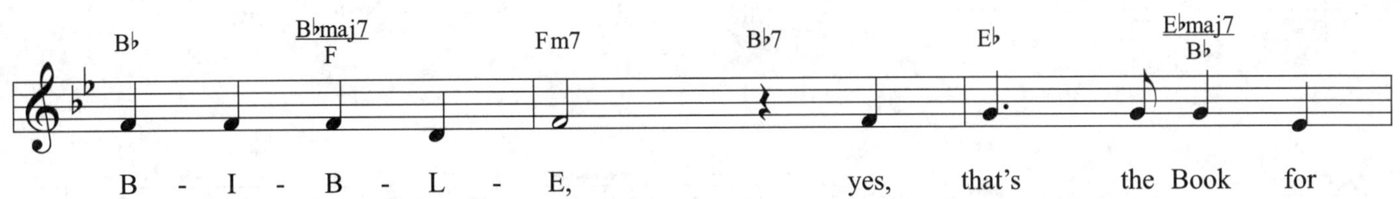
B♭
B♭maj7/F
Fm7
B♭7
E♭
E♭maj7/B♭
B - I - B - L - E, yes, that's the Book for

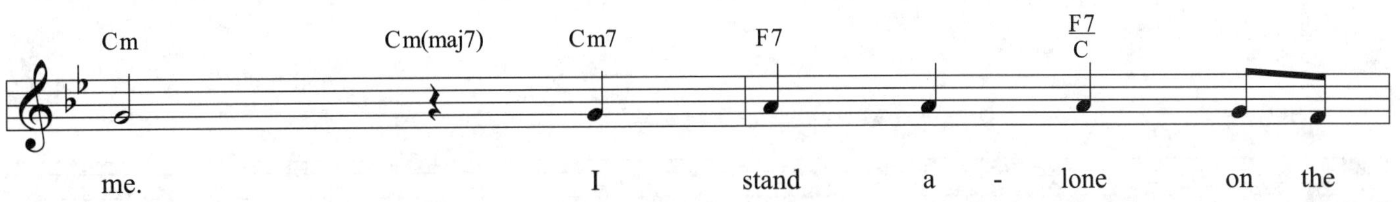
Cm
Cm(maj7)
Cm7
F7
F7/C
me. I stand a - lone on the

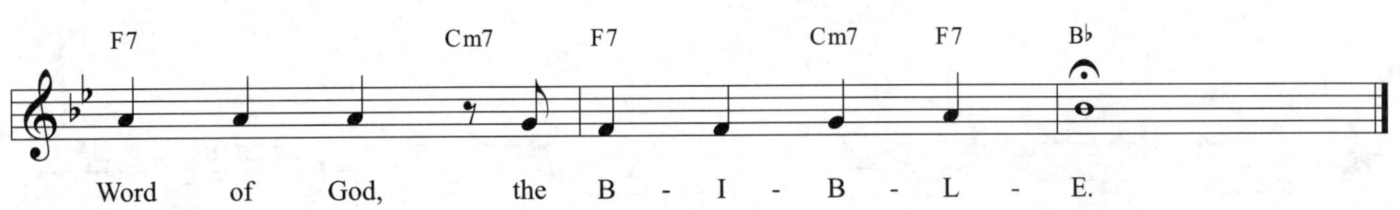
F7
Cm7
F7
Cm7
F7
B♭
Word of God, the B - I - B - L - E.

The Bunny Song

Words and Music by
PHIL VISCHER

Blues shuffle (♩=92)

B♭7
D♭7
C7
F7
The bun - ny, the bun - ny, woh, I ate the bun - ny. I

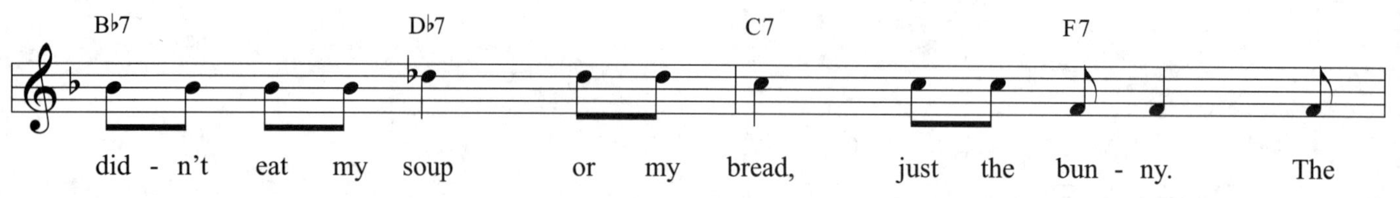
B♭7
D♭7
C7
F7
did - n't eat my soup or my bread, just the bun - ny. The

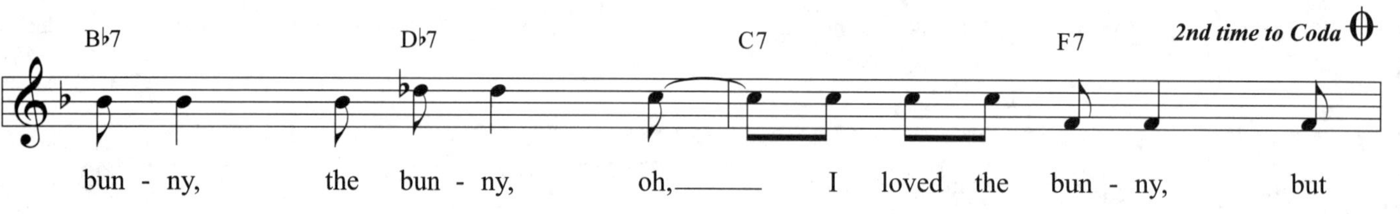
B♭7
D♭7
C7
F7
2nd time to Coda
bun - ny, the bun - ny, oh, I loved the bun - ny, but

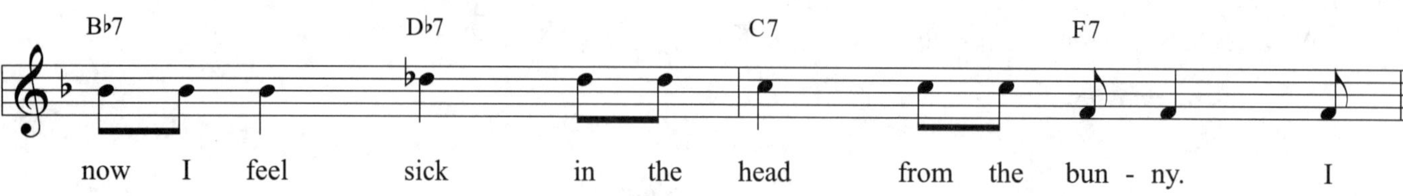
B♭7
D♭7
C7
F7
now I feel sick in the head from the bun - ny. I

B♭7
D♭7
C7
F7
did - n't eat my sal - ad. I did - n't eat my steak. I

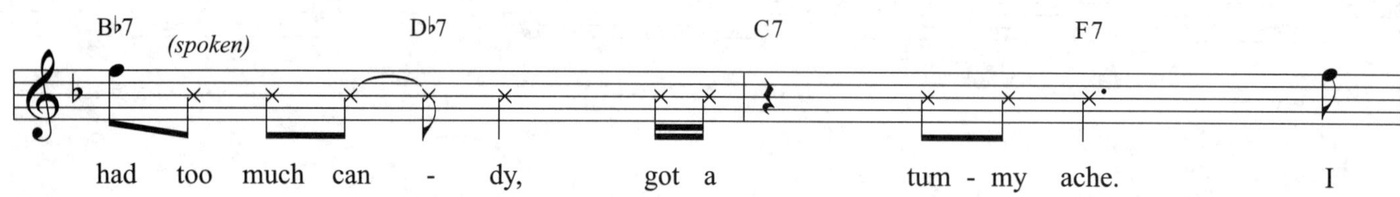
B♭7
(spoken)
D♭7
C7
F7
had too much can - dy, got a tum - my ache. I

B♭7
D♭7
C7
F7
need to eat good food to help me to grow. I'll

B♭7 D♭7 C7 F7
o - bey my mom - ma, 'cause she loves me so. Yeah,
B♭7 D♭7 C7 F7
I'll go to church and I'll go to school. That
B♭7 D♭7 C7 F7
stuff is im - por - tant, and I ain't no fool. I
B♭7 D♭7 C7 F7
don't want no pick-les; I don't want no hon-ey. I just want a plate and a fork and a bun-ny. I
B♭7 D♭7 C7 F7
don't want no tis-sue when my nose is run-ny. I just want a plate and a fork and a bun-ny. I
B♭7 D♭7 C7 F7
don't want to tell you a joke that is fun-ny. I just want a plate and a fork and a bun-ny. I
D.S. al Coda
B♭7 D♭7 C7 F7
don't want to play on a day that is sun-ny. I just want a plate and a fork and a bun - ny. The
CODA
B♭7 rit. D♭7 C7 F7 B♭7
now I feel sick in the head from the bun - ny.

The Burning Bush

(To the tune of The Mulberry Bush)

Words and Music by
RUTH ELAINE SCHRAM

D
Em7
1. Mo - ses was tend - ing a flock of sheep, a flock of sheep, a
2. That's where he saw a burn - ing bush, a burn - ing bush, a
A7
D
flock of sheep. Mo - ses was tend - ing a flock of sheep way
burn - ing bush. That's where he saw a burn - ing bush way
Em7 A7 D
1. Em7 A7 D
up on top of the moun - tain.
up on top of the moun - tain.
2. Em7 A7 D B♭7
E♭
3. God said the place was ho - ly ground,
Fm7 B♭7 E♭
ho - ly ground, ho - ly ground. God said the place was
E♭ Fm7 B♭7 E♭
ho - ly ground, way up on top of the moun - tain.
Fm7 B♭7 E♭ B7
E F♯m7 G♯m C♯m
4. I'm send - ing you to see the king, to
F♯7 G♯m7 F♯7/A♯ B
E F♯m7
see the king, to see the king. I'm send - ing you to

G♯m C♯m F♯ B7 E C7
see the king and lead my peo - ple from E - gypt.
F G Am7 G/B
5. Tell him to let My peo - ple go, My peo - ple go, My
6. You will see man - y mir - a - cles, mir - a - cles,
C C7 F
peo - ple go. Tell him to let My peo - ple go and
mir - a - cles. You will see man - y mir - a - cles and
Gm7 C7 F 1. Gm7 C7 F
lead My peo - ple from E - gypt.
lead My peo - ple from E - gypt.
2. Gm7 C7 F D7 G Am7(4)
7. I'll make a way a -
Bm Em7 A Bm7 A/C♯ D
cross the sea, a - cross the sea, a - cross the sea.
G Am7(4) Bm Em7 Am7 D7
I'll make a way a - cross the sea and lead My peo - ple from
G Am D7 G
E - gypt.

The Devil's My Enemy

Words and Music by
HERB OWEN

Jazzy!
Cm Fm Fm6 G
Sa - tan is my en - e - my; daily he gets
Cm C7 Fm
af - ter me, try - in' to get me to do
F° Cm/G F#°/A G Cm
ev - 'ry lit - tle thing he wants me to. Like the li - ar
Fm G7 Cm
that he is, he tries lots of mon - key biz.
C C7 Fm F° Cm/G
He makes wrong look like it's right; he baits his shin - y hook so
F#°/A G/B Cm C#m F#m G° G#
I will bite! Oh yeah!
C#m F#m G° G# C#m
Sa - tan says he
F#m G#7 C#m
is my friend, and on him I can de - pend;

C♯
C♯7
F♯m
F♯m7
C♯m/G♯
F♯m/A
He and I will have a ball __ if I'll on - ly lis - ten
A♯°
G♯7
C♯m
F♯m
when he calls. __ When I ask him all a - bout sin and stuff, __
G♯
G♯7
C♯m
C♯
he starts real - ly act - in' tough. __ And he says there's
F♯m
C♯m/G♯
F♯m/A
A♯°
G♯/C
C♯m
no such thing and __ it's real - ly O - K __ to do any - y - thing. Uh -
Dm
Gm
G♯°
A
Dm
huh!
Gm
G♯°
A
Dm
Gm
Though my bud - dy he would be, __
A
Dm
D
D7
I know he's my en - e - my; __ and he does - n't
Gm
Dm/A
B♭7
A
care at all __ if in - to a mess __ I trip and fall! __

Dm
Gm
A
A7
So I've got him fig - ured out
and I'm sure there
Dm
D
D7
Gm
is no doubt:
Like a hun - gry li - on, he wants to
Dm
A
B°
A7
C♯
Dm
Gmaj7
A13
gob - ble me up
and swal-low me!
Sa - tan is my
D
Bm7
Em7
A7
D
Am7
D7
en - e - my;
from his pow - er I am free!
And
Gmaj7
A13
D
Bm
it's no more the dev - il and me,
'cause
G
D
F♯
1. Em7 A D
2. Em7 A D
Je - sus is my friend and He set me free!
set me free!
Yes,
G
D
F♯
Em7
A7
D
D
F♯
Je - sus is my friend and He set me free!
G
G♯°
A7
D
N.C.
D
The dev - il's my en - e - my!

The Floating Zoo

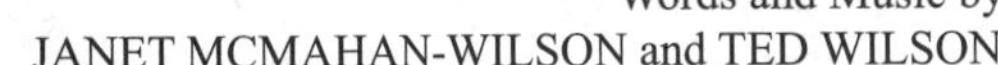

Words and Music by
JANET MCMAHAN-WILSON and TED WILSON

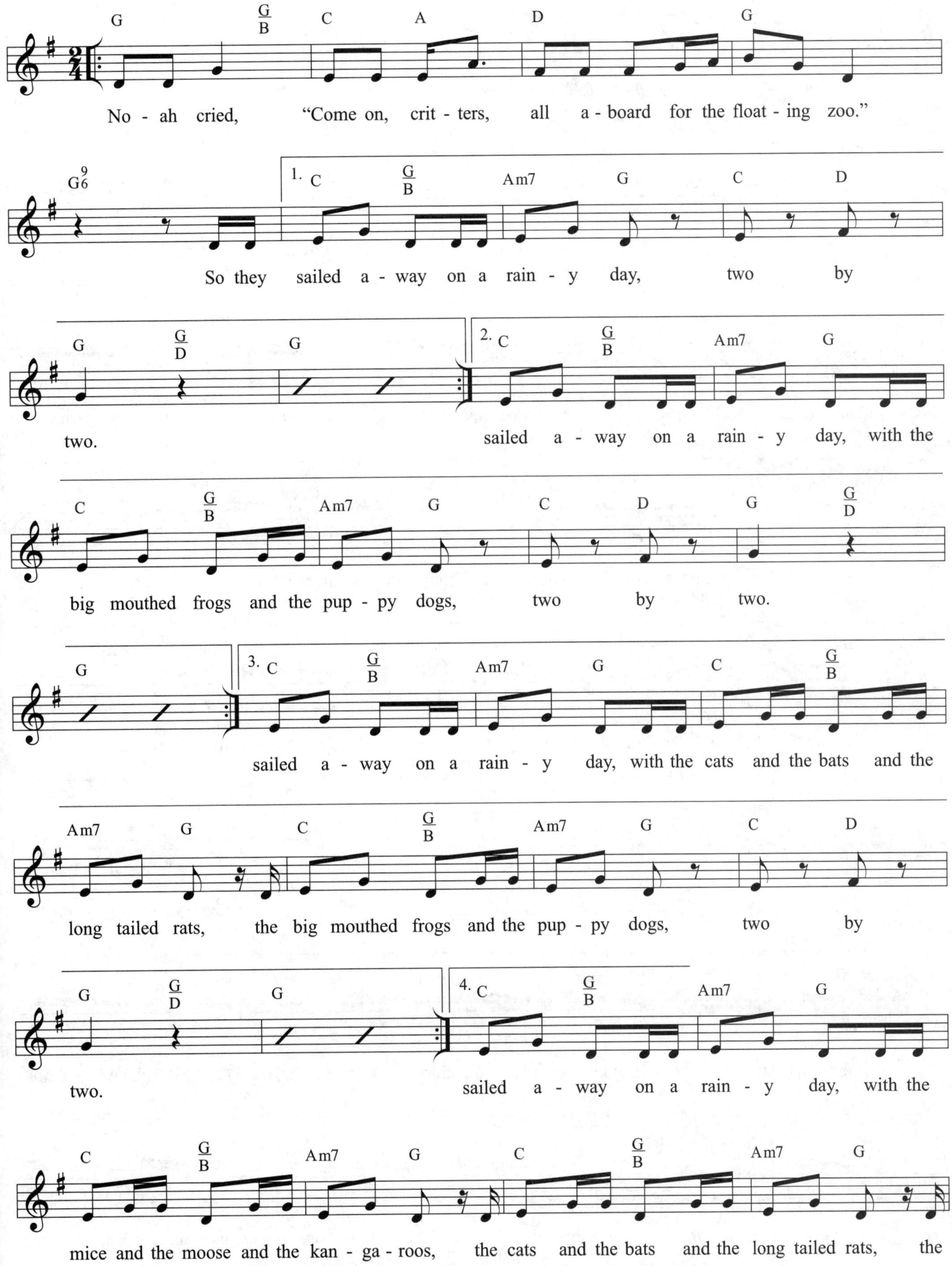
G G/B C A D G
No - ah cried, "Come on, crit - ters, all a - board for the float - ing zoo."
G6/9 1. C G/B Am7 G C D
So they sailed a - way on a rain - y day, two by
G G/D G 2. C G/B Am7 G
two. sailed a - way on a rain - y day, with the
C G/B Am7 G C D G G/D
big mouthed frogs and the pup - py dogs, two by two.
G 3. C G/B Am7 G C G/B
sailed a - way on a rain - y day, with the cats and the bats and the
Am7 G C G/B Am7 G C D
long tailed rats, the big mouthed frogs and the pup - py dogs, two by
G G/D G 4. C G/B Am7 G
two. sailed a - way on a rain - y day, with the
C G/B Am7 G C G/B Am7 G
mice and the moose and the kan - ga - roos, the cats and the bats and the long tailed rats, the

C G/B Am7 G C D G G/F
big mouthed frogs and the pup - py dogs, two by two.
E♭7 D♭/F E♭7/G A♭ A♭/C D♭ B♭ E♭
No - ah cried, "Come on, crit - ters, all a - board for the
A♭ A♭6/9 1. D♭ A♭/C B♭m7 A♭
float - ing zoo." So they sailed a - way on a rain - y day, with the
D♭ A♭/C B♭m7 A♭ D♭ A♭/C B♭m7 A♭
el - e - phants and the pel - i - cans, the mice and the moose and the kan - ga - roos, the
D♭ A♭/C B♭m7 A♭ D♭ A♭/C B♭m7 A♭
cats and the bats and the long tailed rats, the big mouthed frogs and the pup - py dogs,
D♭ E♭ A♭ A♭/E♭ A♭ 2. D♭ A♭/C
two by two. sailed a - way on a
B♭m7 A♭ D♭ A♭/C B♭m7 A♭ D♭ A♭/C
rain - y day, with the hon - ey bees and the chim - pan - zees, the el - e - phants and the
B♭m7 A♭ D♭ A♭/C B♭m7 A♭ D♭ A♭/C
pel - i - cans, the mice and the moose and the kan - ga - roos, the cats and the bats and the

B♭m7 A♭ D♭ A♭/C B♭m7 A♭ D♭ E♭
long tailed rats, the big mouthed frogs and the pup - py dogs two by
A♭ A♭/E♭ A♭
two.
3.
D♭ A♭/C B♭m7 A♭
sailed a - way on a rain - y day, the
D♭ A♭/C B♭m7 A♭ D♭ A♭/C B♭m7 A♭
big and the small, he called them all, the hon - ey bees and the chim - pan - zees, the
D♭ A♭/C B♭m7 A♭ D♭ A♭/C B♭m7 A♭
el - e - phants and the pel - i - cans, the mice and the moose and the kan - ga - roos, the
D♭ A♭/C B♭m7 A♭ D♭ A♭/C
cats and the bats and the long tailed rats, the big mouthed frogs and the
B♭m7 A♭ D♭ E♭ A♭ A♭/E♭ A♭
pup - py dogs, two by two.
A♭/C D♭ B♭ E♭
No - ah cried, "Come on, crit - ters, all a - board for the
A♭ A♭6/9 D♭ A♭/C B♭m7 A♭
float - ing zoo." So they sailed a - way on a rain - y day,
D♭ E♭ A♭6
two by two.

The Flaming Fire

Words and Music by
HERB OWEN

Steady four
F2
Bb2/F
1. Deep with - in the dark - ness of the den of doom, the
2. Deep with - in the pris - on, held by Her - od's men,
C/E
G2 4/D
C
C/Bb
F/A
Bb/C
king of the jun - gle lies and looks a - cross the room.
chained be - tween two sol - diers, Pe - ter looks to God a - gain.
Bb2
Gm7
Dan - iel stands be - fore him as to his God he prays that
All a - cross the cit - y, oth - ers start to pray that
C
F
he might be pro - tect - ed, live to serve Him all his days.
God would de - liv - er him be - fore the break of day.
F2
Bb2/F
High up in the heav - ens the Lord hears Dan - iel's prayer, and
Once a - gain the an - gel, leav - ing heav - en's halls,
C/E
Dm
Dm/C
God sends His an - gel to pro - tect His ser - vant there.
comes to de - liv - er from with - in the pris - on walls.
Bb2
Gm7
Li - on sees the an - gel and hum - bly there he falls be -
Soon the king dis - cov - ers Pe - ter's gone to - day,
C
F
fore the faith of Dan - iel as he to Je - ho - vah calls.
and he learns that God de - liv - ers peo - ple who will pray.

B♭/C
F
Oh, the king of the jun - gle stands in
For the kings of the na - tions stand in
Am7
Dm7
Gm7
awe of the an - gels, for the mes - sen - gers of God are a
F/A
B♭
C
F
Gm7
flam - ing fire.
For the Lord sends His an - gels to de -
F/A
Dm
Gm7
C
2nd time to Coda
liv - er His chil - dren and they all sing His prais - es in a
D.C. al Coda
Gm7
C
F
F/E
Dm
C/D
Dm
C/E
heav'n - ly choir.
CODA
Gm7
C
F
B♭/C
F
heav'n - ly choir.
Oh, the king of the jun - gle stands in
Am7
Dm7
Gm7
awe of the an - gels, for the mes - sen - gers of God are a
F/A
B♭
C
F
Gm7
flam - ing fire.
For the Lord sends His an - gels to de -
F/A
Dm
Gm7
C
Gm7
C7
F
liv - er His chil - dren and they all sing His prais - es in a heav'n - ly choir.

The Forgiveness Song

Words and Music by
KURT HEINECKE and LISA VISCHER

Calypso (♩=132)
B♭
You know that in love we can for - give;
F
it is the on - ly way to live. O - bey God and
C F
see that we can live in har - mo - ny.
B♭
Since God has for - giv - en us, it's true,
F
you for - give me; I'll for - give you. I'm gon - na start
C 1. F
to show for - give - ness from my heart.
2. F Gm/D F/C C7/B♭ F
You know that in love
C
So do your part, and show for -
F Gm/D F/C C7/B♭ F
give - ness from your heart.

The Holy Spirit's Livin' Inside of Me

(To the tune of The Old Gray Mare)

Words and Music by
DOUG SARRETT

The Holy Spirit's livin' inside of me, livin' inside of me,

2nd time to Coda

livin' inside of me. The Holy Spirit's livin' inside of me, showing me the

D.S. al Coda

way, showing me the way, showing me the way. The

CODA

way.

Jesus Christ is livin' inside of me,

livin' inside of me, livin' inside of me. Jesus Christ is

livin' inside of me, showing me the way,

showing me the way, showing me the way. Jesus Christ is

livin' inside of me, livin' inside of me, livin' inside of me.

rit.
Je - sus Christ is liv - in' in - side of me, show - ing me the way.

The Hairbrush Song

Words and Music by
LISA VISCHER, MICHAEL NAWROCKI
and PHIL VISCHER

Dramatically (♩=152)

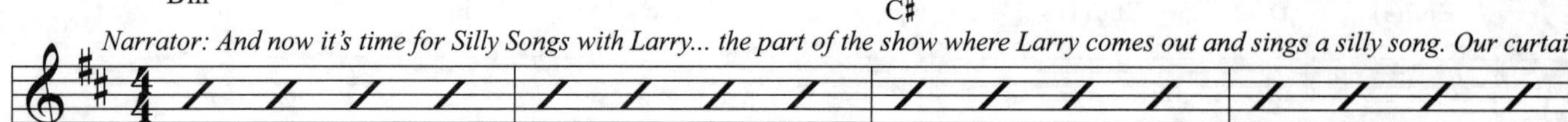
Bm
F♯/C♯
Narrator: And now it's time for Silly Songs with Larry... the part of the show where Larry comes out and sings a silly song. Our curtain

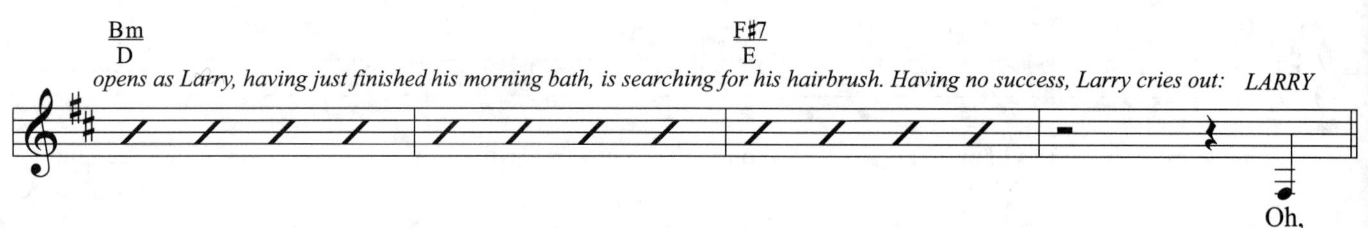
Bm/D
F♯7/E
opens as Larry, having just finished his morning bath, is searching for his hairbrush. Having no success, Larry cries out:
LARRY
Oh,

Bm
Em
where is my hair - brush? Oh, where is my

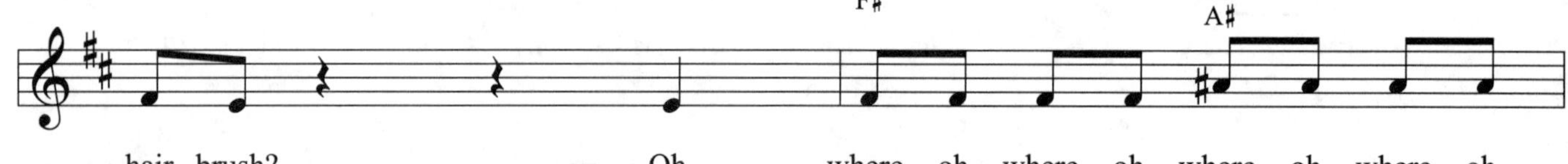
F♯
F♯/A♯
hair - brush? Oh, where, oh, where, oh, where, oh, where, oh,

F♯/C♯
F♯7/E
F♯
where, oh, where, oh, where, oh, where, oh, where is my hair -

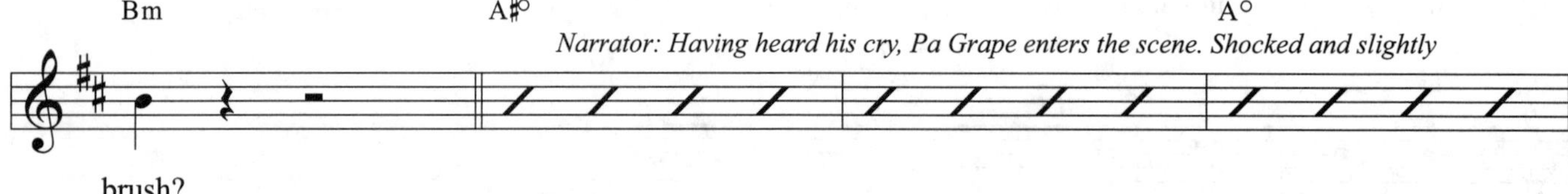
Bm
A♯°
A°
Narrator: Having heard his cry, Pa Grape enters the scene. Shocked and slightly
brush?

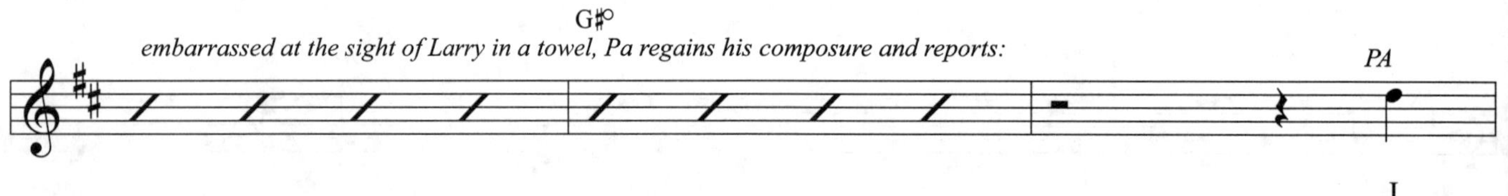
G♯°
embarrassed at the sight of Larry in a towel, Pa regains his composure and reports:
PA
I

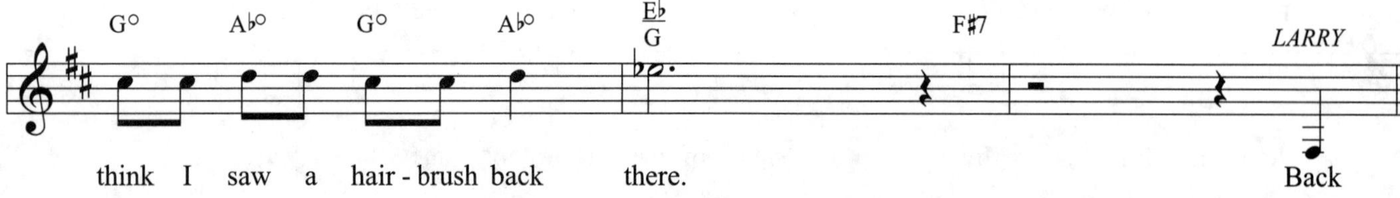
G°
A♭°
G°
A♭°
E♭/G
F♯7
LARRY
think I saw a hair - brush back there. Back

Bm Em
there is my hair - brush. Back there is my
F♯ F♯/A♯
hair - brush. Back there, back there, oh, where, back there, oh,
F♯/C♯ F♯7/E F♯
where, oh, where, back there, back there, back there is my hair -
Bm D Bm
Narrator: Having heard his joyous proclamation, Junior Asparagus enters the scene.
brush.
G G♯°
Shocked and slightly embarrassed at the sight of Larry in a towel, Junior regains his composure and comments:
A Bm/A A Bm/A A Bm/A A
JUNIOR
Why do you need a hair - brush? You don't have an - y hair.
Am Dm/A Am Dm/A Am E/G♯ Em/G
Narrator: Larry is taken aback. The thought had never occurred to him. No hair? What will this mean? What will become of him?
Bm/F♯ F♯sus F♯ Bm
What will become of his hairbrush? Larry wonders:
LARRY
No hair for my

Em
hair - brush. No hair for my hair - brush. No
F♯ F♯/A♯ F♯/C♯ F♯7/E
hair, no hair, no - where, no hair, no hair, no hair, back there, no hair, no
F♯ Bm
hair for my hair - brush.
Bm/F♯ G
Narrator: Having heard his wonderings, Bob the Tomato enters the scene. Shocked and slightly embarrassed at the sight of Larry in a
D/A
towel, Bob regains his composure and confesses:
BOB
Bm
Lar - ry, that old hair - brush of yours, well, you nev - er use it.
B♭+
You don't real - ly need it, so, well, I'm sor - ry, I did - n't know, but I
D/A A♯+
Narrator: Feeling a deep sense of loss, Larry
gave it to the Peach, 'cause he's got hair.
F♯/A♯
stumbles back and laments:
LARRY
Bm Em
Not fair! Oh, my hair - brush. Not fair! My poor

F♯
F♯/A♯
hair - brush. Not fair, not fair, no hair, not fair, no -
F♯/C♯
F♯7/E
F♯
where, no hair, not fair, not fair, not fair! My lit - tle hair -
Bm
F♯/A♯
Narrator: Having heard his lament, the Peach enters the scene. Himself in a towel, both Larry and
brush!
Bm
Bm/D
the Peach are shocked and slightly embarrassed at the sight of each other. But, recognizing Larry's generosity, the Peach is thankful:
F♯7
A
E/G♯
PEACH
Narrator: Yes, good has been done here. The Peach exits the scene. Larry
Thanks for the hair - brush.
F°7
F♯°7
Gsus
G7
smiles, but, still feeling an emotional attachment for the hairbrush, calls out:
LARRY
Take
Cm
Fm
care of my hair - brush. Take care, oh, my hair - brush. Take
G
G/B
G/D
G7/F
care, take care, don't dare not care. Take care. Nice hair. No fair. Take care, take
G
Cm
Narrator: The end.
C
care of my hair - brush.

The Honor Roll

Words and Music by
TROY NILSSON and GENIE NILSSON

March feel (♩=130)
C
Who's on the hon - or roll? Mom and Dad! The most
G7 G Am7/D G
hon - or - a - ble peo - ple that I know. They hug and kiss me
G Am7/D G C G7/B Am7 C/G
when I'm sad and take care of me as I grow, grow, grow. Who's on the
C C7
hon - or roll? Mom and Dad! They're the great - est par - ents in the
F F F♯°7 C/G A7
land. They're the cool - est, neat - est, nif - ty folks and I
Dm7(4) G7 C N.C.
CHEERLEADERS CHOIR CHEERLEADERS
give them hon - or ev - 'ry way I can! Give me an M! M! Give me an
CHOIR CHEERLEADERS CHOIR CHEERLEADERS CHOIR CHEERLEADERS
O! O! Give me an M! M! What's that spell? Mom! Give me a
CHOIR CHEERLEADERS CHOIR CHEERLEADERS CHOIR CHEERLEADERS CHOIR
D! D! Give me an A! A! Give me a D! D! What's that spell? Dad!
CHEERLEADERS CHOIR ALL C
Three cheers for Mom and Dad! Yea! Who's on the hon - or roll?

G7
Mom and Dad! The most hon - or - a - ble peo - ple that I know. They
G Am7/D G G Am7/D G
hug and kiss me when I'm sad and take care of me as I
C G7/B Am7 C/G C
grow, grow, grow. Who's on the hon - or roll? Mom and Dad! They're the
C7 F F F♯°7
great - est par - ents in the land. They're the cool - est, neat - est,
C/G A7 Dm7(4) G7 C A♭7
nif - ty folks and I give them hon - or ev - 'ry way I can! Who's on the
D♭
hon - or roll? Mom and Dad! The most hon - or - a - ble peo - ple that I
A♭7 A♭ B♭m7/E♭ A♭ A♭ B♭m7/E♭ A♭
know. They hug and kiss me when I'm sad and take care of me as I
D♭ A♭7/C B♭m7 D♭/A♭ D♭
grow, grow, grow. Who's on the hon - or roll? Mom and Dad! They're the
D♭7 G♭ G♭ G°7
great - est par - ents in the land. They're the cool - est, neat - est,
D♭/A♭ B♭7 E♭m7(4) A♭7 D♭
nif - ty folks and I give them hon - or ev - 'ry way I can!

The Lovingkindness of the Lord

Words and Music by
JANET MCMAHAN-WILSON

Shuffle
E♭
B♭/D
Cm
B♭
The lov - ing - kind - ness of the Lord lasts for - ev - er and ev - er. In
F
right - eous - ness and glo - ry He reigns.
The lov - ing -
2nd time to Coda
kind - ness of the Lord lasts for - ev - er and ev - er. So
raise your voice in praise to His name.
Sing a
Gm
song of His right - eous - ness. For we His chil - dren have been blessed by
His a - maz - ing deeds. For He has filled our ev - 'ry need.
He has
par - doned our in - iq - ui - ties, re - deemed and healed us from dis - ease. Oh,
C7
D.S. al Coda
that's the lov - ing - kind - ness of the Lord.
The lov - ing -
CODA
raise your voice in praise to His name.
Raise your voice and praise His ho - ly name!

The River Nile

(To the tune of Paw Paw Patch)

Words and Music by
RUTH ELAINE SCHRAM

The Perfect 10

Words and Music by
KATHIE HILL and JANET MCMAHAN-WILSON

(♩=120)
In a cloud of fire and smoke a might - y voice of thun - der broke as
God de - scend - ed to the moun - tain - top.
High up - on Mt. Si - n - ai He gave the rules we should live by as
Slower, a tempo (♩=100)
Rall.
God gave out the "shalts" and "thou shalt nots."
Num - ber one, we've just be - gun: God should be first in your life.
Num - ber two's the i - dol rule: Those grav - en im - a - ges aren't nice.
Num - ber three: God's name should be nev - er spo - ken in jest.
Num - ber four: The Sab - bath's for our wor - ship and for rest.
Num - ber five: We all should strive to hon - or fa - ther and moth - er.

Num - ber six: Don't get your kicks from kill - ing one an - oth - er.
Num - ber sev - en: Life is heav - en when you're true to your mate.
Num - ber eight: Don't steal and break this rule for good - ness sake!
Num - ber nine: Don't be the kind who goes a - round tell - ing lies.
Num - ber ten: Don't cov - et when you see your neigh - bor's house or wife.
That's the list and God in - sists we stay a - way from these sins.
That is why we mem - o - rize com - mand - ments one through ten. The Per - fect Ten, the
Per - fect Ten; They're just as true as they were way back when God gave the
Per - fect Ten, the Per - fect Ten. God gave the Per - fect
Ten. The gave the Per - fect Ten.

The Son of God

(To the tune of The Muffin Man)

Words and Music by
RUTH ELAINE SCHRAM and ED KEE

F
G
Am7(4)
G/B
1. Do you know the Son of God, the Son of God, the
2. Yes, I know the Son of God, the Son of God, the

C
Dm7(4)
C/E
F
Dm
Dm7
Son of God? Do you know the Son of God who
Son of God? Yes, I know the Son of God who

Gm7
C7
1. Fsus
F
2. F
Dsus
D7
died and rose a - gain?
gain.
died and rose a -

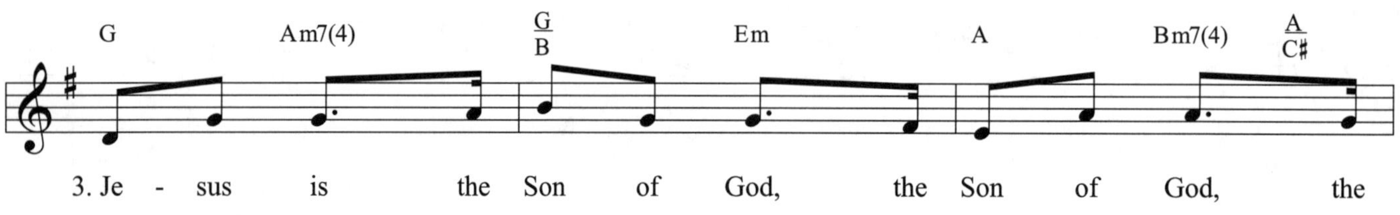
G
Am7(4)
G/B
Em
A
Bm7(4)
A/C♯
3. Je - sus is the Son of God, the Son of God, the

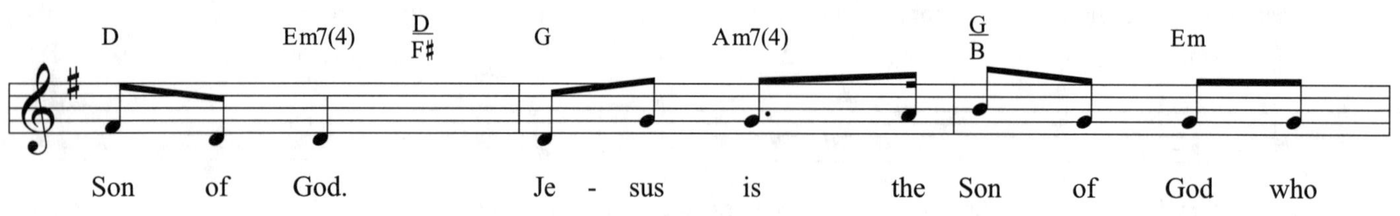
D
Em7(4)
D/F♯
G
Am7(4)
G/B
Em
Son of God. Je - sus is the Son of God who

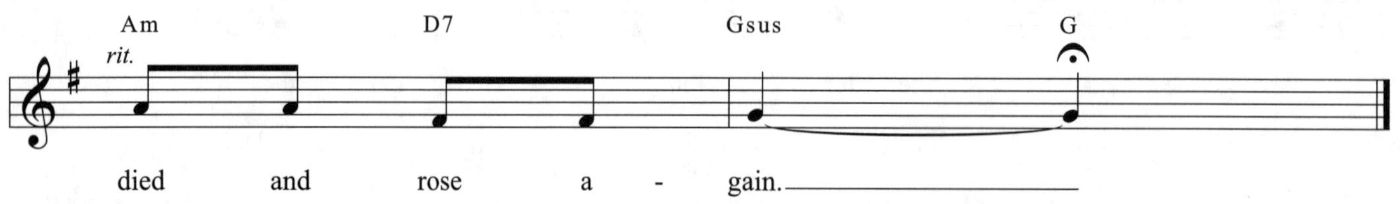
Am
D7
Gsus
G
rit.
died and rose a - gain.

The Wise Man and the Foolish Man

Traditional

1. The wise man built his house up-on the rock. The
(2. The) fool - ish man built his house up-on the sand. The
wise man built his house up-on the rock. The wise man built his
fool - ish man built his house up-on the sand. The fool - ish man built his
house up-on the rock, and the rains came tumb - ling down.
house up-on the sand, and the rains came tumb - ling down.
The
rains came down and the floods came up. The rains came down and the
floods came up. The rains came down and the floods came up, and the
1.
house on the rock stood fast!
2. The
2. Slowing
house on the sand went smash! (shouted)
N.C.

The Spirit

Words and Music by
HERB OWEN

Reggae
F
F/A
B♭
Gm7
The Spir - it em - pow - ers me that I might be
C
C7
B♭/F
F
F°
ex - act - ly just what He wants me to be;
F7
3rd time to Coda
guid - ing me day by day in all I do or say,
help - ing me know that the Lord loves me so. The Spir - it
F7/A
teach - es His Word that I've read or I've heard, help - ing
me un - der - stand how I fit in His plan;
tak - ing the truth I hear, mak - ing it all so clear,

C C7 F F7
shin - ing God's Light on His Word. Just like a
B♭ F
lov - ing moth - er He com - forts me so, and when I
B♭ F
do some - thing wrong, He helps me to grow. And if I
B♭ F
won - der if God real - ly cares for me,
G9 D♭7 C7
D.S. (twice) al Coda
He tells me Je - sus loves me, this I know! The Spir - it
CODA C
help - ing me un - der - stand how I fit in His plan,
C7 Gm7 C7 F
let - ting me know that God loves me!

The Wisdom of the Lord

Words and Music by
JANET MCMAHAN-WILSON

Happy! (♩=112)
C A/C♯ Dm
With our ears we can hear the wis - dom of the
G7 Dm G7 C
Lord, the wis - dom of the Lord, the wis - dom of the
A7/C♯ Dm
Lord. With our ears we can hear the wis - dom of the
G7 G C
Lord. So hear, hear, hear the wis - dom of the Lord.
A D
With our eyes we can
B/D♯ Em A7 Em
read the wis - dom of the Lord, the wis - dom of the
A7 D
Lord, the wis - dom of the Lord. With our eyes we can

B/D♯
Em
A7
A
read the wis - dom of the Lord. So read, read, read the
D
wis - dom of the Lord.
B
E
C♯/F
F♯m
With our hearts we can seek the wis - dom of the
B7
F♯m
B7
E
Lord, the wis - dom of the Lord, the wis - dom of the
C♯/F
F♯m
Lord. With our hearts we can seek the wis - dom of the
B7
B
Lord. 1. So seek, seek, seek the wis - dom of the
2. Read, read, read the wis - dom of the
3. Hear, hear, hear the wis - dom of the
1.2.
E
C♯m7
3.
E
Lord.
Lord.
Lord.

The Woman at the Well

(To the tune of The Farmer in the Dell)

Words and Music by
RUTH ELAINE SCHRAM

1. The wom - an at the well, the wom - an at the well,
Je - sus Christ would change her life, the wom - an at the well.
2. He
(3. He)
asked her for a drink. He asked her for a drink.
knew what she had done. He knew what she had done.
Je - sus Christ would change her life. He asked her for a drink. 3. He
Je - sus Christ would change her life. He knew what she had
done. 4. She had a change of heart. She had a change of
heart. Je - sus Christ had changed her life. She had a change of heart. 5. She
went and told her friends. She went and told her friends.
Je - sus Christ had changed her life. She went and told her friends.

The Words of the Lord

Words and Music by
JANET MCMAHAN-WILSON

Smoothly (♩=84)
C Am Dm G
1. The words of the Lord are true. The
(2.) words of the Lord on your heart. Write the
Dm7 G C C7 F C/E
words of the Lord are true. They're great-er than sil-ver,
words of the Lord on your heart. They're great-er than sil-ver,
Dm G7 C Am7 Fmaj7 G 1. C2
great-er than gold. The words of the Lord are true.
great-er than gold. Write the words of the Lord on your
2. C Asus A
2. Write the heart. 3. Let the
D Bm Em A Em7 A
words of the Lord lead your life. Let the words of the Lord lead your
D D7 G D/F♯ Em A7 D Bm7
life. They're great-er than sil-ver, great-er than gold. Let the
Gmaj7 A D Gmaj7 A
words of the Lord lead your life. Write the words of the Lord on your
D Gmaj7 A D
heart, for the words of the Lord are true.

There Is Power in the Name of Jesus

Words and Music by
ARNOLD MANKE

G
G/D
1. There is pow - er in the
(2.) glo - ry in the
G G/B D7 D7/A
name of Je - sus. There is pow - er in the
name of Je - sus. There is glo - ry in the
G C/D G C/G G G/D
name of Je - sus. There is pow - er in the
name of Je - sus. There is glo - ry in the
B7 Em Em7 Am7 Am7/D C/D
name of Je - sus. There is pow - er in that won - der - ful name.
name of Je - sus. There is glo - ry in that won - der - ful name.
1. G C/D 2. G D♭/E♭
2. There is
3. There is
A♭ D♭/A♭ A♭ B♭m/E♭ A♭/E♭ A♭ B♭m/A♭ A♭
heal - ing in the name of Je - sus. There is
B♭m7 E♭7 D♭/E♭ A♭ B♭m/A♭ A♭ D♭/E♭
heal - ing in the name of Je - sus. There is

A♭
D♭/A♭
A♭
B♭m/E♭
A♭/E♭
A♭
Fm7
heal - ing in the name of Je - sus. There is
B♭m7
B♭m7/E♭
A♭
D/E
heal - ing in that won - der - ful name.
4. There's sal -
A
D/A
A7
D/E
A
F♯m7
va - tion in the name of Je - sus. There's sal -
Bm7
E/B
D/E
E7
A
Bm/E
D/E
va - tion in the name of Je - sus. There's sal -
A
A7
D/A
D
C♯7
F♯m7
va - tion in the name of Je - sus. There's sal -
Bm7
Bm7/E
A
A/G♯
F♯m
F♯m7
va - tion in that won - der - ful name.
There's sal -
Bm7
Bm/E
A
A/E
A
va - tion in that won - der - ful name.

There Was a Man

(To the tune of Itsy, Bitsy Spider)

Words and Music by
JANET MCMAHAN-WILSON,
DAVITA HUNGATE and TED WILSON

In two
E♭ Fm7 B♭
There was a man named No - ah who built a great big
E♭ E♭
boat. For for - ty days and nights God
Fm7 B♭7 E♭ E♭
kept the boat a - float. And when the storm was
Fm7 B♭ E♭
o - ver and all the land was dry, God's
Fm7 B♭
prom - ise could be seen by His rain - bow in the
E♭ B7 E B7
sky. There
E F♯m7 B
was a man named Mo - ses who was part of the
E
plan to lead God's cho - sen peo - ple

F♯m7 B7 E
to the prom - ised land. But Pha - roah would - n't
F♯m7 B E B7
free them. He made them toe the line 'til
E F♯m7 B
God sent plagues up - on him to help him change his
E C7 F C7
mind. There
F Gm7 C
was a man named Jo - nah and God com - mand - ed
F
him to go to Nin - e - veh and
Gm7 C7 F F
tell them of their sin. But Jo - nah dis - o -
Gm7 C F C7
beyed and was swal - lowed by a fish. Be - ing
F Gm7 C F
sor - ry, Jo - nah prayed, then o - beyed God's ev - 'ry wish.

This Is My Commandment

Traditional

Eb Eb/Bb Eb Bb Eb Eb/Bb
This is my com - mand - ment, that you love one an -
Eb Eb/G Ab Eb/Bb Fm7/Bb Bb7
oth - er, that your joy may be
1. Eb Ab/Bb 2. Eb Ab/Bb
full. full, that your
Eb Ab Eb Eb/Bb
joy may be full, that your
Eb Gm7 Ab Bbsus Bb7 Ab/C Bb7/D
joy may be full.
Eb Eb/D Cm Eb/Bb Bb Eb Eb7/G
This is my com - mand - ment, that you love one an -
Ab Eb/Bb Eb+/Bb Fm7/Bb Bb7
oth - er, that your joy may be
1. Eb Ab/Bb D.S. 2. Eb Eb7/G Ab
full, that your full, that your
Eb/Bb Eb+/Bb Fm7/Bb Bb7 Eb Eb/Bb Eb
joy may be full!

This Is the Day

Words and Music by
LES GARRETT

Eb Eb/Bb Bb Eb Eb/Bb Eb Eb/Bb Bb Eb
This is the day, this is the day that the
Gm/Bb Bb7/F Bb7 Fm7 Bb7 Fm7
Lord hath made, that the Lord hath made.
Bb Bb/F Eb/F Bb7 Fm7 Bb Bb/F Eb/F Bb7
I will re - joice, I will re - joice and be
Fm/Eb Eb/Bb Eb Eb/Bb Fm/Eb Eb/Bb Eb Bbm7 Eb7
glad in it, and be glad in it
Ab Ab/Eb Ab Eb Eb/Bb Eb Eb7/G
This is the day that the Lord hath made.
Ab Abmaj7 A° Eb/Bb Ab/Bb
I will re - joice and be glad in it!
Eb Eb/Bb Bb Eb Eb/Bb Eb Eb/D C7(b9)
This is the day, this is the day that the
F13 F9(#5) Fm7/Bb Bb7
Lord hath
1. Eb Ab/Bb
made.
2. Eb Eb/Bb Eb
made.

This Little Light of Mine

Traditional

C Cmaj7/G C6 C/G C Cmaj7/G C7 B♭/D C7/E
1. This lit - tle light of mine, I'm gon - na let it shine.
F Fmaj7/C F6 F/C F6 F♯° C/G F♯°
This lit - tle light of mine, I'm gon - na let it shine, Let it
C/G C/E F C/G G7 C Dm7 Dm7/G
shine, let it shine, let it shine.
C C6/G Cmaj7 C6/G C Cmaj7/G Gm7 C7
2. Hide it un - der a bush - el, no! I'm gon - na let it shine.
F F6/C Fmaj7 F6 F C/E F
Hide it un - der a bush - el, no! I'm gon - na let it shine, Let it
C/E F C/G G7 C F/G
shine, let it shine, let it shine.
C Cmaj7/G C6 Cmaj7/G C Cmaj7/G C7 Gm7/D
3. Don't let Sa - tan blow it out, I'm gon - na let it shine.

F Fmaj7/C F6 F/C F F6 F♯° C/G F♯°
Don't let Sa - tan blow it out, I'm gon - na let it shine, Let it
C/G C/E F C/G G7 C E♭m7/A♭ A♭13(9)
shine, let it shine, let it shine.
D♭ D♭maj7 G♭maj7 D♭ D♭maj7/A♭ A♭m7 D♭7
4. Let it shine 'til Je - sus comes, I'm gon - na let it shine.
G♭ G♭/D♭ G♭ G♭6 Gm7(♭5) G° D♭/A♭ D♭maj7/A♭
Let it shine 'til Je - sus comes, I'm gon - na let it shine, Let it
B♭7(♭9) E♭9 E♭m9/A♭ A♭7 D♭ E♭m7 E♭m7/A♭
shine, let it shine, let it shine.
D♭ D♭maj7/A♭ D♭6 D♭/A♭ D♭ D♭maj7/A♭ D♭7 C♭/E♭ D♭7/F
This lit - tle light of mine, I'm gon - na let it shine.
G♭ G♭maj7/D♭ G♭ G♭/D♭ G♭6 G° D♭/A♭ G°
This lit - tle light of mine, I'm gon - na let it shine, Let it
D♭/A♭ D♭/F G♭ D♭/A♭ A♭7 D♭
shine, let it shine, let it shine!

This Old Saint

(To the tune of This Old Man)

Words and Music by
TRISH MENDOZA and ED KEE

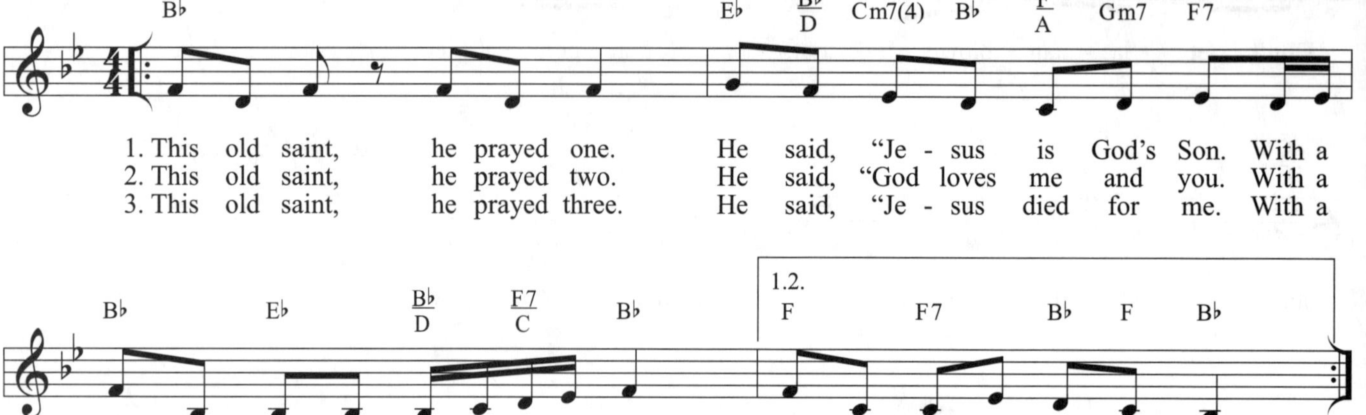
B♭
E♭
B♭/D
Cm7(4)
B♭
F/A
Gm7
F7
1. This old saint, he prayed one. He said, "Je - sus is God's Son. With a
2. This old saint, he prayed two. He said, "God loves me and you. With a
3. This old saint, he prayed three. He said, "Je - sus died for me. With a
B♭
E♭
B♭/D
F7/C
B♭
1.2.
F
F7
B♭
F
B♭
new life, clean heart, liv - in' for the Lord, great in heav'n is my re - ward."

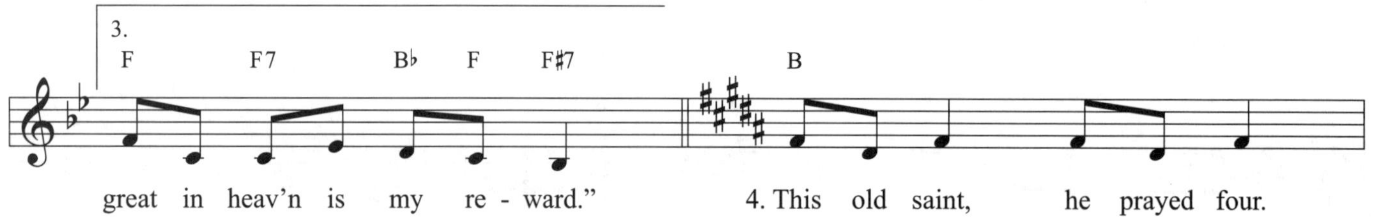
3.
F
F7
B♭
F
F♯7
B
great in heav'n is my re - ward." 4. This old saint, he prayed four.

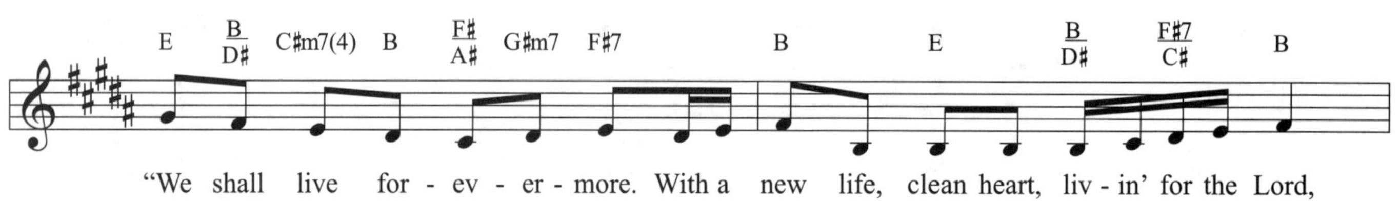
E
B/D♯
C♯m7(4)
B
F♯/A♯
G♯m7
F♯7
B
E
B/D♯
F♯7/C♯
B
"We shall live for - ev - er - more. With a new life, clean heart, liv - in' for the Lord,

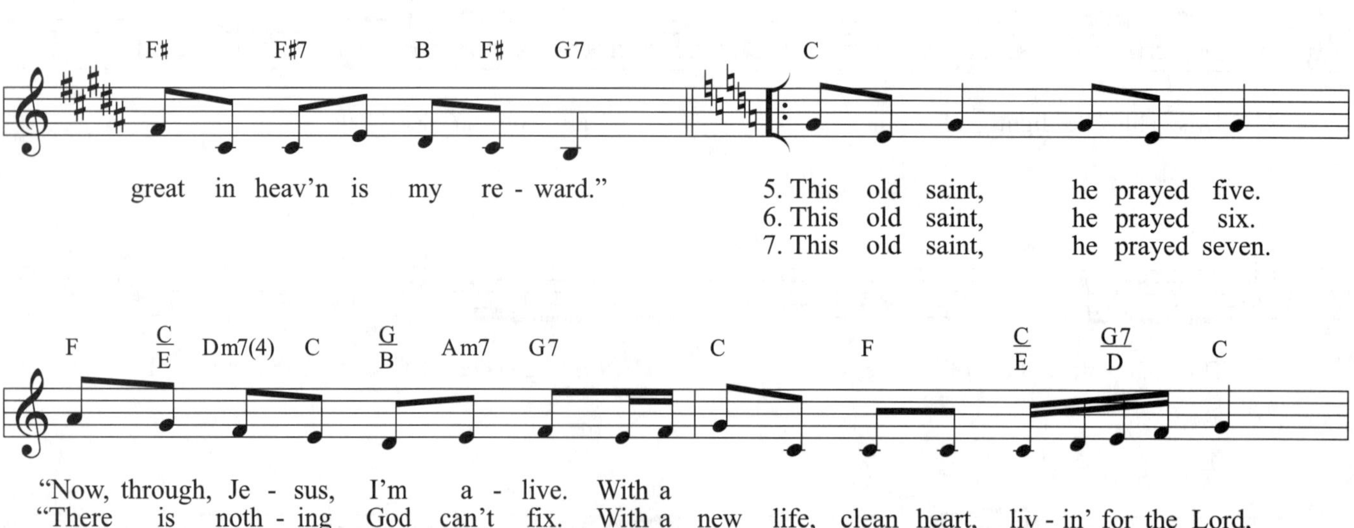
F♯
F♯7
B
F♯
G7
C
great in heav'n is my re - ward." 5. This old saint, he prayed five.
6. This old saint, he prayed six.
7. This old saint, he prayed seven.
F
C/E
Dm7(4)
C
G/B
Am7
G7
C
F
C/E
G7/D
C
"Now, through, Je - sus, I'm a - live. With a
"There is noth - ing God can't fix. With a new life, clean heart, liv - in' for the Lord,
"We will live with God in heav'n. With a

1.2.
G G7 C G C
great in heav'n is my re - ward."
3.
G G7 C G7 A♭7
great in heav'n is my re - ward."
D♭ G♭ D♭/F E♭m7(4) D♭ A♭/C B♭m7 A♭7
8. This old saint, he prayed eight. "Truth we love and lies we hate. With a
D♭ G♭ D♭/F A♭7/E♭ D♭ A♭ A♭7 D♭ A♭ A7
new life, clean heart, liv - in' for the Lord, great in heav'n is my re - ward."
D G D/F♯ Em7(4) D A/C♯ Bm7(4) A7
9. This old saint, he prayed nine. "God is good and God is kind. With a
10. This old saint, he prayed ten. "Je - sus Christ will come a - gain. With a
D G D/F♯ A7/E D
new life, clean heart, liv - in' for the Lord,
1.
A A7 D A D
great in heav'n is my re - ward."
2.
A A7 Em9 A7 D Em7 A7 D
great in heav'n is my re - ward."

Thou Shalt Not Steal!

Words and Music by
TROY NILSSON and GENIE NILSSON

Bright Circus feel (♩=150)
D A D Bm E A
Don't take Mol - ly's dol - ly. Don't take To - ny's ba - lo - ney or Mike's bike or Ike's kite, Fred's sled or an - y - thing from Ed.
D A D Bm E Slowly A7
Don't take An - dy's can - dy. Don't take Bar - ry's ber - ries or Sam's ham or Lou's lamb, Jake's snake or Sal - ly's piece of cake.
D A
Steal - ing is bad; steal - ing is wrong. That is why we're sing - ing this song.
D A D
Steal - ing is wrong; steal - ing is bad. Just be hap - py with what you have.
Faster tempo, even 8ths
Don't take Son - ny's bun - ny. Don't take Gar - ret's
A D Bm E
car - rot, Scat's cat or Bob's bat, Joan's phone;
A D
just leave it a - lone! Don't take Sher - ry's cher - ries. Don't take Ed - dy's spa -

A D Bm E
ghet - ti, Kate's skates, Gail's snail, Dale's pail or
A7 Slowly D
you'll end up in jail. Steal - ing is bad; steal - ing is wrong.
A D
That is why we're sing - ing this song. Steal - ing is wrong; steal - ing is bad.
A D E♭ Faster tempo, even 8ths
Just be hap - py with what you have. Don't take Jo - ey's toys.
B♭ E♭ Cm
Don't take Ry - an's li - on, Zack's yak, Mack's back - pack,
F B♭ E♭
Lee's skis or E - die's pret - ty bead - ies. Don't take Og - gie's
B♭
dog - gie. Don't steal To - ny's po - ny, Chuck's truck,
E♭ Cm F Slowly B♭7
Bud's bucks, Paul's ball or an - y - thing at all!
E♭ B♭
Steal - ing is bad; steal - ing is wrong. That is why we're sing - ing this song.
E♭ B♭ E♭
Steal - ing is wrong; steal - ing is bad. Just be hap - py with what you have.

Three Wise Men

(To the tune of Three Blind Mice)

Words and Music by
JANET MCMAHAN-WILSON
and RHETT PARRISH

Three wise men, three wise men, trav - 'ling a - far,
see - ing the star. They found the Sav - ior in Beth - le - hem. They
fell on their knees and they wor - shipped Him. "Nev - er be - fore had there ev - er been a
child like Him," said three wise men.
Three wise men, three wise men, trav - 'ling a - far,
see - ing the star. They found the Sav - ior in Beth - le - hem. They
fell on their knees and they wor - shipped Him. "Nev - er be - fore had there ev - er been a
child like Him," said three wise men.

Thy Word Have I Hid in My Heart

Psalm 119:11

Traditional

G7
C
Thy Word have I hid in my

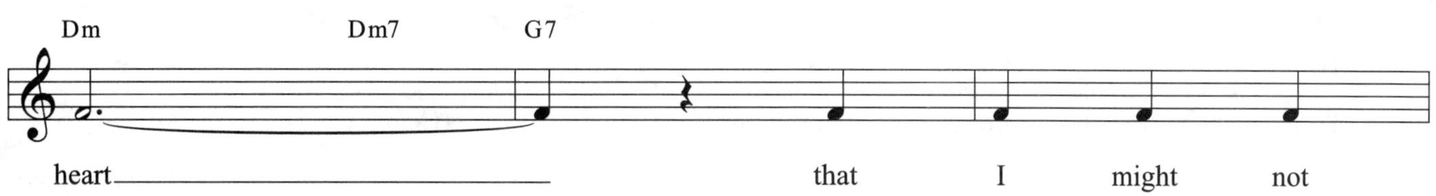
Dm
Dm7
G7
heart
that I might not

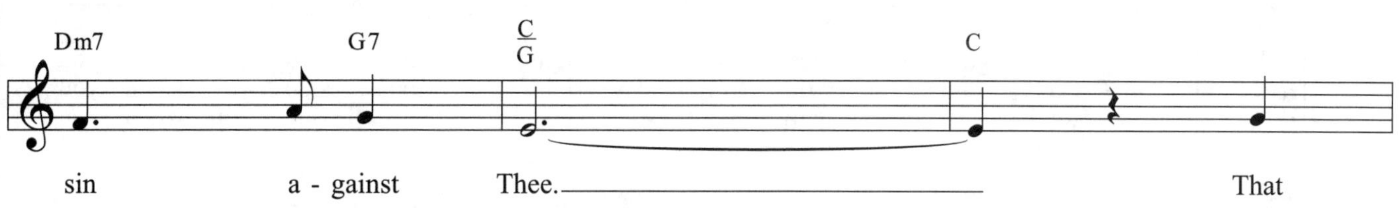
Dm7
G7
C/G
C
sin a - gainst Thee.
That

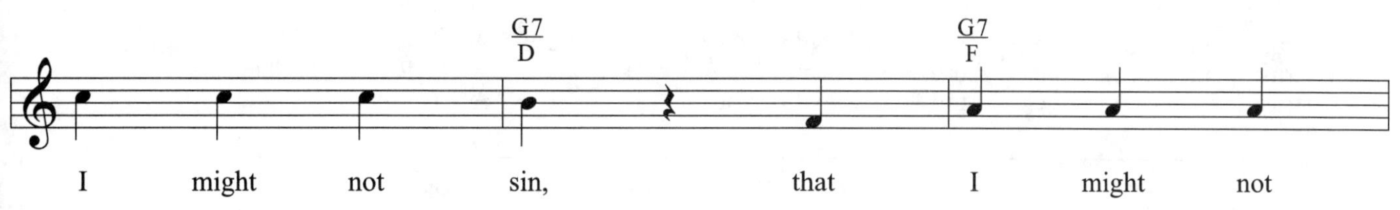
G7/D
G7/F
I might not sin, that I might not

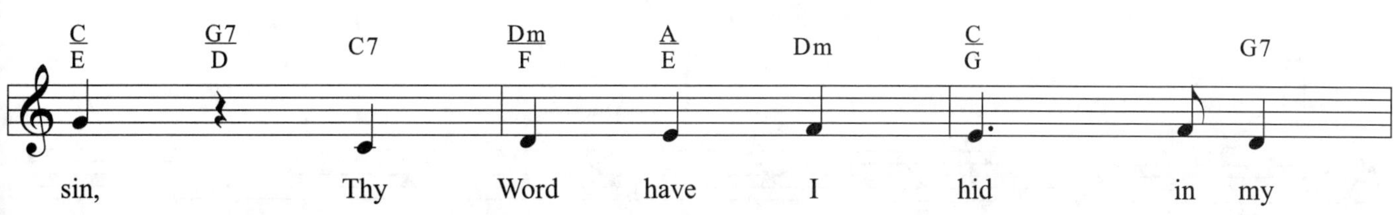
C/E
G7/D
C7
Dm/F
A/E
Dm
C/G
G7
sin, Thy Word have I hid in my

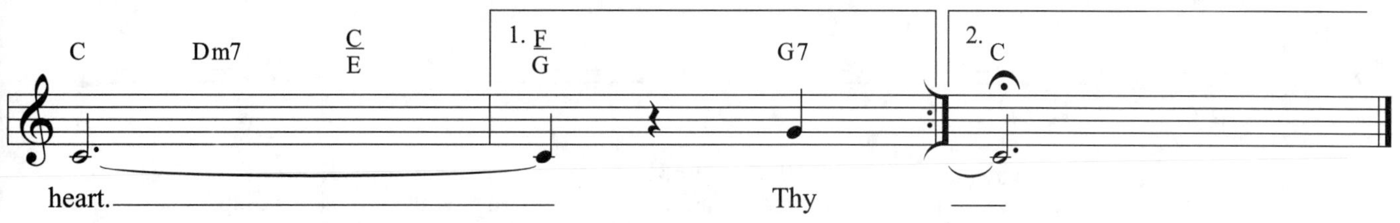
C
Dm7
C/E
1. F/G
G7
2. C
heart.
Thy

Trust in the Lord

Words and Music by
JANET MCMAHAN-WILSON

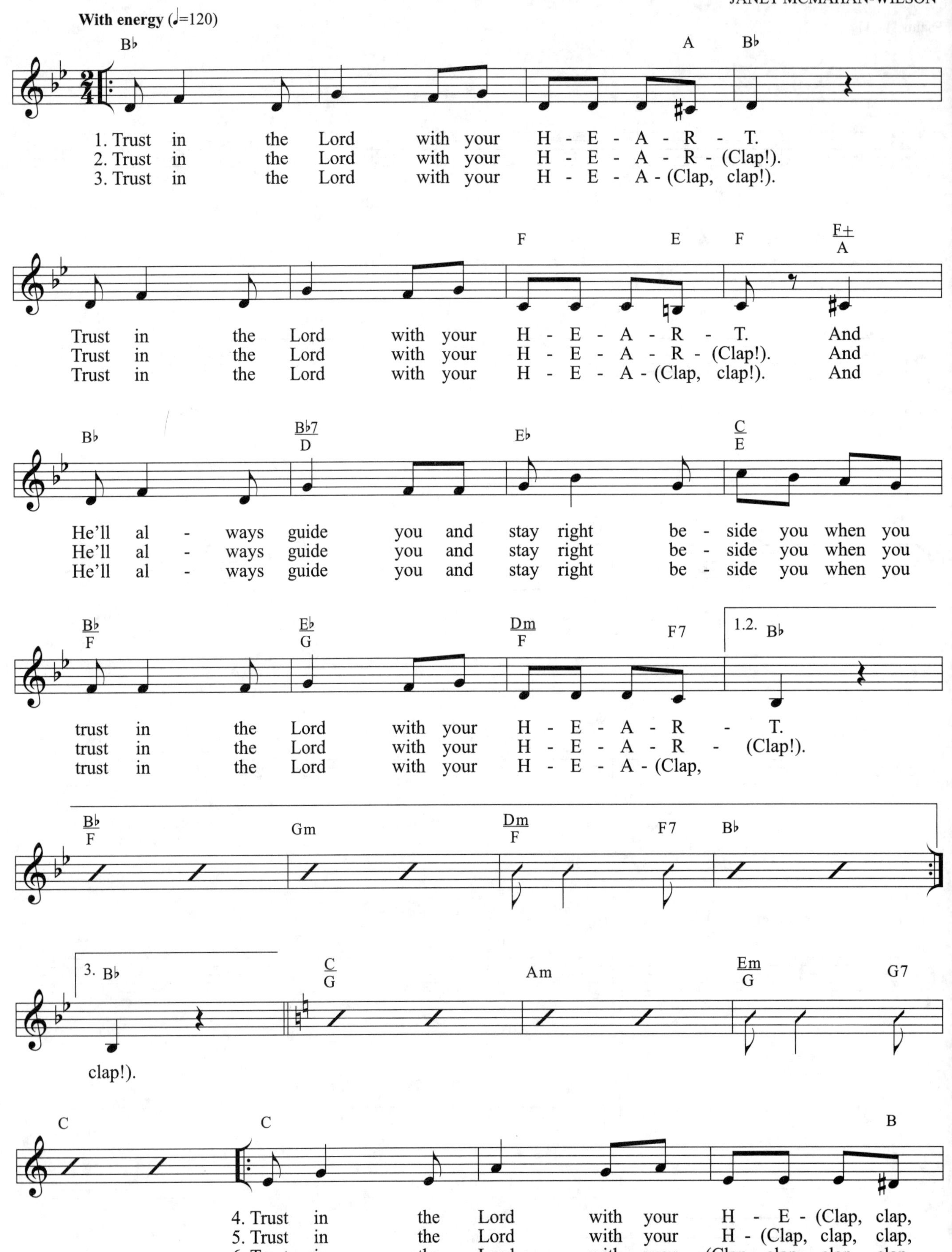
With energy (♩=120)
B♭ A B♭
1. Trust in the Lord with your H - E - A - R - T.
2. Trust in the Lord with your H - E - A - R - (Clap!).
3. Trust in the Lord with your H - E - A - (Clap, clap!).
F E F F+/A
Trust in the Lord with your H - E - A - R - T. And
Trust in the Lord with your H - E - A - R - (Clap!). And
Trust in the Lord with your H - E - A - (Clap, clap!). And
B♭ B♭7/D E♭ C/E
He'll al - ways guide you and stay right be - side you when you
He'll al - ways guide you and stay right be - side you when you
He'll al - ways guide you and stay right be - side you when you
B♭/F E♭/G Dm/F F7 1.2. B♭
trust in the Lord with your H - E - A - R - T.
trust in the Lord with your H - E - A - R - (Clap!).
trust in the Lord with your H - E - A - (Clap,
B♭/F Gm Dm/F F7 B♭
3. B♭ C/G Am Em/G G7
clap!).
C C B
4. Trust in the Lord with your H - E - (Clap, clap,
5. Trust in the Lord with your H - (Clap, clap, clap,
6. Trust in the Lord with your (Clap, clap, clap, clap,

clap!). Trust in the Lord with your H - E - (Clap, clap,
clap!). Trust in the Lord with your H - (Clap, clap, clap,
clap!). Trust in the Lord with your (Clap, clap, clap, clap,
clap!). And He'll al - ways guide you and stay right be -
clap!). And He'll al - ways guide you and stay right be -
clap!). And He'll al - ways guide you and stay right be -
side you when you trust in the Lord with your H - E - (Clap, clap,
side you when you trust in the Lord with your H - (Clap, clap, clap,
side you when you trust in the Lord with your (Clap, clap, clap, clap,
1.2.
clap!)
clap!)
3.
clap!) He'll al - ways guide you and
stay right be - side you when you trust in the Lord with your
H - (Clap!) E - (Clap!) A - (Clap!) R - (Clap!)
T, heart!

Trust in the Lord with All Your Heart

Words and Music by
TROY NILSSON and GENIE NILSSON

Steady four (♩=96)
G C G/B D G C G/B D
Na, na, na, na, na, na. Na, na, na, na, na, na.
G C G/B D G C G/B D
Na, na, na, na, na, na. Na, na, na, na, na, na.
G C2 D Dsus D
Trust in the Lord with all Your heart.
G C2 D Dsus D D2 D
Lean not on your own un - der - stand - ing.
G C2 D Dsus D D2 D
In all your ways ac - know - ledge Him, and He will make your
4th time to Coda
C D 1. G C D 2.3. G
pa - ee - aths straight. straight.
C G D G
1. Straight path through dark night, got a clean line of sight. Your
2. Trust God in all your ways; He will guide you all your days.
C G A D D.S. (twice) al Coda
head is clear; the fu - ture's bright. Ev - 'ry - thing will be al - right if you
He will re - new your strength as you walk the road of faith.

CODA
G Eb Ab Db2
straight. Trust in the Lord with all Your
Eb Ab Db2
heart. Lean not on your own un - der - stand -
Eb Ab Db2
- ing. In all your ways ac - know - ledge
Eb Ebsus Eb Db Eb
Him, and He will make your pa - ee - aths
Fm Db Eb
straight. He will make your pa - ee - aths
Ab Db Ab/C Eb Ab Db Ab/C
straight. Na, na, na, na, na. Na, na, na, na, na,
Eb Ab Db Ab/C Eb
na. Na, na, na, na, na, na.
Ab Db Ab/C Eb Ab
Na, na, na, na, na, na.

Truth

Words and Music by
HERB OWEN

C
Dm/C
Em/G
C
Dm/C
Em/G
Am
G
C
C/G
G
1. Don't look left, don't look right, Look straight a - head at the Guid - ing Light.
2. Don't be - lieve all you hear, False - hood and e - vil you'll learn to fear.

C
Dm/C
Em/G
C
Dm/C
Em/G
Am
G
C
C/E
Don't get off of the track, Keep go - ing on - ward and don't look back, For
Put a - way e - vil words, Care - ful - ly judge ev - 'ry - thing you hear. For

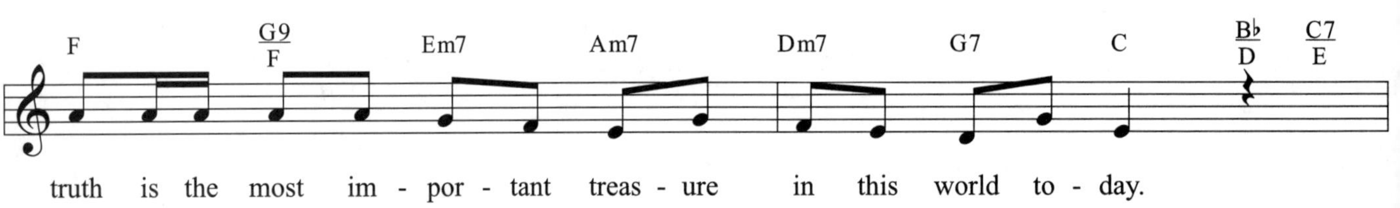
F
G9/F
Em7
Am7
Dm7
G7
C
B♭/D
C7/E
truth is the most im - por - tant treas - ure in this world to - day.

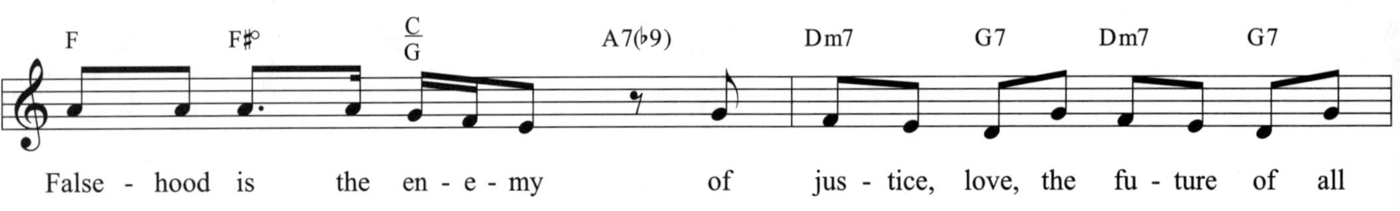
F
F♯°
C/G
A7(♭9)
Dm7
G7
Dm7
G7
False - hood is the en - e - my of jus - tice, love, the fu - ture of all

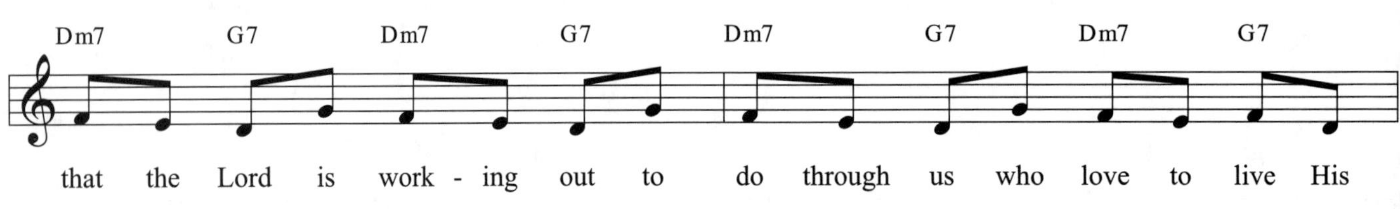
Dm7
G7
Dm7
G7
Dm7
G7
Dm7
G7
that the Lord is work - ing out to do through us who love to live His

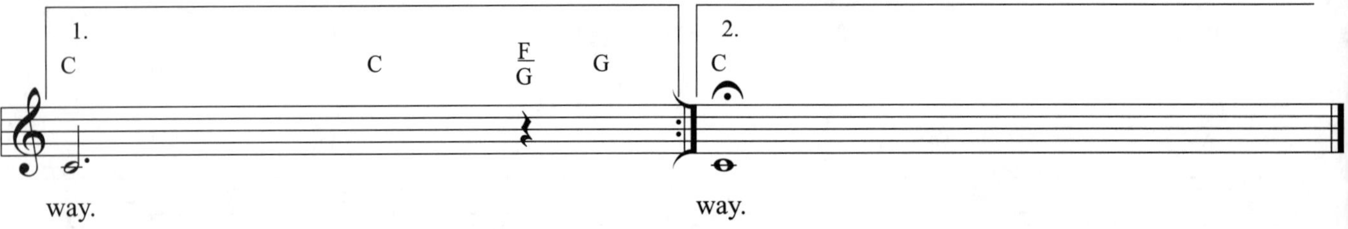
1.
C
C
F/G
G
way.
2.
C
way.

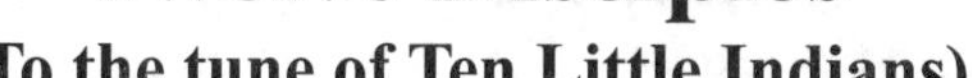

Twelve Disciples

(To the tune of Ten Little Indians)

Words and Music by
DENNIS SCOTT

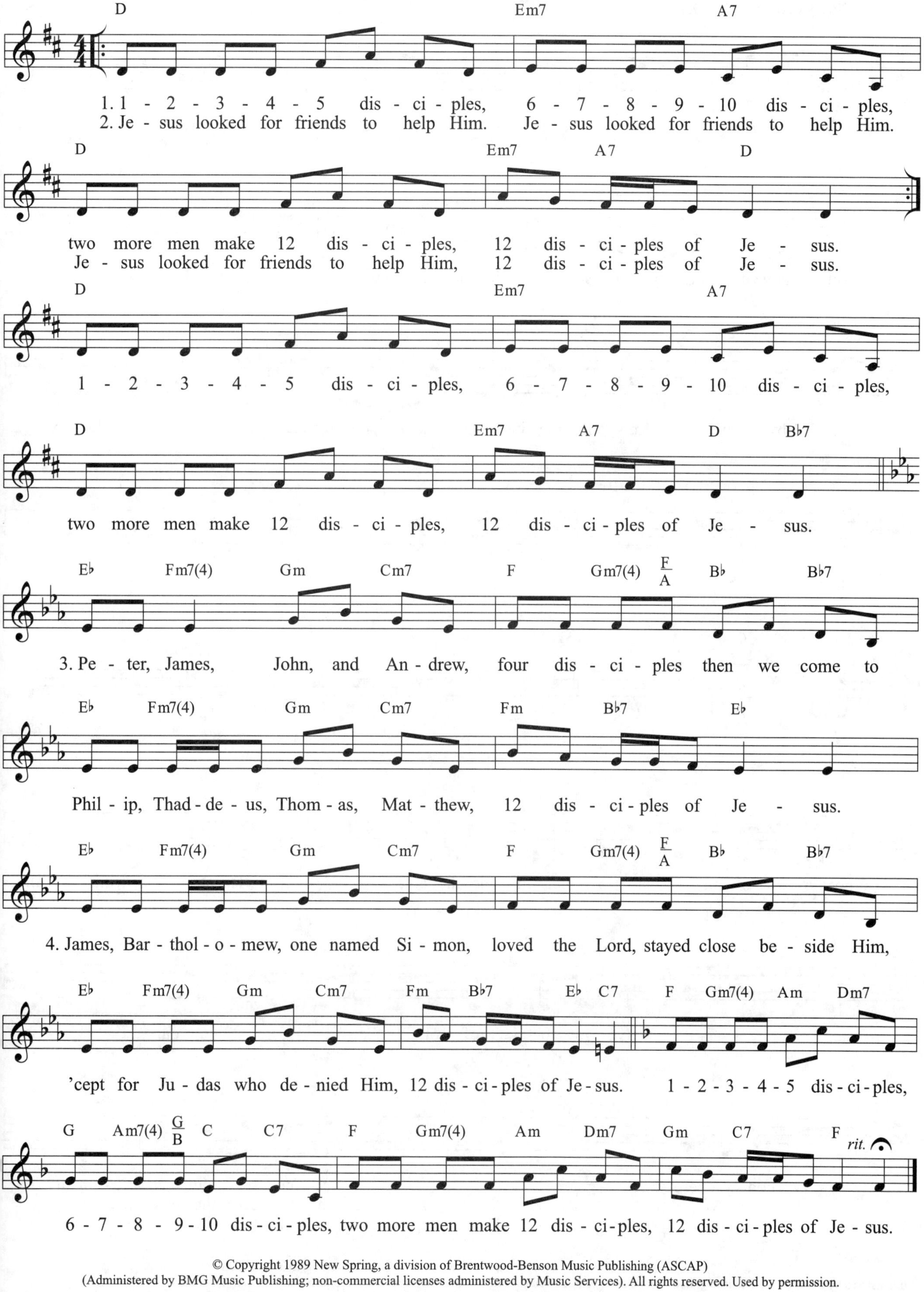
D Em7 A7
1. 1 - 2 - 3 - 4 - 5 dis - ci - ples, 6 - 7 - 8 - 9 - 10 dis - ci - ples,
2. Je - sus looked for friends to help Him. Je - sus looked for friends to help Him.
D Em7 A7 D
two more men make 12 dis - ci - ples, 12 dis - ci - ples of Je - sus.
Je - sus looked for friends to help Him, 12 dis - ci - ples of Je - sus.
D Em7 A7
1 - 2 - 3 - 4 - 5 dis - ci - ples, 6 - 7 - 8 - 9 - 10 dis - ci - ples,
D Em7 A7 D B♭7
two more men make 12 dis - ci - ples, 12 dis - ci - ples of Je - sus.
E♭ Fm7(4) Gm Cm7 F Gm7(4) F/A B♭ B♭7
3. Pe - ter, James, John, and An - drew, four dis - ci - ples then we come to
E♭ Fm7(4) Gm Cm7 Fm B♭7 E♭
Phil - ip, Thad - de - us, Thom - as, Mat - thew, 12 dis - ci - ples of Je - sus.
E♭ Fm7(4) Gm Cm7 F Gm7(4) F/A B♭ B♭7
4. James, Bar - thol - o - mew, one named Si - mon, loved the Lord, stayed close be - side Him,
E♭ Fm7(4) Gm Cm7 Fm B♭7 E♭ C7 F Gm7(4) Am Dm7
'cept for Ju - das who de - nied Him, 12 dis - ci - ples of Je - sus. 1 - 2 - 3 - 4 - 5 dis - ci - ples,
G Am7(4) G/B C C7 F Gm7(4) Am Dm7 Gm C7 F
rit.
6 - 7 - 8 - 9 - 10 dis - ci - ples, two more men make 12 dis - ci - ples, 12 dis - ci - ples of Je - sus.

Two by Two

Words and Music by
ANDY GULLAHORN and DAVE HUNT

Bluesy rock (♩=114)
D
Bm
Two by two, two by two,
G
F
G
D
Bm
God showed mer - cy to No - ah and his crew. Two by two, two
by two, He's do - ing just the same for me and you.
C
We've
got a lot of an - i - mals to get in - side the ark. Bet - ter start tak - ing roll.
We've got a lot of work to do be - fore it gets dark, so
A
ev - 'ry - bod - y, here we go.
1. Let me see the el - e - phants.
2. Let me see the sheep.
3. Let me see the bears.

G F D A
*(Kids respond with sounds and motions)
Let__ me see the chick-ens. * Let__
Let__ me see the crick-ets. Let__
Let__ me see the dog-gies. Let__
D G F A7
__ me see the mon-keys. * Let__ me see the coy-o-tes.__
__ me see the al-li-ga-tors. Let__ me see the ow-ls.__
__ me see the pen-guins. Let__ me see the laugh-ing hy-e-
D Bm
__ * Two__ by two, two__ by two,
- nas.
G F G D Bm
God showed mer-cy to No-ah and his crew. Two by two, two__
G
Last time to Coda
__ by two, He's do-ing just the same__ for me__
1.2. F G D Bm
__ and you.__
G B♭ C
3. F G
D.S. al Coda
__ and two__
CODA F G D Bm
__ and you.__
G B♭ C D

Under the Sun

Words and Music by
BEN RYAN

Fun 60's rock (♩=128)
F
Eb
La - de - dah, dah, dah, dah, dah, dah.
F
1.
Eb
2.3.
Eb
La - de - dah, dah, dah, dah, dah, dah. dah, dah, dah.
F
Eb
1. A bear likes his fun un - der the sun.
2. A liz - ard loves his rock un - der the sun.
3. A pos - sum loves the night un - der the stars.
F
Eb
Hors - es like to run un - der the sun.
A par - rot loves to squawk un - der the sun.
Bats, they all take flight un - der the stars.
F
Ab
All God's crea - tures take de - light
All God's crea - tures take de - light
All God's crea - tures take de - light
Db
C
1. Db
C
play - ing in the warm sun - light.
play - ing in the warm sun - light.
play - ing un - der - neath star - light.
2.3. Db
C
Db
Don't you know that there's

E♭ Cm
a joy to liv - ing in the
Fm/C Fm E♭ D♭
light of love. All crea - tures great
E♭ Cm C
and small are known by God; He sees
Fm E♭ D♭ D♭/C
them all in day and night.
1st time: D.C.
2nd time: Go on
B♭m Csus C Csus C
He's in con - trol un - der the sun.
Repeat as desired
F E♭
La - de - dah, dah, dah, dah, dah, dah.
F E♭
La - de - dah, dah, dah, dah, dah, dah.
Last time
E♭ F
dah, dah, dah. Un - der the sun.

Up, Down, Zacchaeus

(To the tune of Pop! Goes the Weasel)

Words and Music by
RUTH ELAINE SCHRAM

C G C G
All a - round Jer - i - cho town he looked and looked for
C C G C
Je - sus. He hap - pened to see a syc - a - more tree.
Dm7 G C Am D
Up went Zac - chae - us. Well, Zac went up and
G Am D G
Zac came down the day that he met Je - sus.
N.C. Dm7 G7
Then his life was turned a - round, up, down, Zac -
C Dm7 G7 C A♭7
chae - us. When
D♭ A♭ D♭ A♭
Je - sus got right to the spot, He said to old Zac -
D♭ D♭ A♭ D♭
chae - us, "I'm gon - na stay at your house to - day."
E♭m7 A♭7 D♭ B♭m E♭
Down came Zac - chae - us! Well, Zac went up and

A♭
B♭m
E♭
A♭
Zac came down the day that he met Je - sus.
N.C.
E♭m7
A♭7
Then his life was turned a - round, up, down, Zac -
D♭
E♭m7
A♭7
D♭
A7
chae - us.
A
D
A
D
A
brand new heart, a brand new start, he gave them back their
D
A
D
tax - es. And God can do the same for you,
Em7
A7
D
Bm
E
turned 'round like Zac is! Well, Zac went up and
A
Bm
E
A
Zac came down the day that he met Je - sus.
N.C.
Em7
A7
Then his life was turned a - round, up, down, Zac -
D
Em7
A7
D
chae - us.

Wait on the Lord

Words and Music by
JANET MCMAHAN-WILSON
and GRETA GARNER-HART

Strong four (♩=144)
A
D
E
When there's some - thing bug - gin' you and you're not quite sure what
A
D
you should do, don't wor - ry. Don't fret.
E
A
D
Here's one thing to nev - er for - get: Wait on the Lord.
A
E
A
Wait on the Lord. He'll
D
A
Esus
B
E
A
give you all you need and more. So wait on the Lord.
3rd time to Coda
D
Fol - low Him and He'll show you the
A
B7
way. He'll be there to guide
E
D.S. al Coda
you ev - 'ry day. So
CODA
Esus
B
E
A
Esus
B
E
A
Wait on the Lord. Wait on the Lord.

Walk in the Light of the Lord

Words and Music by
JANET MCMAHAN-WILSON
Shuffle (♩=132)
Dm
Don't stum - ble down the road of dark - ness. Walk
A A7 Dm
in the light of the Lord. Don't tum - ble in - to a
A A7 Dm
big mess. Walk in the light of the Lord, not
Gm Dm E
to the left or to the right, but straight a - head, do - in'
A G F Em Dm
what is right. Don't stum - ble down the road of
A A7 1. Dm C Dm
dark - ness. Walk in the light of the Lord.
C Dm C A 2. Dm
Don't Walk
A A7 Dm A A7
in the light of the Lord. Walk in the light of the Lord.
Dm C Dm C Dm C Dm

Walking in the Light of God

Writer Unknown

With sincerity (𝅗𝅥=98)
F Bb Csus
It's a great day to praise the Lord. It's a great day to
F Dm7 Gm7
praise the Lord. It's a great day to praise the Lord,
C F F
1. walk - in' in the light of God. So walk, walk, walk, walk
2. jump - in' in the light of God. So jump, jump, jump, jump
3. hop - pin' in the light of God. So hop, hop, hop, hop
4. slid - in' in the light of God. So slide, slide, slide, slide
(5.) walk, walk, walk, walk
Bb C F C/E
in the light, walk, walk, walk, walk in the light,
in the light, jump, jump, jump, jump in the light,
in the light, hop, hop, hop, hop in the light,
in the light, slide, slide, slide, slide in the light,
in the light, jump, jump, jump, jump in the light,
Dm7 Gm7 C Last time to Coda
walk, walk, walk, walk in the light, walk - in' in the light of
jump, jump, jump, jump in the light, jump - in' in the light of
hop, hop, hop, hop in the light, hop - pin' in the light of
slide, slide, slide, slide in the light, slid - in' in the light of
hop, hop, hop, hop in the light, slid - in' in the light of
1.2.3. F 4. F D.S. al Coda
God. It's a God. So
God.
God.
CODA
F C F C F
God, walk-in' in the light of God, walk-in' in the light of God.

Wanna

Words and Music by
HERB OWEN

F F/A B♭6 Gm Gm7
1. I wan - na, wan - na, wan - na, wan - na, wan - na, wan - na, Real - ly wan - na
2. Man - y, man - y, man - y, man - y, man - y, man - y, ver - y man - y
C7 Gm7 C7 F B♭/C F F7/A
be just like the Lord. So ev - 'ry day I'm gon - na, gon - na
times with - in His Word, He said that an - y, an - y, an - y
B♭6 Gm Gm7 C7 Gm7 C7 F B♭/C
read the Book and rest up - on - a God's own Ho - ly Word. Of
time I'll pray and seek Him Then He'll see that I am heard. I
F F7/A B♭ Gm7
good in me there's none - a, none - a, That's o - kay be - cause I'm gon - na
know that when He, when He, when He said that an - y, an - y, an - y
C7 Gm7 C7 F F/C
trust up - on the work that's done - a on the cross. And
time I'll stop and pray to Him He planned to keep His
Dm Dm/C Gm/B♭ Gm Gm7
Je - sus is the One - a One - a God the Fa - ther's Son - a Son - a
Word He and He real - ly meant, He meant to keep His prom - ise and He
1. C7 Gm7 C7 F B♭/C 2. C7 Gm7 C7 F F/A A♭°
And my sin He cured! has my heart as - sured, He
C7/G B♭/C C7 F F/A A♭° C9/G C7/G Gm7/C C7 F
has my heart as - sured; He has my heart as - sured!

We Are United

Words and Music by
JOELINE MCGREGOR and MANUEL MCGREGOR

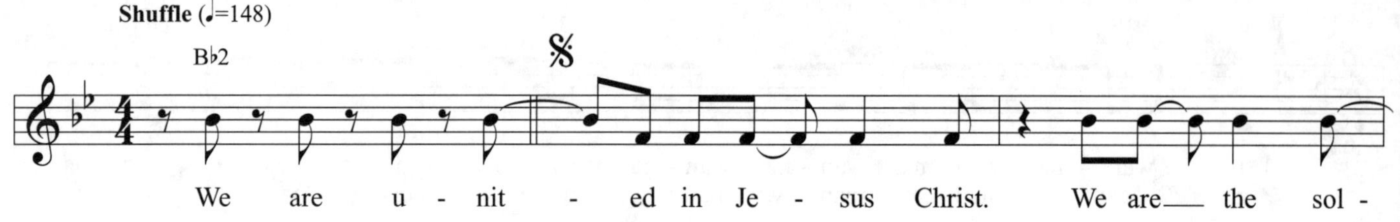
Shuffle (♩=148)
B♭2
We are u - nit - ed in Je - sus Christ. We are the sol -

E♭
F6
Cm/F
- diers of the Light. We don't wres - tle flesh and blood

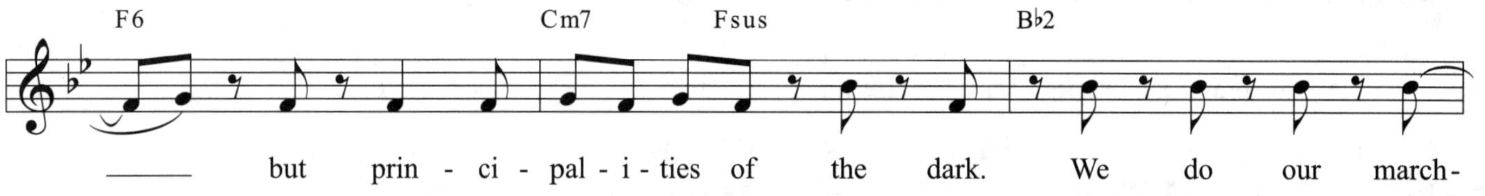
F6
Cm7
Fsus
B♭2
but prin - ci - pal - i - ties of the dark. We do our march -

E♭
- ing to one beat, crush - ing the en - e - my un - der our feet.

F6
Cm/F
F6
We are might - y in our stand with God's Word

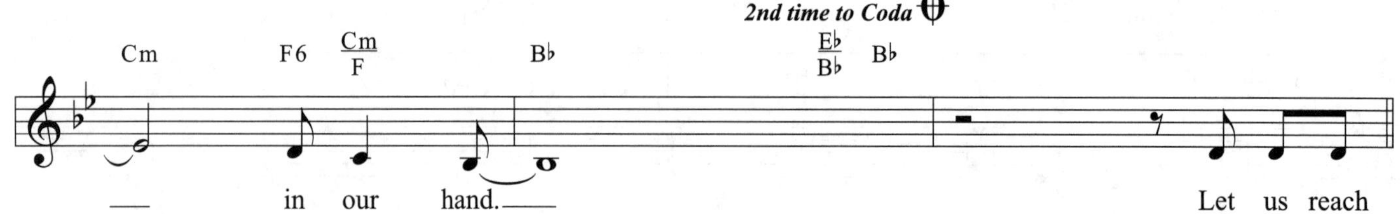
2nd time to Coda
Cm
F6
Cm/F
B♭
E♭/B♭
B♭
in our hand. Let us reach

Gm
Gm(maj7)
Gm7
this gen - er - a - tion, ev - 'ry tribe and ev - 'ry na -

Gm6
Eb
-tion, for we've o-ver-come the world by the
F
Bb2
D.S. al Coda
blood of Christ the Lamb. We are u-nit-
CODA
Bb
Cm7
F7
The Lord our God is a sword and shield. We
Cm
F7
Cm7
fight our bat-tles on our knees. The Lord our God is a sword
F7
Cm7
F7
and shield. We fight our bat-tles on our knees. The
Cm7
F7
Cm7
Lord our God is a sword and shield. We fight our bat-tles on
F
G
our knees.
C2
We are u-nit-ed in Je-sus Christ. We are the sol-

F G6 Dm/G
- diers of the Light. We don't wres - tle flesh and blood
G6 Dm7 Gsus C2
but prin - ci - pal - i - ties of the dark. We do our march -
F
- ing to one beat, crush - ing the en - e - my un - der our feet.
G6 Dm/G G6
We are might - y in our stand with God's Word
Dm G6 Dm/G C F G6 Dm/G
in our hand. We are might - y in our stand
G6 Dm G6 Dm/G C F
with God's Word in our hand. We are might -
G6 Dm/G G6 Dm G6 Dm/G
- y in our stand with God's Word in our hand.
C F/C C G7 C
We are might - y!

We Agree to Agree

We Agree to Agree
Words and Music by
PAM ANDREWS and JOHNATHAN CRUMPTON
With an "Island" feel (♩=83)
When_ we a - gree_ to a - gree, we'll work to-geth - er in
har - mo - ny. It's_ not the "I"_ but the "we." We a-gree_ to a -
gree. When_ gree. Like a fish and a rod and a pea in a pod and a
Fine
ham - mer and a nail, to - geth - er they do so much more
than all by them - selves. When_ we a-gree_ to a -
gree, we'll work to-geth - er in har - mo - ny. It's_ not the "I"_ but the
"we." We a-gree_ to a - gree. Can I help? Yes, I can. Reach - ing
out, take my hand. I need you, and you need me. To - geth - er we do
so much more when we're in u - ni - ty. When_
D.S. al Fine

We Are the People of the Lord

Words and Music by
JANET MCMAHAN-WILSON

March tempo (♩=116)
E♭
We are the peo - ple of the Lord.
We are the peo - ple of the Lord.
E♭7
We'll
A♭
stomp out the en - e - my, for
E♭
God gives the vic - tor - y.
Cm7
Fm
B♭
We are the peo - ple of the
E♭
Lord.
E
We are the peo - ple of the
Lord.
We are the peo - ple of the
Lord.
E7
We'll
A
march in with all our might and

E
C♯m7
F♯m7
B
He'll help us win the fight. We are the peo - ple of the

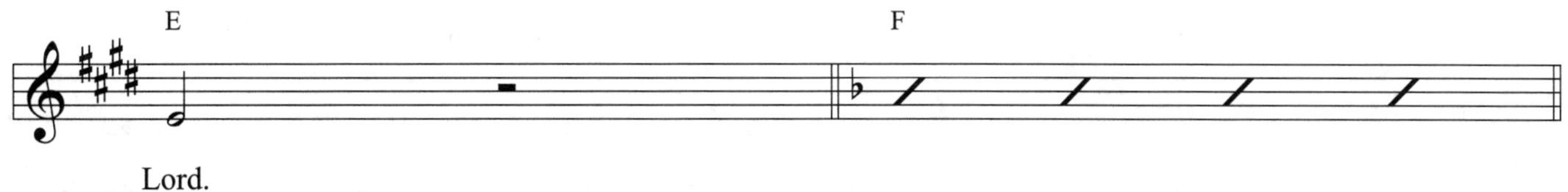
E
F
Lord.

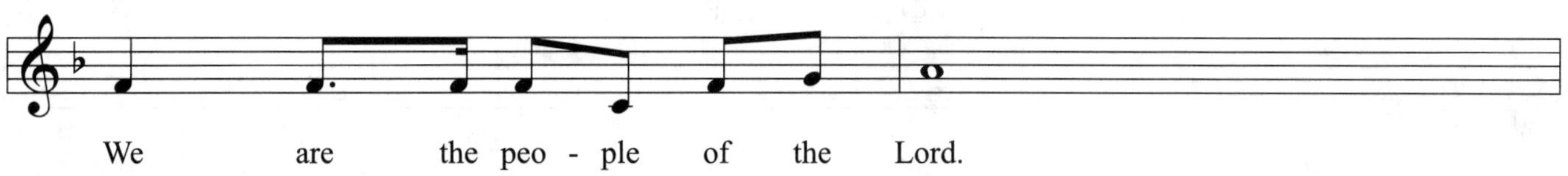
We are the peo - ple of the Lord.

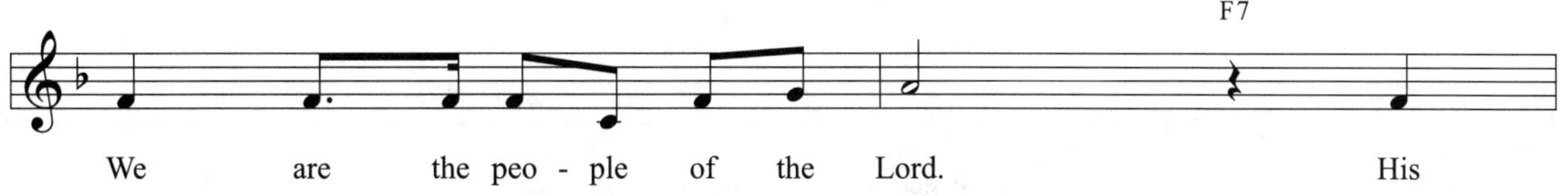
F7
We are the peo - ple of the Lord. His

B♭
F
Dm7
word is our bat - tle cry, V - I - C - T - O - R - Y.

Gm
C
F
D7
We are the peo - ple of the Lord.

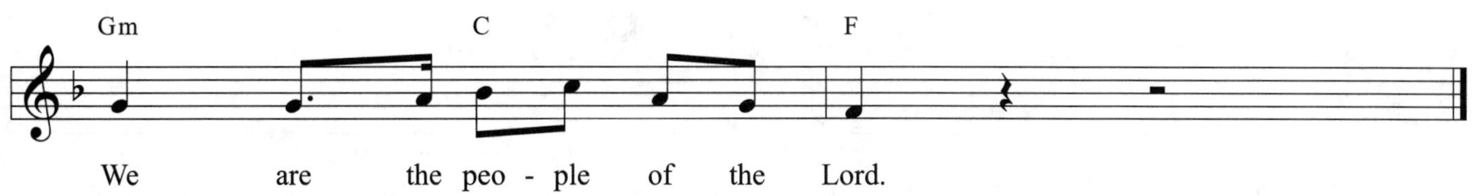
Gm
C
F
We are the peo - ple of the Lord.

We'll Call Him Jesus

Words and Music by
KAREN DEAN

E♭
Fm7
Fm7/C
A♭/B♭
Gm/B♭
Fm/B♭
We'll call Him Je - sus, the name the an - gels

A♭/E♭
E♭
B♭/D
Cm
C7(♭9)
Fm7
Fm7/C
whis - pered. We'll call Him Je - sus, come from

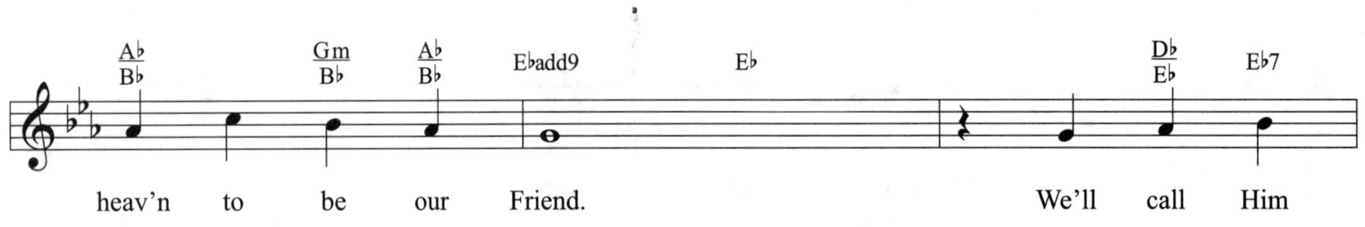
A♭/B♭
Gm/B♭
A♭/B♭
E♭add9
E♭
D♭/E♭
E♭7
heav'n to be our Friend. We'll call Him

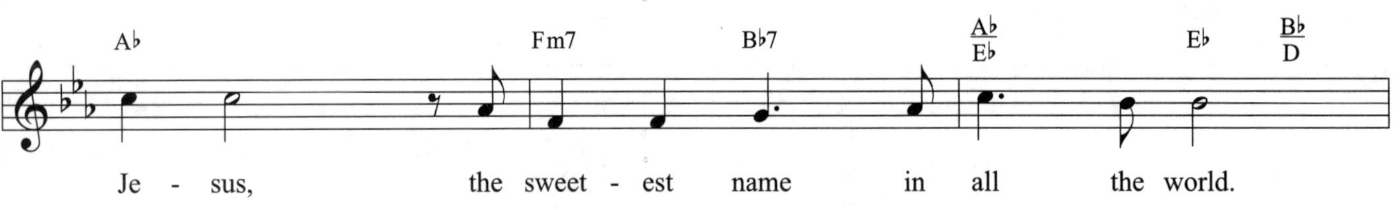
A♭
Fm7
B♭7
A♭/E♭
E♭
B♭/D
Je - sus, the sweet - est name in all the world.

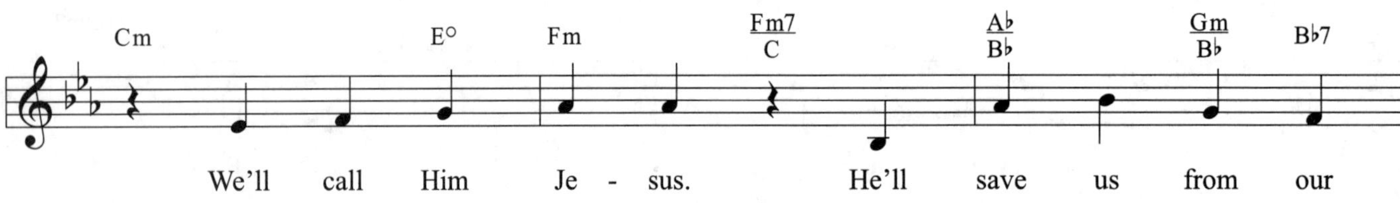
Cm
E°
Fm
Fm7/C
A♭/B♭
Gm/B♭
B♭7
We'll call Him Je - sus. He'll save us from our

1. E♭
2. E♭
E♭/D
Cm
E°
sin. We'll call Him sin. We'll call Him

Fm
Fm7/C
A♭/B♭
Gm/B♭
B♭7
E♭sus
E♭sus/B♭
E♭
Je - sus. He'll save us from our sin.

Whisper a Prayer

Traditional

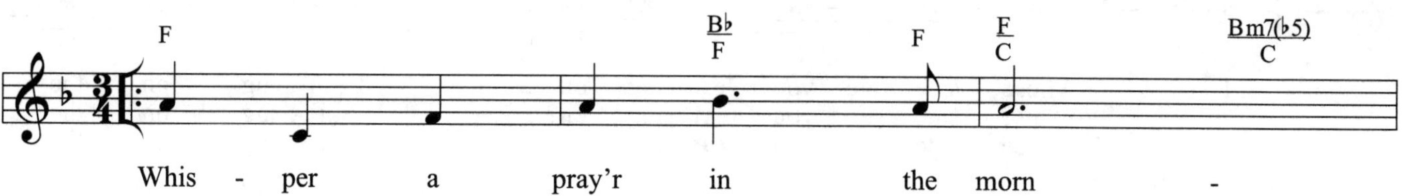
F
B♭/F
F
F/C
Bm7(♭5)/C
Whis - per a pray'r in the morn -

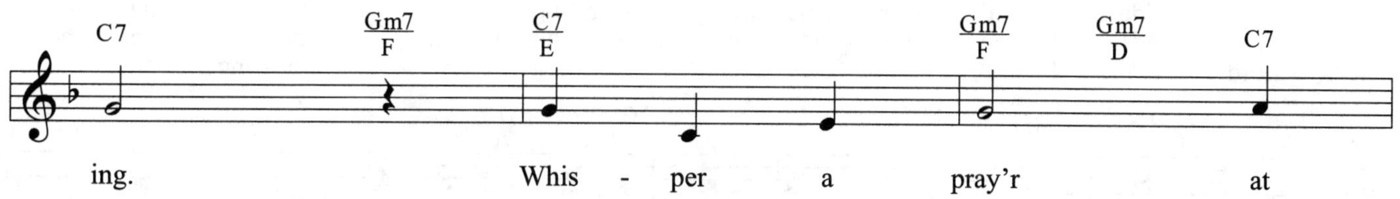
C7
Gm7/F
C7/E
Gm7/F
Gm7/D
C7
ing. Whis - per a pray'r at

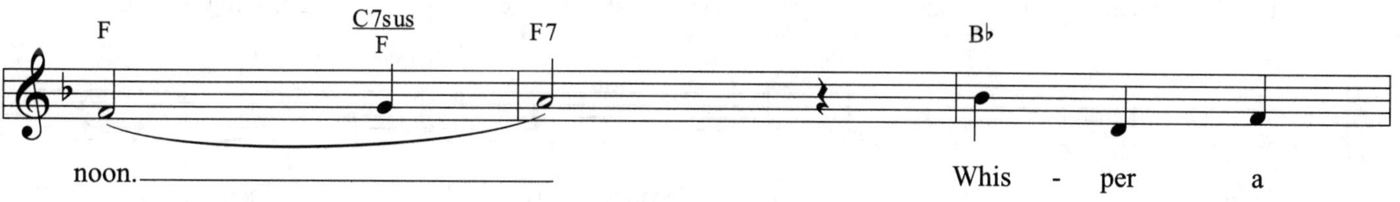
F
C7sus/F
F7
B♭
noon. Whis - per a

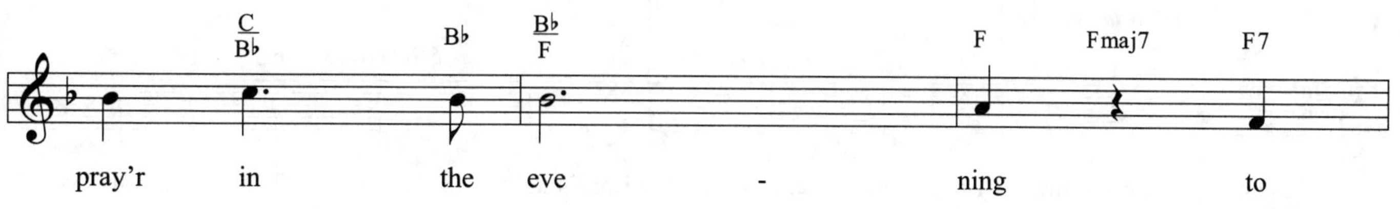
C/B♭
B♭
B♭/F
F
Fmaj7
F7
pray'r in the eve - ning to

Gm/B♭
D/A
Gm7(♭5)
F/C
B♭maj7/C
C7
keep your heart in

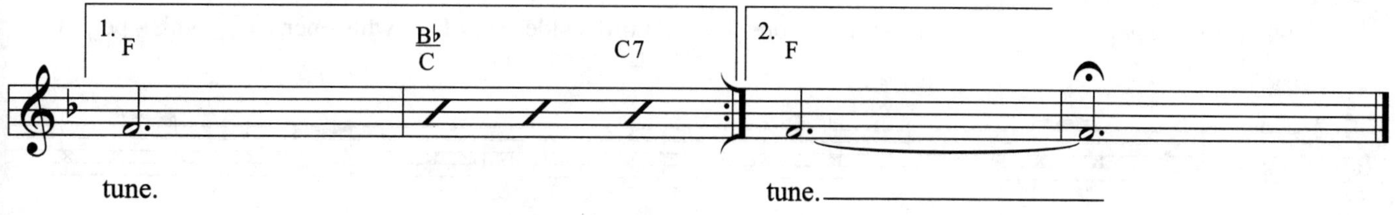
1.
F
B♭/C
C7
2.
F
tune.
tune.

Whose Side Are You Leaning On?

Writer Unknown

SOLO
D
whis-per, I whis-per. Whis-p'ring on the Lord's side. 4. I said, Whose side are you
G D CHOIR A D SOLO
yell-ing on? Yell-ing on the Lord's side. I said, Whose side are you
G D CHOIR A D ALL (go crazy!)
yell-ing on? Yell-ing on the Lord's side. I yell, I yell, I
G D A D
yell, I yell. Yell-ing on the Lord's side. I yell, I yell, I
G D A D D.S. al Coda
yell, I yell. Yell-ing on the Lord's side.
CODA
A D SOLO CHOIR
Lord's side. 6. I said, Whose side are you lean-ing on? Lean-ing on the
SOLO CHOIR
Lord's side. I said, Whose side are you lean-ing on? Lean-ing on the
ALL D G D
Lord's side. I lean, I lean, I lean, I lean. Lean-ing on the
A D D G D
Lord's side. I lean, I lean, I lean, I lean.
1. A D 2. F♯m/A A7 D
Lean-ing on the Lord's side. I Lord's side.

Wide as the Ocean

Words and Music by
C. AUSTIN MILES

B♭ E♭ B♭ B♭maj7/F B♭6/F B♭ B♭/F B♭7 A♭/C B♭7/D
Wide, wide as the o - cean, high as the heav - ens a -
E♭ Cm7 F7 B♭ B♭/D B♭m6/D♭
bove, deep, deep as the deep - est sea is
F/C Gm9 C7 Cm7/F F7 E♭/G F7/A B♭ B♭/D E♭ F/E♭ E♭
my Sav - ior's love. I, though so un -
B♭ B♭maj7/F B♭6/F B♭ B♭7 A♭/C B♭7/D E♭ E♭/B♭
wor - thy, still am a child of His care,
E♭ E♭maj7 E° B♭/F Gm7 Cm7 F7
for His Word teach - es me that His love reach - es me ev - 'ry -
1. B♭ F7 E♭/G F7/A 2. B♭ F7/C B♭/D E♭ E♭maj7 E°
where. where, for His Word teach - es me
B♭/F Gm7 C13 C7 F7 B♭ B♭/F B♭
that His love reach - es me ev - 'ry - where!

Wisdom's Havin' a Party

Words and Music by
JANET MCMAHAN-WILSON

Swing feel (♩=144)
If you'd like to learn a-bout God's book and feast up-on His truth,
then o-pen your eyes and take a look. There's a
big sur-prise for you. Wis-dom's hav-in' a
par-ty o-pen to ev-'ry-one.
Some kind of fab-u-lous par-ty, come on and
join the fun. Hear what wis-dom has to say.
Read the word and find the way to wis-dom's fab-u-lous
par-ty. Join in the fun to-day.
Come on and find the way. Read the word and o-bey.

Wisdom

Words and Music by
HERB OWEN

1. God has prom - ised me wis - dom from a - bove.
2. If I choose to make wis - dom my life's goal,
I will have suc - cess if un - der - stand - ing I will love.
He will then re - ward me with much hon - or as I grow.
1.
2.
Hear now ye chil - dren the wis - dom of God.
"I teach you well, so for - sake not my law."
Wis - dom is see - ing the world as God sees,
do - ing what He does, so Him I can please.
In the Word of God treas - ures there I find,

G Bm7 G/B C C#7(♭5) C#°7 D7 C/D D7 G G/B C D
un - der - stand - ing for my heart, and knowl - edge for my mind.
G Bm7 G/B C Am7 D7 Am7 D7 G D7sus
God has prom - ised me wis - dom from a - bove.
G Bm7 G/B C G6/B Am7 D C/D D7 G G/B C D
I will have suc - cess if un - der - stand - ing I will love.
G Bm7 G/B C Am7 Bm C D7 C/D D7
If I choose to make wis - dom my life's
G C D Em Dm7 G7/D A/C# Cm6 D C/D D7
goal, He will then re - ward me with much hon - or as I
G G/B C D G Bm7 G/B C Am7
grow. Don't let me for - get
D7 C/D D7 G G/B Em Dm7 G7/D
les - sons I have learned. Keep them all with -
A/C# Cm6 D C/D D D7 G G/B C D
in my heart as to them I re - turn.
Em D6 G6/D C G6/B Am7 C#°7 D C/D D7 G N.C.
Keep them all with - in my heart as to them I re - turn.

With All My Heart

Words and Music by
AMI SANDSTROM-SHROYER

Broad ballad (♩=87)
B♭2
Cm7
Lord, I love You with all my heart.
E♭
E♭m
B♭
Thank You for the things You've giv - en me.
B♭2/D
E♭maj9
E♭m6
Je - sus, I know that You are near. I will
B♭/F
F7sus
B♭/F
praise You. I will love You. I will fol - low You
F7sus
1. B♭
E♭2/G
for - ev - er.
B♭
E♭2/G
2. B♭
F
E♭maj9
For - ev - er, for - ev - er,
F
for - ev - er, His

1. Gm7 E♭2 F
love en - dures for - ev - er.
2. Gm7 E♭2 F G
love en - dures for - ev - er.
C2 Dm7
Lord, I love You with all my heart.
F Fm C
Thank You for the things You've giv - en me.
C2/E Fmaj9 Fm6
You are near. I will
C/G G7sus
praise You. I will love You. I will
1.2. C/G G7sus
fol - low You. I will serve You. I will
3. C/G C
fol - low You for - ev - er.

With My Whole Heart

Words and Music by
BILLY CROCKETT and KENNY WOOD

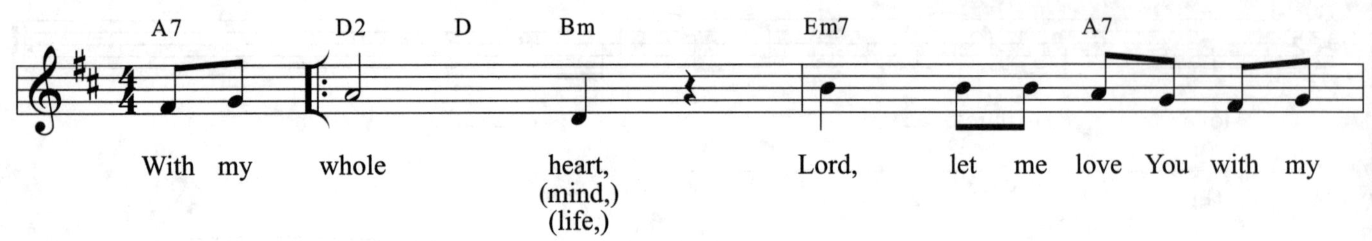
A7
D2
D
Bm
Em7
A7
With my whole heart, Lord, let me love You with my
(mind,)
(life,)

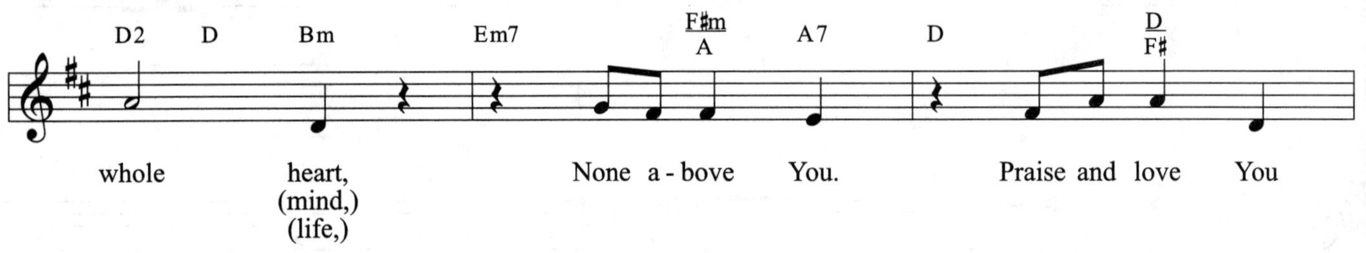
D2
D
Bm
Em7
F#m/A
A7
D
D/F#
whole heart, None a-bove You. Praise and love You
(mind,)
(life,)

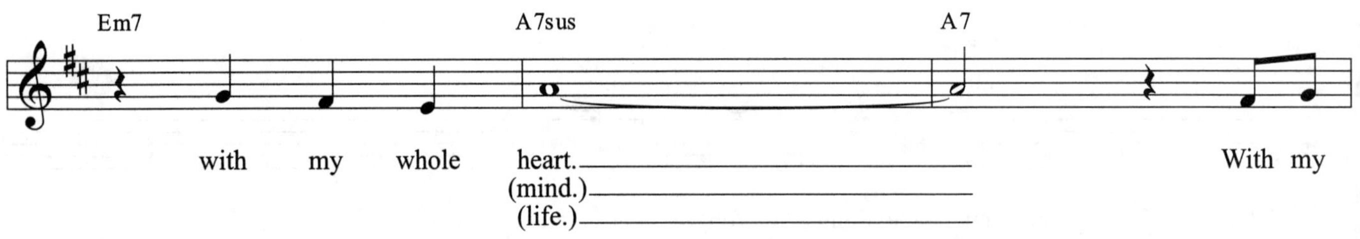
Em7
A7sus
A7
with my whole heart. With my
(mind.)
(life.)

D2
D
Bm
Em7
A7
D2
D
Bm
whole heart, Lord, let me hear You with my whole heart,
(mind,)
(life,)
(mind,)
(life,)

Em7
F#m/A
A7
D
G
D/F#
Em7
F#m/A
A7
Ev - er near You. Help me hear You with my whole

1.2.
D
G/A
A7
3.
D
heart. With my life.
(mind.)

Wonderful to Be in the Family of God

Words and Music by
HERB OWEN

1. In a world sur - round - ed by God's en - e - mies, con - found - ed by the
2. By His Spir - it born a - gain He plac - es us, His church with - in, that
prob - lems that we face here ev - 'ry day,
we might then to - geth - er serve the Lord.
pon - der - ing His mer - cies new while
From the church we all then go to
won - der - ing just what to do, how great it is to praise Him and say:
tell the world He loves them so and work to - geth - er in one ac - cord.
Don't cha know it's
won - der - ful to be in the fam - 'ly of God,
im - pos - si - ble to count all the
bless - ings He's giv - en, re - mark - a - ble to know that He loves us so, and
com - fort - ing He's pa - tient as we learn and grow,
awe - some just to see His
love for you and me, and
1. glo - ri - ous that we are His e - ter - nal - ly!
2. glo - ri - ous that we are His e - ter - nal - ly! And
glo - ri - ous that we are His e - ter - nal - ly!

Written on My Heart

Words and Music by
JANET MCMAHAN-WILSON

Lively (♩=126)
B♭
A
B♭
The words of the Lord are writ - ten on my heart. The
F
E
F
words of the Lord are writ - ten on my heart and
B♭
B♭7
E♭
C7/E
I will keep them in the deep - est part of me. His
B♭/F
F
B♭
A/F
B♭
F7
words are writ - ten on my heart.
B♭
A/F
B
The truth of the Lord is
A♯
B
writ - ten on my heart. The truth of the Lord is
F♯
F
F♯
B
B7
writ - ten on my heart and I will keep it

E C#/F B/F# F#
in the deep - est part of me. His truth is writ - ten on my
B A#/F# B F#7 B A#/F# C
heart. The
B C
laws of the Lord are writ - ten on my heart. The
G F# G
laws of the Lord are writ - ten on my heart and
C C7 F D/F#
I will keep them in the deep - est part of me. His
C/G G C
laws are writ - ten on my heart. His
C/G G C
truth is writ - ten on my heart. The
C/G G C B/G C G7 C G C
words of the Lord are writ - ten on my heart.

You Are Lord

Words and Music by
JANET MCMAHAN-WILSON

Soft rock feel

G
F
G
F
Lord, You are the shield a-round me.

G
F
G
F
Though my en - e - mies sur-round me,

Bm7(♭5)
Am7
F/G
G
Bm7(♭5)/E
Fmaj7
C/D
Dsus
I am safe with - in Your care. I can feel Your pres - ence ev - 'ry - where.

G
F
G
F
Lord, You are the shield a-round me.

A♭
G♭
Lord, You are the arms that hold me. Your

A♭
G♭
might - y wings of love en-fold me.

Cm7(♭5)
B♭maj7
G♭/A♭
A♭
Cm7(♭5)/F
G♭maj7
D♭/E♭
E♭sus
I am safe with - in Your care. I can feel Your pres - ence ev - 'ry - where.

A♭ G♭
Lord, You are the arms that hold me.
A G
Lord, You are the peace within me. I
A G
find my hiding place within Thee.
C♯m7(♭5) Bm7 G/A A C♯m7(♭5)/F♯ Gmaj7 D/E Esus
I am safe within Your care. I can feel Your presence ev'ry-where.
A G
Lord, You are the peace within me.
B♭ A♭ B♭ A♭
Lord, You are the arms that hold me.
B♭ A♭ B♭ A♭
Lord, You are the shield around me.
D♭/E♭ Cm/F G♭m7 A♭ B♭
You are Lord. You are Lord!

You'd Better Get Ready

Words and Music by
HERB OWEN

Moderato
E♭ B♭
He will come a - gain for me to
Fm7 B♭ E♭ Gm/D Cm G7 Cm G7
take me home with Him; an - y day now He'll break through the clouds, and you won't be -
Cm G7 Cm B♭7/D E♭ Fm7 E♭/G A♭
lieve the cheer - ing crowds who wel - come back the Son of God to
E♭/B♭ B♭7 E♭ E♭ B♭
plan - et earth a - gain. All the dead in Christ shall rise to
Fm7 B♭7 E♭ Gm/D Cm G7 Cm G7
live for - ev - er - more. And we'll see so man - y friends a - gain in a cel - e -
Cm G7 Cm B♭/D E♭ Fm7 E♭/G A♭
bra - tion with - out end, for sin, temp - ta - tion, cloud - y days, will
E♭/B♭ B♭7 E♭ B7
be there nev - er - more. It will be a

E B F♯m7 B E G♯m/D♯
hap - py day___ when we will see the Lord; we will thank Him
C♯m G♯7 C♯m G♯7 C♯m G♯7 C♯m B/D♯
for the things He's done; we will sing our praise to God the Son. He'll
E F♯m7 E/G♯ A E/B B E
wel - come us to our new home and give us our re - ward.
C7 F C
Are you read - y for that day___ when
Gm7 C F Am/E Dm A7 Dm A7
Je - sus will re - turn? It is when we place our trust in Him, He for - gives and
Dm A7 Dm C/E F Gm7 F/A B♭
takes a - way our sin. So, you'd bet - ter get read - y 'cause Je - sus is com - ing to
F/C Dm Gm7 C7 F B♭/C F B♭/C F B♭/C F
take us all a - way!___

You're the One

Words and Music by
AMI SANDSTROM-SHROYER

Driving rock (♩=104)
A
D
I love You, Lord, You are mine. I
F#m
E
A
love You for - ev - er. I love You, Lord,
D
F#m
E
You are mine. I love You for - ev - er. You're the
D
E
D
E
One for me. You're the One for me.
3rd time to Coda
You're the One for me. You're the
1. N.C.
2. A
One. I One.
A(no3)
N.C.
A(no3)
N.C.
D.S. al Coda
I
CODA
A
D
One. God, come and

A D A D
live in my heart. God, come and live in my heart. God, come and
A E N.C. D
live in my heart to - day. God, come and
A D A D
live in my heart. God, come and live in my heart. God, come and
A E 1. N.C. 2. N.C.
live in my heart al - ways. I
A E F♯m E
love You, Lord, You are mine. I love You for - ev - er. I
A D F♯m E
love You, Lord, You are mine. I love You for - ev - er. You're the
D E D E
One for me. You're the One for me. You're the
D E 1. A
One for me. You're the One. You're the
2. N.C. A
You're the One.

Your Wondrous Ways

Words and Music by
JANET MCMAHAN-WILSON

Smoothly
A
G/A
1. Ev - 'ry ti - ny grain of sand
2. Ev - 'ry dawn that greets the day
A
G/A
fash - ioned by Your lov - ing hand
with the sun - shine's gol - den rays
Dmaj7
C♯m
F♯m
speaks of the mar - vel - ous mys - ter - y
speaks of the glo - ri - ous mir - a - cles
Bm7
E
A
of Your plan. Ev - 'ry star that
You have made. Ev - 'ry drop of
G/A
A
lights the night, ev - 'ry flock of
morn - ing dew, ev - 'ry sum - mer
G/A
Dmaj7
birds in flight speaks of the
sky of blue speaks of the
C♯m
F♯m
Bm7
splen - dor and joy of Your pow'r and might.
beau - ty and won - der we find in You.

E
Dmaj7
Oh Lord, Your won - drous ways are wor - thy
C♯m
F♯m
Bm7
of our praise. Let all cre - a - tion raise
E
A
its voice and sing! Let ev - 'ry
Dmaj7
C♯m
F♯
tongue pro - claim Your name a - bove all names.
Bm7
E
You are Je - ho - vah God, our Lord and
1.
A
G/A
King.
2.
Dmaj7
King.
C♯m
F♯
You are Je -
Bm7
ho - vah God, our Lord and King.

Your Word

Words and Music by
GARY FORSYTHE

Dm Gm
Your Word is a lamp un - to my feet, un -
Dm A7 Dm
to my feet, un - to my feet. Your Word is a lamp un -
Gm Dm/A A7
to my feet and a light un - to my
1. Dm 2. Dm C/E
path. Your path.
F C Dm
I will hide it in my heart so I will al - ways
A Bm7 A7/C♯ F C A7/C♯
do what's right. I will hide it in my heart so
Dm A 2nd time to Coda Dm
I will walk in the light. Your
Dm Gm Dm
Word is a lamp un - to my feet, un - to my feet, un -
A Dm Gm
to my feet. Your Word is a lamp un - to my feet and a

1.
2.
D.S. al Coda
B♭ C Dm Dm C/E
light un - to my path. Your path.
CODA Dm B♭7 E♭m
light. Your Word is a lamp un -
A♭m E♭m B♭7
to my feet, un - to my feet, un - to my feet. Your
E♭m A♭m C♭ D♭
Word is a lamp un - to my feet and a light un - to my
E♭m B7 Em Am
path Your Word is a lamp un - to my feet, un -
Em B7 Em
to my feet, un - to my feet. Your Word is a lamp un -
Am C D Em
to my feet and a light un - to my path, and a
C D Em C
light un - to my path, and a light un -
D Em
to my path.
3

You Are Always in His Sight
Words and Music by
JANET MCMAHAN-WILSON
Reverently
G Am/G
All through the day and through the night,
Am C/D D G
you are al-ways in His sight. No need to fear, for
Am/G Am C/D D7 G
God is here all through the day and night. No
Em Bm7 Em D C A/C♯
mat - ter where you are, He holds you close
D E
to His heart. All
A Bm/A Bm D/E E
through the day and through the night, you are al-ways in His
A Bm/A
sight. No need to fear, for God is here all
Bm D/E E7 A A/E
through the day and night. You are al - ways
E7 A
in His sight.

Zacchaeus Was a Wee Little Man

Traditional

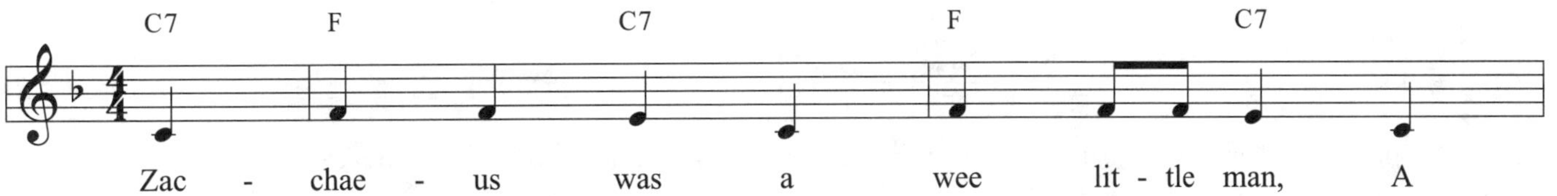
C7
F
C7
F
C7
Zac - chae - us was a wee lit - tle man, A

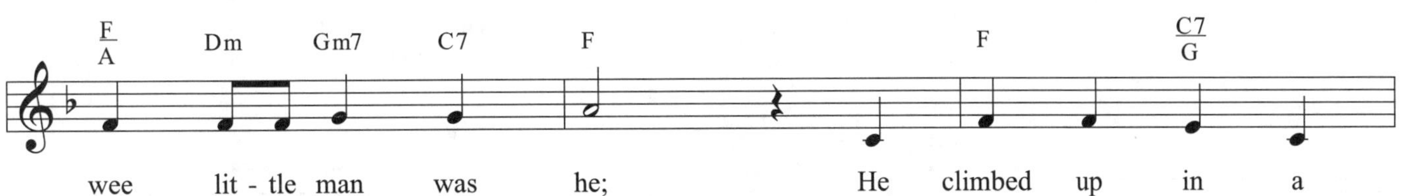
F/A
Dm
Gm7
C7
F
F
C7/G
wee lit - tle man was he; He climbed up in a

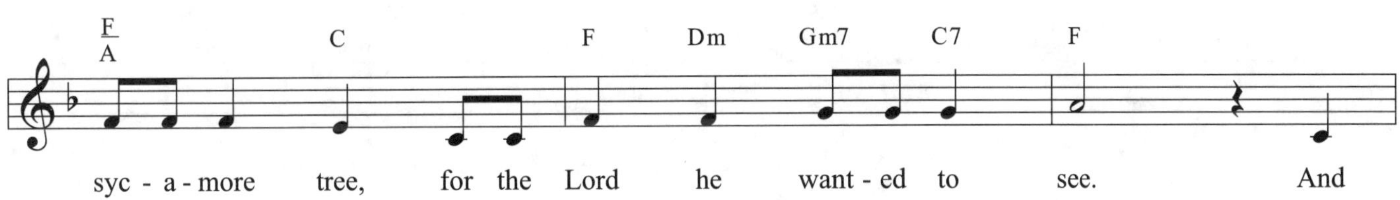
F/A
C
F
Dm
Gm7
C7
F
syc - a - more tree, for the Lord he want - ed to see. And

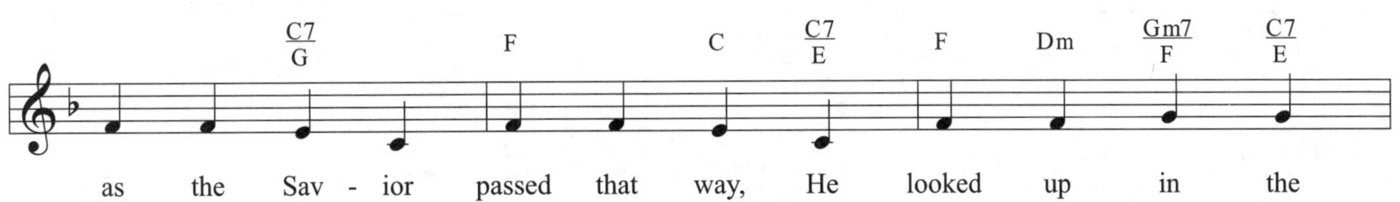
C7/G
F
C
C7/E
F
Dm
Gm7/F
C7/E
as the Sav - ior passed that way, He looked up in the

F
(Spoken:) And He said,
"Zacchaeus, you come down!"
F
Dm
Gm7
C7
tree. For I'm go - ing to your house to -

F
C/E
Dm
G7
Gm7
C7
F
day, For I'm go - ing to your house to - day."

Zip Zip Zippity Zip
Words and Music by
JANET MCMAHAN-WILSON
and GRETA GARNER-HART
Bright shuffle (♩=152)
Some - times you've got to zip your lip be - fore you let some - thing that should - n't slip. Don't
blow your top or flip your lid. Just zip zip zip - pi - ty zip your lip.
2nd time to Coda
Swal - low your pride. (Gulp!) Let the love of the Lord be your guide. Some -
D.S. al Coda
CODA
zip your lip. Zip zip zip - pi - ty zip your lip. Zip zip zip - pi - ty zip.

Alphabetical Index of Songs

Index by Themes/Topics

FRIENDS

FRUIT OF THE SPIRIT

FUN SONGS

GOD'S ARMY

GOD'S LOVE FOR US

GOD'S WORD

GOSPEL

GRACE / MERCY

GUIDANCE AND CARE

HOLY SPIRIT

INVITATION

JESUS CHRIST

JOY

LOVING OTHERS

MISSIONS / EVANGELISM / SERVICE

NOAH AND THE FLOOD

OUR LOVE FOR GOD

SUFFICIENCY OF GOD

SURRENDER AND SUBMISSION

TEN COMMANDMENTS

THANKS / THANKFULNESS

TRINITY

TRUST / OBEDIENCE

TRUTH

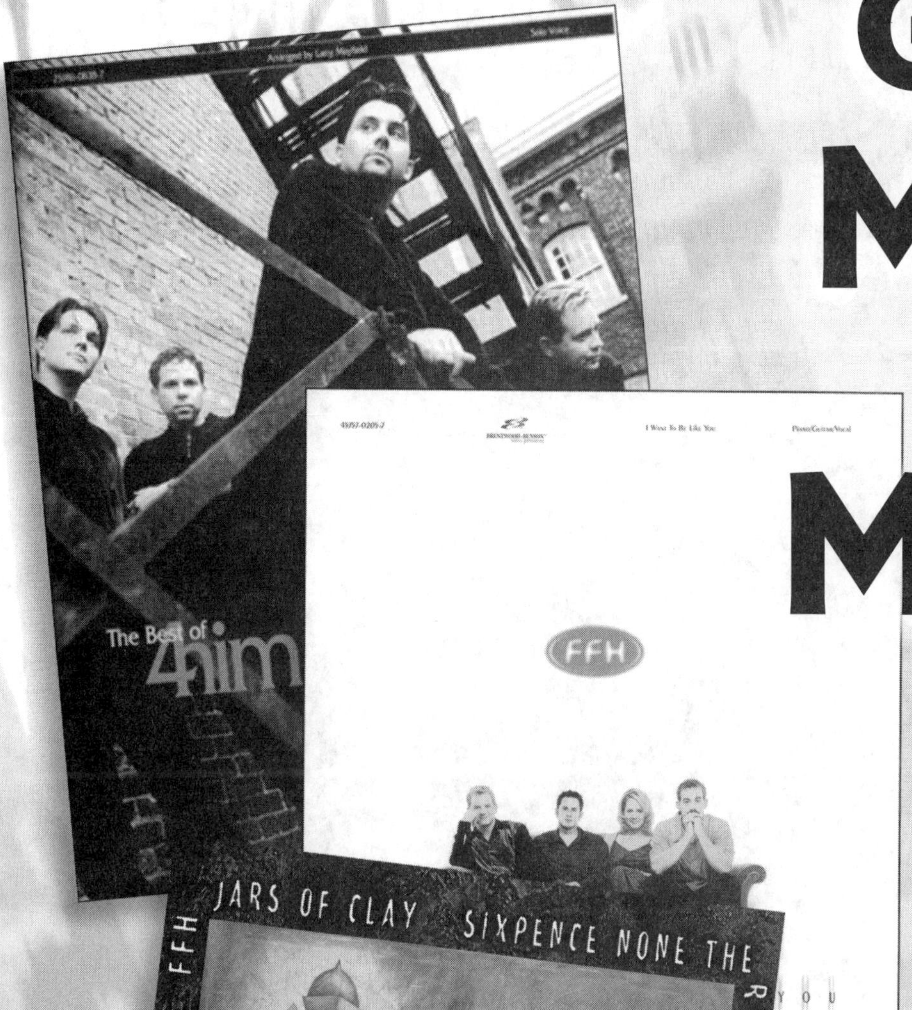